GETTING AND SPENDING

£3·95

MAINSTREAM SERIES

Editors: Lord Blake, Leon Brittan, Jo Grimond,
John Patten and Alan Peacock

LEO PLIATZKY

Getting and Spending

Public Expenditure, Employment and Inflation

Basil Blackwell

First published 1982
Revised edition 1984
Basil Blackwell Publisher Limited
108 Cowley Road, Oxford OX4 1JF, England

British Library Cataloguing in Publication Data

Pliatzky, Leo
    Getting and spending.
    1. Government spending policy – Great Britain
    – History – 20th century   2. Great Britain –
    Appropriations and expenditures
    I. Title
    336.3′9′0941   HJ2096
    ISBN 0-631-13589-8

Printed in Great Britain by The Camelot Press, Southampton

In memory of Jean

Getting and spending, we lay waste our powers . . .

Wordsworth

Fate takes many forms,
And destiny produces many surprises.
Forecasts are not fulfilled,
But god finds a way for results not in the forecasts.
That is how it has turned out in this case.

Euripides, *Alcestis*
(translated by the author)

Contents

1

The Post-war Years

This book is about public expenditure in Britain from the end of the second world war, and especially about the years in the sixties and seventies when I was myself increasingly involved. It is also about my time in the civil service, and so the book touches here and there on subjects other than public expenditure. Throughout the post-war period, up to the watershed of the Conservative government's return to power in 1979, policy in this field was dominated by the pursuit of two objectives which had been conceived during the war itself – full employment and the welfare state.

My years as a civil servant corresponded roughly with this period. Having passed the post-war Reconstruction Competition in the summer of 1946, I put off joining the civil service for six months while making up my mind about it, and then became an Assistant Principal in the Ministry of Food in February 1947.

Everything about the initial experience was depressing. The contrast between the brave new society planned for the future and the austerity of the present was stark. Outside there was ice and snow everywhere. The country was in a fuel crisis because the long freeze-up had stopped distribution of coal, on which the economy largely depended at that time. North Sea oil and gas had not yet been discovered, and the use of oil generally was still relatively limited.

The particular Ministry of Food office in Portman Square to which I was sent, a building long since replaced by a modern block, was cold, dismal and unsuitable for office use. It appeared to have been a block of flats or perhaps a hotel, converted in a makeshift way. I was put in a sort of cubby hole, where a wash basin took up a good deal of the limited space. I did not at first have a great deal of work to do in Alcohol and Yeast Division, to which I was assigned, and filled in time

by entering for *New Statesman* literary competitions, in which at one
stage I had quite a good winning streak.

During those early days I attended a week's induction course for
new entrants to the Ministry of Food. Practically every lecturer
referred with pride to the fact that the Ministry was spending £1
million a day on food subsidies. Since I did not see everything in
public expenditure terms in those days, I did not react in any
particular way to this information. There was still a physical shortage
of food in the war-devastated world, and food subsidies were part of
the apparatus of controls and rationing designed to ensure a fair
distribution of supplies.

In retrospect I came to see the food subsidies as a budgetary
millstone round the post-war government's neck. At early 1983
prices, that £1 million a day would have been about £11 million a day
or roughly £4000 million a year, a major expenditure programme
exceeded by only the few largest programmes. In the impoverished
circumstances of 1947, it was an enormous amount to find. I have no
doubt that there were people in the Ministry who understood this
better than I did at the time and who would have liked to get away
from this policy of subsidising food prices for rich and poor alike. But
once a government is involved in controlling and subsidising prices or
rents, it is difficult to cut the subsidy off, because price increases are
unpopular. This sets up a pressure for subsidies, once introduced, to
grow, as rising costs are not matched by price increases, until sooner
or later budgetary counter-pressures compel the government to face
the unpopularity of a change of policy.

Events in Poland have provided the most dramatic illustration of
this problem. At a Cambridge conference in 1979 a Polish official
described the food subsidies as Poland's biggest economic problem,
and I did not doubt that they were a crippling burden on the Polish
budget. Yet in 1970, when the Polish government had made their first
attempt to reduce the subsidies, it had provided the occasion, in the
face of all the apparatus of totalitarian repression, for popular
demonstrations against the régime. Though the demonstrations were
bloodily put down, the government had to make some economic
concessions.

This appeared to be a case of the popular pressures for public
expenditure, with which we are familiar as part of the democratic
process, making themselves felt even in a police state backed by
Soviet tanks – instruments of control not available to Her Majesty's
Treasury. Something similar took place in Egypt in 1977 when there
were riots against increases in food prices, designed to reduce the

subsidy bill, following the Egyptian government's negotiations with the International Monetary Fund.

When the Polish government made a later attempt to cut food subsidies, in 1980, the situation was aggravated by a shortage of food, resulting from the diversion of goods to export markets so as to earn foreign currency and help service the country's massive overseas debts. But though it was price increases which once again triggered off a popular reaction, this time the protest movement soon became directed towards the further objective of some relaxation of the oppressive régime and the establishment of independent trade unions. There was little doubt that a degree of freedom in their lives ranked even higher in the priorities of the Polish people than the issue of prices and subsidies. Those twin issues of food and freedom in Poland continued, astonishingly, to hold the stage throughout the months in which the writing of this book first took place.

Let me revert now to the Ministry of Food in 1947. It was a large Department with about 50,000 staff, some at the various head-quarters offices in London and the rest spread over the country in area and local offices and at the port organisations. Created from scratch during the war, it was by now a well run-in machine. It had some very good people, including some who would not have had a chance to prove their potential but for the war-time expansion of government. There were others who had been promoted far beyond their abilities in this expansion. Even at the most elementary level of routine work, the huge requirement for clerical staff meant that many were engaged on rationing and such like who were not really suitable for any kind of desk work. The Department compensated for the mixed quality of its staff by being well organised and having well-established procedures, all directed to the function of very detailed control of the supply and distribution of foodstuffs. People who talk of a siege economy without experience of one have little idea of the degree of regimentation which was involved in the running of the country during the war and even in the years after the war.

After Alcohol and Yeast Division, and a spell in Home Grown Cereals Division, I moved out to the so-called temporary office buildings at Stanmore, on the edge of London, to be Head of Branch in Animal Feeding Stuffs Division. *Rien ne dure comme le provisoire.* Those single-storeyed, box-like offices outlasted the more solid structure in Portman Square.

To start with I was still graded in my new post as an Assistant Principal, which was a meagrely paid grade, and received a modest allowance on top for being Head of Branch. By the time I was 28 and had served in the Assistant Principal grade for eighteen months, which satisfied the conditions governing the promotion of reconstruction entrants, I became eligible for promotion to Principal and felt well enough off to get married.

My work was concerned not merely with the rationing, licensing and price control of such obviously essential animal feeding stuffs as National Cattle Food No. 1, National Cattle Food No. 2, National Calf Food, Ewe Nuts and so on, but also with more unexpected aspects of control such as the Domestic Poultry Keepers' Scheme, the Commercial Rabbit Breeders' Scheme – what, I wondered, did a commercial rabbit look like? – and National Pigeon Food for the National Pigeon Service. Apart from occasionally signing enormous cheques for purchases of feeding stuffs, I was not involved in the bulk buying, importing and selling of these commodities. This part of the work was run personally by the Director of Animal Feeding Stuffs in Portman Square, assisted by a number of others who, like him, had been seconded to the Ministry from the feeding stuffs trade.

Every so often I took the tube from Stanmore to call on the Director of Animal Feeding Stuffs and discuss my side of the Division's affairs with him. We hit it off quite well and I enjoyed the work. He was a rough diamond who, before coming to the Ministry of Food, had worked his way up from the bottom in the feeding stuffs industry. He had not had much formal education but he knew everything there was to know about buying and selling coarse grains, oil cake and seed and such like. His technical knowledge of these and all the many other products and by-products which can be fed to animals – they are omnivorous creatures – was encyclopaedic. There was one remark of his which stuck in my mind: 'When a commodity is short, people think that it is always going to be short. When a commodity is long, people think that it is always going to be long.' Which meant, of course, how wrong people are to think this.

After a time, in spite of continuing shortages of supply, the minds of the policy makers in Whitehall, very senior and remote people, began to turn to possibilities of decontrol. Harold Wilson, as President of the Board of Trade, was having what was described as a bonfire of controls. But Hugh Gaitskell, as Economic Secretary to the Treasury, was reported to be concerned about the pace of decontrol, and we were told that any proposal to do away with a piece of control had to be cleared with the Treasury.

Although the feeding stuffs trade used to complain about the Labour government's controls, when it came to the point neither they nor the trade men seconded to the Ministry to help operate the controls were enthusiastic for decontrol. They had got used to their chains. In Animal Feeding Stuffs Division we conceived of National Pigeon Food as a prime candidate for decontrol. This feeding stuff was composed of maple peas and maple beans, imported from Australia and New Zealand, which were in scarce supply in Britain during the war, like all imported commodities. Supplies were still short after the war, partly because Australia and New Zealand were hard currency countries. (In those days, when sterling was not fully convertible into other currencies, foreign currencies were divided into a category of soft currencies, which were relatively freely available for imports, and a category of hard currencies, which were scarce and allocated for imports only with great stringency. Maple peas and beans were in the category of hard currency imports.)

During the war National Pigeon Food had been allocated, at controlled prices, only for members of the various homing unions, as they were called, who registered their racing pigeons as available to fly missions for the country in the National Pigeon Service. Whether or not any pigeon had ever been put at physical risk, now, years after the war, these privileged birds remained the only pigeons entitled to this special price controlled food. It seemed to us that the time had come for them to take their chance in competition with other pigeons.

Supported by someone from the Ministry of Food's Finance Division, I presented myself at the Treasury and put the case for decontrol of pigeon food. On the basis that we would not seek a bigger import programme for maple peas and beans, the measure was agreed. This was one of the few times that I had set foot in the Treasury up till then, and I had of course no premonition that I would later spend twenty-seven years of my working life there.

When this measure of decontrol was announced, there was strenuous resistance to it from the homing unions. Concerned at the possibility of higher prices and perhaps even a forced change of diet for their birds, they had 50,000 standard letters of protest printed, so that each of their members could sign one and send it to his Member of Parliament, appealing against this measure of decontrol. The homing unions were particularly strong in coal-mining areas and, as the miners were held to have a good deal of clout, there were those who spoke gravely of this move. Members of Parliament simply sent these printed letters on in bunches to the Minister of Food so that he could let them have replies to send back to their constituents. All the letters were passed on to me so that I could provide the Minister's office with draft replies. The Ministry as a whole were used to dealing with an average of a thousand letters of complaint a day – another statistic much quoted at the time, like the million pounds a day on food subsidies – but to me this avalanche of complaints was new. However, I prepared a standard draft reply to the standard letter of complaint and had the required number of draft replies duplicated. The furore died down and National Pigeon Food became a thing of the past.

At some stage I paid another visit to the Treasury building to be interviewed as a possible recruit for the Economic Section. This organisation was at that time part of the Cabinet Office although it later became part of the Treasury, but even then it was in the same building as the Treasury, as was the whole of the Cabinet Office in those days. My name had been given to Robert Hall, who was then Chief Economic Adviser and head of the Economic Section, by Tony Crosland, who was still a close friend of mine from Oxford days. However, I was not found suitable for the Economic Section. I am sure that this was a good judgment both from their point of view and, as it turned out, from the standpoint of my own interests.

In 1950 the Ministry of Food's Establishment Division suggested me to the regular Treasury as suitable to work there for a couple of years on loan from the Ministry. I was interviewed by the Assistant Secretary who was Deputy Establishment Officer in the Treasury, Richard Griffiths, and by another Assistant Secretary, Ronald Harris, who was head of the Treasury's Establishments Manning Division. This Division dealt with manpower questions relating to the civil service as a whole.

It was explained to me that the Treasury as a whole was divided into a number of parts – Home Finance, Overseas Finance, Supply Divisions, Establishment Divisions, Central Economic Planning Staff and Organisation and Methods – and I was asked about my order of preference. I gave Overseas Finance as my first choice. I had always had a penchant for international affairs, and also I had for some time become rather obsessed with the problem of the balance of payments. The austerity of those years would have been something far worse if the United States, having abruptly discontinued their help under the war-time lend-lease arrangements, had not provided fresh help to our balance of payments through the post-war loan to Britain and then the Marshall Plan for American aid to Europe. I put Supply work, that is, public expenditure, somewhere in the middle and Establishments work last.

The interview went quite well and presently I was sent on loan to the Treasury. Naturally I was put on Establishments work first, and later went on to the public expenditure side. But before I get on to the subject of the Treasury and public expenditure control, let me say something about the earlier history of public expenditure.

THE RISE OF PUBLIC EXPENDITURE

What we now call public expenditure consisted, for the greater part of history, very largely of the cost of wars and armies – in present-day parlance, defence expenditure. It is true that even in early times there were some other items which nowadays would find a place in the appropriate programme in our public expenditure White Papers – public buildings, for instance, such as King Solomon's great temple, which appears to have created a financing problem in its time. Prisons and law courts also go back a long way, and the bread and circuses of ancient Rome were an early example of food subsidies. But throughout early history it was the cost of wars and armies which created the big problems of resources and financing.

Until about the middle of the last century paying for defence still accounted for the larger part of public expenditure in Britain. Before the Napoleonic wars total government expenditure was 11 per cent of gross national product. On the eve of Waterloo it had risen to 29 per cent, an astonishing figure for those times. After the wars with Napoleon the figure fell back again to 11 per cent.

For some time after the Napoleonic era, interest on public debt, greatly swollen by the war, became the largest single item of government expenditure, accounting at one time for almost half of the total, until it was overtaken later in the century by direct military expenditure.[1] The other principal item of public expenditure at that time was poor relief provided by local government.

Defence still has pride of place as Programme 1 in UK public expenditure White Papers, and the size of the defence budget has remained, as we shall see, one of the recurring issues in the post-war period. Even so, the defence budget is now only one among a number of large blocks of expenditure, and not even the largest single block.

Until relatively recent times, a large part of what are now public services, such as education or health care or sponsorship of the arts and sciences, was provided, if at all, only through private charity or patronage or by religious institutions. There are today in Britain followers of Milton Friedman's view that a large part of the public

[1] *The Growth of Public Expenditure in the United Kingdom,* by Alan T. Peacock and Jack Wiseman, Unwin University Books, 1967.

services should revert to voluntary organisations or private enterprise; and this school of thought has made itself heard rather more in
the last few years than before.

However, in the latter part of the nineteenth century the tide was
flowing the other way. A major extension of the role of the state in
Britain had begun. Industrialisation and new technology, and the
enfranchisement of new classes of voters, were part of the process
which at the same time created the demand for new public services
and the resources to make them possible. In the public debates
leading to the Education Act of 1870 Robert Lowe, Chancellor of the
Exchequer in Gladstone's first Ministry, made the famous 'we must
educate our masters' speech. (The Education Acts of 1870 and 1880
introduced universal school education in Britain.)

The process went on in this country until the setback of the great
slump of the 1930s. In some other countries the mass unemployment
of that period led to a further expansion of the role of the state – in the
United States, for instance, to Roosevelt's New Deal, in fascist Italy
to the creation in 1933 of the Istituto per la Ricostruzione Industriale
(IRI) to rescue Italian industries from insolvency, in Nazi Germany to
the corporate state and rearmament. Nothing comparable took place
in Britain in spite of various calls for new forms of government
intervention – from Lloyd George, for instance, who called for a New
Deal of our own, and Oswald Mosley, who subsequently founded his
own fascist party. There were, it is true, the beginnings of regional
policy in measures to help what were then called the derelict areas,
including financial help for production in those areas which would be
used in schemes to help the colonies. But the principal instrument of
government support for British industry was neither subsidisation nor
import controls, such as have been adopted since the second world
war, but tariff protection.

The main response to the great slump prescribed by pre-Keynesian
economic policy was to cut salaries and government expenditure. This
was regarded as an inevitable condition for raising a foreign loan, and
led to the break-up of the Labour government of the day and its
replacement by a National Government – a piece of history which
came irresistibly to mind when Mr Callaghan's Labour government
was so divided over the need for public expenditure cuts as a
prerequisite for a loan from the International Monetary Fund in 1976.
However, this time the government held together in the end.

The tables in Peacock and Wiseman show that between 1928 and
1933 government expenditure was reduced by about 2½ per cent in
money terms, from £1094 million to £1066 million, in spite of a large

increase in payments to the unemployed.[2] It is ironical that, because of the fall in prices brought about by the slump, in constant price terms these reduced money figures produce an increase of about 10 per cent, and government expenditure rose as a proportion of GDP from 24.2 per cent to 25.9 per cent over that five-year period. Here again history has come close to repeating itself, because the Conservative government elected in 1979 faced the difficulty of reducing public expenditure as a proportion of GDP in a slump when GDP was falling and social security benefits were increasing; the difference this time was that prices were rising in spite of the slump.

In the slump of the 1930s, it took rearmament, in response to the threat from Nazi Germany, to restore the rising trend in government expenditure in Britain in absolute terms and not merely as a proportion of GDP. This helped to reduce unemployment, but it took the war itself to produce full employment.

In the literature on the subject there is some discussion why, in modern times, public expenditure in the industrialised countries has grown not merely in line with national wealth but as a percentage of it. Peacock and Wiseman comment that the two world wars had a ratchet effect on the growth of public expenditure; people became accustomed to an enlarged role for the state and changed their ideas about the limits of taxable capacity. Though this is true enough, the change in attitudes between the thirties and forties went deeper than that, I think. There was a profound feeling that, after the great common effort in fighting the war, the country could not go back to the kind of society which it had had in the thirties. The concepts of full employment and the welfare state were a reaction against the miseries of the slump years.

That plans for the post-war welfare state were being drawn up during the war, while Britain was a beleaguered country, reflected a confidence in the future which no longer exists in Britain. I recall that, when the Beveridge Report on a post-war scheme of social insurance was issued in a White Paper in November 1942 (Cmnd. 6404), I was a junior officer in the army in Egypt and learned about the Beveridge plan from a pamphlet issued by the Army Bureau of Current Affairs. It fell to me, as the unit's ABCA officer, to give a talk about the scheme, knowing no more about it than was in the pamphlet, to the men in the unit sitting around in the hot desert sun and listening attentively. Later, when the Education Act to introduce universal

---

[2] The figures of unemployment benefit are to be found in the Beveridge Report on Social Insurance, Appendix B, Table XVIII.

secondary education after the war was passed in 1944, the war was still a long way from being won.

The White Paper on *Employment Policy* (Cmnd. 6527, presented to Parliament by the Minister of Reconstruction in May 1944), with its historic opening statement that 'the Government accept as one of their primary aims and responsibilities the maintenance of a high and stable level of employment after the war', was an even more remarkable landmark.

Only a few years earlier the Keynesian palace revolution which captured the Treasury during the war would have seemed unthinkable. As it was, Keynesian economics prevailed from that time on, and had a profound effect on public expenditure policies, until the intellectual counter-revolution more than thirty years later, during their time out of office, among the Conservative economic policy makers who later came into power in 1979. At this point the commitment to full employment lapsed, and public expenditure ceased to be treated as a principal instrument for securing it.

But in the meanwhile the commitment to a high and stable level of employment had become progressively more difficult to honour. It should be said that the economists who headed the Economic Section of the Cabinet Office, and who produced the early drafts of the 1944 White Paper before handing it over to the Treasury, probably had at the back of their minds a possible unemployment rate of 5 to 6 per cent rather than the 2 per cent which later came to be thought of as representing full employment. (Keynes himself was not in the Economic Section but in the Treasury which, curiously, did not involve him in the preparation of the White Paper which was the embodiment of his doctrine. Beveridge, who had produced a sort of freelance report on full employment, with a major input from Nicki Kaldor, was outside Whitehall and did not manage to get into the White Paper act.) If that was their thinking, they underestimated the employment levels which were to be achieved in the 1950s and 1960s. But from our present perspective, when those levels are a thing of the past and we would be glad to get unemployment down to even 5 or 6 per cent, one of the interesting things about the 1944 White Paper is the confidence underlying the assumption that the required conditions for success, including wage and price stability, would exist; that, given international economic stability, Britain would be competitive enough to take advantage of it; and that governments would be able, through the limited instruments envisaged in the White Paper (essentially public works programmes), to secure a high and stable level of employment. No government could reassert that White Paper commitment with any confidence now.

TREASURY ESTABLISHMENTS

The Treasury, in contrast to the Ministry of Food, was a small Department with a high proportion of good graduates and not much in the way of organisation. Later on, that part of the Treasury which dealt with civil service matters was hived off to form the nucleus of a separate Civil Service Department, after which there were no more than a thousand or so staff in the Treasury, including secretaries, messengers and so on. In 1950, when the Establishments side of the Treasury was still responsible for civil service numbers and pay and such like, it would have had a few hundred more than that.

I was assigned to a Principal post in one of these Establishment Divisions. It was located, not in the main Treasury building by Parliament Square, but in what was then called the Treasury Old Building, overlooking Downing Street on one side and Whitehall on another. It was a rambling place of staircases and passages, one of which led into No. 10 Downing Street. My own office was an old-fashioned, well-proportioned room, reputed once to have been Nell Gwynn's bedroom. Some years later, the interior of the Treasury Old Building was reconstructed, behind the same facade, to become the new home of the Cabinet Office.

In Departmental Establishments Division One – ED1 for short – I found myself dealing with the staff matters of a group of Departments of which the largest were the Ministry of Agriculture, the Forestry Commission and the Ordnance Survey, and the smallest was the Development Commission, with a complement of twenty-one. I negotiated with their Establishment Officers on such matters as staff numbers, gradings and pay claims for Departmental classes of staff such as vets, foresters and cartographic draughtsmen.

This was in the period following the devaluation of the pound, during the Chancellorship of Stafford Cripps. A rigid pay freeze was in force so that the improved competitiveness of our exports, which the devaluation was meant to bring about, should not be eroded through higher wage costs. The Treasury had a standard reply to civil service wage claims – 'In the words of the Chancellor, nothing, literally nothing.'

The pace of events on the Establishments side of the Treasury was slow. Attitudes towards the lot of the civil service were cautious and niggardly. As well as people like myself, doing a stint on this work in the course of a career mostly spent on other things, the Establishment Divisions had a higher proportion than the rest of the Treasury of Higher Executive Officers, Senior Executive Officers and Principals who had earned class-to-class promotion from the executive grades. These provided a more permanent corps of staff versed in Establishments work, who were custodians of the book of rules called Estacode. Negotiations with the civil service trade unions loomed large. There was no room in this work for unorthodoxy or flexibility. Any concession to one individual or group would evoke a demand from the staff side for a similar concession to everyone. Consistency was all. The smallest inconsistency would produce embarrassment and repercussions. Kant's injunction – act so that the maxim of thy action may be universalised – came into its own.

Though I did not care for the pedestrian character of Establishments work, and was irked by its excessive slowness, I took naturally to the austere Treasury ethos towards the use of public money. This Treasury attitude towards the civil service of which it was itself a part was well described as a hair shirt policy. Once during this time, when I won a prize of £10 in a competition run by the *Observer* for an essay on the subject of Eyes, the Forestry Commission's Establishment Officer commented bitterly that it should have been Noes.

The expenditure of government Departments on matters other than staff, and the policies which gave rise to this expenditure, were dealt with by a different set of Treasury divisions called Supply Divisions,[3] a term I shall explain later on. There was occasional *ad hoc* contact between the two sides of the Treasury. I would, for instance, ask the Supply side whether a Department's proposals on staff numbers corresponded to what was happening on the policy front. But for the most part we worked in separate, fairly watertight compartments. Although I was in the Treasury, which was responsible for the management of the economy, I was no better informed than the man in the street about what was happening in the fields of financial and economic policy.

Each year, in the months before the Budget, a basic function of Treasury Principals and their Executive Officers, in both the Supply Divisions and the Establishment Divisions, was to scrutinise the Estimates of the Departments with which they dealt and recommend

[3] As an exception to this split of the work, there were two 'mixed Divisions', one called Law and Order, the other called Imperial and Foreign, which dealt with both Supply expenditure and the Establishment matters of, respectively, the Home Office and the Foreign Office, Colonial Office and Commonwealth Relations Office.

them for approval as the basis for the expenditure of those Departments in the coming financial year. At this time of year an Estimates Circular used to be issued, in pretty well identical terms each time, reiterating the traditional procedure to be followed and calling for economy and stringency in the preparation of Estimates. Each Treasury Principal was left to apply this injunction according to his own good sense and judgment and his knowledge of his spending Departments, but without any wider frame of reference. I would scrutinise the Establishment Subheads of an Estimate in isolation from even the other expenditure Subheads of the same Estimate, which were dealt with by the Supply Division concerned. The figures recommended by the various Principals would be sent, as they still are, to another Treasury Principal in the post of Estimates Clerk, who put them all together to form the expenditure side of the Budget arithmetic. Principals generally knew nothing of the total arithmetic. I shall have more to say about this system in a later chapter.

Every Friday there was a joint meeting of the Treasury Establishment Divisions attended by the Principals and equivalent grades and by the Assistant Secretaries who headed these Divisions. The two Under Secretaries in charge of all the Establishments work presided. These meetings talked about pay policy, the size of the civil service and such like. We did not have joint meetings with the Supply Divisions.

In those days the Treasury grade above Under Secretary was Third Secretary, now restyled Deputy Secretary. All the Third Secretaries got knighthoods then, though later on you had to become a Permanent Secretary to get a knighthood. I cannot remember even setting eyes on a Treasury knight during my time on the Establishments side, apart from one occasion when the Permanent Secretary to the Treasury, Sir Edward Bridges, had myself and a couple of other new recruits to tea.

Apart from my dealings with the Ministry of Agriculture and the rest, I was also involved in a certain amount of coordinating work on the appointments and pay of the chairmen and Board members of the nationalised industries which had come into public ownership since the war. This work included a new series of annual White Papers on Public Boards of a Commercial Character. Thirty years later, when I carried out a special review of public bodies, as my last assignment in the civil service, I found this series of White Papers still running.

Another addition to my little empire was the newly created Ministry of Materials. This was set up because of the shortages of essential minerals and other materials at the time of the war in Korea, when we supported the United States in resisting the invasion of non-communist South Korea by the communist régime in North Korea and embarked on a rearmament programme of our own. There was a belief, exemplified by an American document called the Paley Report, that the world was in for a long period of shortages of essential materials. This was a classic example of people thinking that, because a commodity is short, it will always be short. In fact the shortages turned before long to surpluses. The stockpiles which the Ministry of Materials had just built up were disposed of – at a loss, I should imagine. The Ministry of Materials itself was dissolved.

Apart from this matter of the staffing of the Ministry of Materials, I had no involvement in the problems arising from the Korean war, and no idea of the soul-searching which must have been going on elsewhere in the Treasury about the effect which rearmament was going to have on the Budget and the economy. It was a good many years later, when I was deeply involved in the defence budget and the defence review, that I saw this situation in perspective.

One of the achievements of the post-war Labour government had been the rapid reconversion of the economy to a peace-time footing. I imagine that previous planning under the war-time coalition government also had something to do with this. In 1946–47 defence expenditure was 16.2 per cent of GDP. By the following year it was less than half this percentage, and by 1949–50 not much more than a third. But in 1950–51, when the process of beating swords into plough-shares had been reversed, the figure started to rise year by year, reaching a new peak of 8.7 per cent in 1952–53. The diversion of physical resources to military use probably achieved its maximum effect somewhat in advance of that. (The full series of figures of defence expenditure as a percentage of GDP at market prices is set out in table 1.1. Higher percentages result if GDP is reckoned at factor cost.)

Britain had emerged from the war as the leading country in Europe and the second strongest military power in the Western world. But we had suffered enormous losses of shipping and destruction of homes. We had sold off overseas assets to pay for imports before American war-time lend-lease began, and we had accumulated huge debts in the form of the sterling holdings of countries such as India and Egypt, where our armies had been during the war. Production had been diverted from exports, and civilian standards of living had been reduced, in order to fight the war. With the war won, now was the time to rebuild a peace-time economy, regain export markets and improve standards of living.

Table 1.1: Defence expenditure as a percentage of
GDP, 1946–47 to 1979–80

	% GDP at market prices		% GDP at market prices
1946–47	16.2	1966–67	5.6
1947–48	7.8	1967–68	5.4
1948–49	6.3	1968–69	5.1
1949–50	5.8	1969–70	4.8
1950–51	6.1	1970–71	4.8
1951–52	7.6	1971–72	4.8
1952–53	8.7	1972–73	4.7
1953–54	7.9	1973–74	4.7
1954–55	7.9	1974–75	4.7
1955–56	7.2	1975–76	4.8
1956–57	7.2	1976–77	4.8
1957–58	6.5	1977–78	4.6
1958–59	6.4	1978–79	4.5
1959–60	6.1	1979–80	4.6
1960–61	6.2	1980–81	4.8
1961–62	6.0	1981–82	4.9
1962–63	6.0	1982–83	5.1
1963–64	5.9	1983–84	5.3
1964–65	5.9	(planned)	
1965–66	5.9		

When we consider that in 1980 there was still a tug-of-war between the Treasury and the Ministry of Defence over a defence budget accounting for around 4½ per cent of GDP, we can see what a drastic reverse it was for our post-war recovery when defence expenditure was raised to nearly twice that percentage of a much smaller GDP. The situation was quite different from the 1930s, when rearmament took up part of the slack in the economy. Now there was no slack to take up. The Korean war rearmament programme ran clean counter to the devaluation strategy of steering resources into the balance of payments. The political and strategic case for rearmament must have seemed overwhelming at the time to Hugh Gaitskell, who had succeeded Stafford Cripps as Chancellor of the Exchequer. In the event, because of the time-lags involved, which are the bugbear of all economic planning and management, by the time that rearmament came on stream it was too late to make any difference to the Korean war, and it was more or less irrelevant to the wider East–West confrontation.

After three years on Establishments work I was reassigned to a Principal post in a Supply Division. Meanwhile Labour had lost the 1951 general election and Clement Attlee's government, the first Labour administration with a working majority in Parliament, had fallen. During their time in office, all but one of the major themes had been sounded which were to recur again and again under successive governments. Some of these I have already mentioned – sterling and the balance of payments, public ownership, incomes policy and, of course, public expenditure and the defence budget.

Two other recurring issues deserve special mention. One is the problem of regional policy and how to redress the imbalance between the growth areas in the South and the Midlands, and the declining areas of high unemployment in the North and in Scotland, Wales and Northern Ireland. There were at that time high hopes for the policy of taking work to the workers in development areas, or development districts as they were once called, through building industrial estates and advance factories and giving incentives to employers to go there. These financial incentives were still relatively modest compared to the increased financial support which was to be given by later governments as the problems got worse rather than better.

And then there was the problem of industrial productivity. Ministers in subsequent governments, each in their turn, appeared almost to believe that they were the first to identify this basic weakness of the British economy and that they had hit on novel remedies for it. But the disparity, in some cases as much as 100 per cent, between productivity in British and in American industry was established by Anglo-US productivity teams in those early post-war years; and various measures were taken, and a variety of bodies set up, to help in putting this right. Among these measures was legislation to enable Development Councils to be created to deal with the problems of individual industries. The left criticised the government for not setting up enough of these councils, but those which were established were not great successes and disappeared in due course. The last of them, the Furniture Development Council, was finally wound up in 1980 as a result of the review of public bodies in which I was then involved.

The one great issue which had not yet come to the fore in Britain was the question of Europe. On the Continent the ideas had already been sown which were to lead to the European Economic Community, but Britain did not respond to them. Americans such as General Eisenhower were urging the Europeans to become a United States of Europe. But in the early post-war years an economic marriage with, say, a country such as Germany, even more devastated by the war than Britain, would have had little economic attraction for the British. And politically Whitehall gave a higher priority to the Commonwealth and to the special relationship with the United States than to Europe. In any event, the EEC had not yet emerged as a concrete proposition on which we had to take a decision. When, in 1950, the French launched the more limited scheme for a European Coal and Steel Community, the British government did not grasp its significance, and were preoccupied with their mounting problems on other fronts, and so the ECSC went ahead without us.

Some of the measures carried out by the Attlee government, such as the new social security scheme and the new secondary school system, gave effect tó planning which had taken place under the war-time coalition government. But many of the others added up to a distinctively Labour programme. They included the repeal of the Trade Disputes Act of 1926 which, among other things, had outlawed general strikes, the creation of the National Health Service, and the nationalisation of the Bank of England, of the coal, gas and electricity supply industries, of the railways and a large part of road haulage, and above all of the iron and steel industry. This measure was opposed with particular bitterness by the Opposition but was seen on the Labour side as the capture, in Aneurin Bevan's words, of 'the commanding heights of the economy' India and Pakistan were given their independence, at the cost of a great deal of bloodshed between them, and the process of decolonisation in Africa was started.

This programme was translated into administrative action by the civil service, carrying out its role of serving the elected government of the day. The notion had at one time gained some currency that the higher civil service, educated mainly outside the state school system, with a high proportion of Oxford and Cambridge graduates, and containing in its upper reaches hardly anyone of working-class background, would prove uncooperative or worse in carrying out a radical Labour programme of this kind. The experience of the post-war Labour government should have been evidence enough to the contrary.

Throughout these years the country had full or over-full employment. Money was kept cheap; those lucky enough to get local authority mortgages paid a fixed interest rate of 2 per cent. Although there was persistent inflation in the old-fashioned sense of too much money chasing too few goods, we did not yet have cost-push inflation driving wage and price increases up to the levels of the 1960s and 1970s. But the period ended, as it had begun, as a time of austerity in personal living standards, and some public sector programmes were still starved of funds. Life was bound still to be difficult because of continuing physical shortages and the time needed to make good the losses of the war; but the budgetary problem would have been eased if the food subsidies had been phased out, and the period might have ended on a quite different note but for the Korean war which caused the conversion of the economy to a peace-time basis to be put into reverse.

2

Thirteen Tory Years

The Supply Division to which I was posted was called TI, standing for Trade and Industry. I shared an office with another Principal in the main Treasury building. The Assistant Secretary in charge of the Division was Frank Figgures, who reminded me irresistibly, in physical appearance and in the ebullience of his style, of the well-known actor Robert Morley. Later in his career he went to the European Free Trade Area as its Secretary General, then returned to the Treasury and became Second Permanent Secretary in charge of the Finance side. He left the Treasury again, when Mr Heath was Prime Minister, to become Director General of the National Economic Development Office, and later still chairman of the short-lived Pay Board. Frank Figgures worked and thought quickly, as I am said to do, and liked to conduct business to a large extent through meetings and conversations rather than on paper. In this way we got through a lot of work, without putting in excessively long hours. Not everyone and everything on the Supply side moved as quickly as this, but it was nevertheless a great change for the better after my previous post.

My main spending Departments were the Board of Trade, the Ministry of Transport and the Ministry of Fuel and Power, together with their nationalised industries. The denationalisation of the iron and steel industry and of road haulage was also part of this work.

In the short period that they had been nationalised, the individual steel companies had not yet lost their separate identities. Now their shares were transferred from the Iron and Steel Corporation, which had been set up by the Labour government, to a new Iron and Steel Holding and Realisation Agency, which had the job of selling the

shares back to the public. The selling price and the other arrangements for each issue had to be approved by the Treasury. The first
shares sold were those of the United Steel Company. Others such as
the Lancashire Steel Company and Stewarts and Lloyds followed. I
played no part in the policy decisions but I became quite expert in the
administrative mechanics of these operations.

The Labour Party would of course have opposed the denationalisation of the steel industry anyway, but two features of the exercise
aroused particular objections. First, only the ordinary shares, which
gave control, were sold at the outset. The Agency retained the prior
charge securities – that is, the debentures and preference shares – for
later disposal, which never in fact took place. Thus it could be argued
that the public purse was still providing a large part of the industry's
capital, while the private investor was enabled to buy control cheaply.
Second, the government had set up a parallel body to the Agency
called the Iron and Steel Board, with responsibility for such things as
price control, and also with power to lend public funds to the denationalised companies. There was an outcry on the Labour side
about a large loan to a denationalised company called Colvilles.

It was made part of Labour's programme that the steel industry
should be re-nationalised when they regained power. After their
success in a by-election at, I believe, North Derby, which was
regarded as a pointer for the next general election, selling the shares
of the companies still in the Agency's hands became harder, while
new capital investment in the denationalised companies languished.

This was the first of what was to become a spiralling series of
reversals and counter-reversals by successive governments of their
predecessors' policies. The civil servants, of course, worked out the
detailed measures and prepared the legislation with equal competence in each case.

But at that time, notwithstanding denationalisation of steel and
road haulage, there was no wholesale reversal of the Labour government's measures. With R. A. Butler replacing Hugh Gaitskell as
Chancellor of the Exchequer, it was the period of Butskellite consensus. The Board of Trade's programmes for the development
districts, which were part of my sphere of interest, were not cut back.
Within a few years – though I had by then moved on to another
Division – they were in fact stepped up, and a new tax incentive was
introduced for investment in these areas, in the form of free depreciation which enabled companies to charge the whole of the capital
expenditure, and not merely a single year's depreciation, against tax
in the year that the money was spent. This was a response to a

temporary increase in unemployment in the country as a whole, which always produces a disproportionate increase in the outlying regions, but even so the numbers of unemployed were small compared to the unemployment figures which were to come in the 1970s.

Food subsidies were phased out, along with food rationing, but this, together with the unwinding of the rearmament programme, enabled some other programmes to be expanded. Harold Macmillan, who was at that time Minister for Housing and Local Government, and who before the election had set a target of 300,000 new homes to be built in a year, presided over the achievement of that figure, taking council houses and owner-occupied houses together.

One of the fields of expenditure in my little province was the road programme, which consisted at that time solely of maintenance and minor improvements, because not a single mile of new road was built for ten years after the war. The motoring and road haulage associations plied us with documentation of the appalling congestion which was developing on the roads as the number of vehicles grew, but Mr Butler and his Financial Secretary, John Boyd-Carpenter, did not believe that the time had yet come for a major programme of road construction. However, the situation changed when Boyd-Carpenter moved from the Treasury to become Minister of Transport. His conversion may well have struck the Chancellor as a classic case of gamekeeper turned poacher.

There was a similar backlog as regards hospitals, until a major programme of hospital-building was put in hand during the 1950s. These were the first new hospitals built for the National Health Service, which the Conservatives kept in being although they had opposed its introduction.

So a considerable degree of *de facto* consensus on full employment and the welfare state coexisted with confrontation on such issues as public ownership and the distribution of wealth. And even in the matter of denationalisation the Conservative government did not go the whole hog and attempt to sell off any of the newly nationalised industries apart from steel and road haulage. In fact, after part of the nationalised road haulage fleet had been sold back to the private sector, and the rest was proving rather difficult to sell, I was rather gratified when Reginald Maudling, who was at that time Economic Secretary to the Treasury, but whom I had never met, having read a minute of mine in which I wondered whether the government might settle for this mixture of public and private ownership, wrote to the Minister of Transport to put this thought to him. It was an agreeable surprise to find that the minutes which one sent up the chain of command to remote superiors might actually be read and taken notice of, even if on relatively minor matters.

This reaction on Maudling's part was characteristic of his intellectual flexibility and lack of dogma. Later on he came to have the reputation of being a lazy Minister, but I think that this misconstrued his low threshold of boredom with formal proceedings, dull meetings and routine thinking. He was more responsive to departures from the conventional wisdom, even if the ideas came from a junior official, than most senior officials were. I found it sad that, towards the end of his career, his reputation suffered from events in which he was involved while out of office.

Along with the remaining nationalised industries, the Conservatives inherited the problems of relationships and control vis-à-vis the public sector of industry, which were still rather novel then but which have remained with us to this day. At that time the nationalised industries used to raise investment capital from the market by issuing stock with a Treasury guarantee. A limit on the total amount of borrowings which each industry could raise, and which the Treasury could guarantee, was specified in an Act of Parliament. When this limit was reached, the Minister concerned with the industry in question had to put a further Bill to Parliament in order to get increased borrowing and guarantee powers. These pieces of legislation were liable to get Conservative Ministers into trouble with their own supporters, who were unreconciled anyway to the continued existence of the nationalised industries and objected in particular to giving Parliamentary approval for guarantees to finance expenditure over which Parliament had no control.

After one debate on a borrowing powers Bill, in which the Conservative backbenchers had been particularly rebellious, I remember being involved in a little council of war in the House of Commons in the office of Aubrey Jones, then Minister for Fuel and Power, together with Edward Boyle, who had by now taken over as Economic Secretary to the Treasury – an exceptionally fair-minded man, who had endeared himself to economic advisers in the Treasury by taking an interest in their work not often found in Ministers, but whose non-partisan approach was not much appreciated by the Conservative backbenchers. The meeting was joined by R. A. Butler, who was now Leader of the House of Commons, and Edward Heath, at that time a government Whip, and ways of handling the criticisms from their supporters were discussed.

One subsequent development was that Harold Macmillan, who had succeeded Butler as Chancellor of the Exchequer, was deputed to talk to a private meeting of the Conservative backbenchers in a committee room in the House of Commons. Apart from hearing him speak some years earlier at a debate in the Oxford Union, the only time I had ever set eyes on Macmillan was at an *ad hoc* meeting of Ministers about a proposal for underground car parks in one of the London squares, to which I went with John Boyd-Carpenter. This had been during Macmillan's time as Minister for Housing and Local Government, a Departmental Minister like the others at the meeting, but I was struck by the way they deferred to him even then.

For the meeting with his party rebels, I wrote him a brief, explaining that the backbenchers seemed to me to want to apply the procedures for controlling Vote expenditure of Departments to the capital expenditure of the nationalised industries, which was not Voted money and to which these procedures could not be applied. I learned afterwards that he had informed the meeting that he held in his hand a learned technical document which he threatened to read out if necessary. The rebellion was quelled, for the time being at any rate, without the need for that, but there was continuing dissatisfaction at the fact that the nationalised industries were not effectively accountable to Parliament. The eventual creation of the Select Committee on the Nationalised Industries was a partial response to this disquiet.

Some time after this an edict came from Home Finance Division (which – under the tutelage of the Bank of England – played a central role in the arrangements for the borrowings of the nationalised industries) that the system of stock issues by the industries with Treasury guarantee was to be discontinued. Instead, the Treasury would raise all the money itself and on-lend it to the nationalised industries. The reason for this was that it would improve the management of the capital markets by the Bank of England, which, under the old arrangements, had the task of marshalling the queue of public bodies awaiting access to the London market. Also the government could borrow at a fractionally cheaper rate of interest than the nationalised industries could, even with a Treasury guarantee.

The new system came into effect in 1956. The government loans provided in this way to the nationalised industries were not part of Supply expenditure but were, in the parlance of the times, a 'below-the-line' item. The distinction, to oversimplify somewhat, is this. When Departments spend taxpayers' money on providing services to the public, traditionally known as Supply Services, they draw the money from the Consolidated Fund; to get authority for this, Estimates for the expenditure have to be approved, first by the Treasury, and then by Parliament under the procedures for 'voting Supply'. But capital expenditure which the government finances by borrowing is channelled through what is today called the National Loans Fund, and comes under looser Parliamentary control. Readers interested in more detail should turn to 'The Mechanics of Public Expenditure', now relegated to Appendix III so as not to hold up the narrative.

OVERSEAS FINANCE: SUEZ

In 1956, I moved again, this time to a Principal post on the Overseas Finance side of the Treasury, thus achieving my original preference – rather like the biblical character who worked seven years for his prospective father-in-law in order to win the hand of his beautiful daughter, only to find himself fobbed off with her plain sister, after which he worked a further seven-year stint before finally marrying the beautiful daughter. My stints had been three years on Establishments and three years on Supply, and during this time the loan arrangement under which I first went to the Treasury was converted to a permanent posting. Thus, when the rump of the Ministry of Food was absorbed by the Ministry of Agriculture, Fisheries and Food, I did not go into MAFF, as the new joint Department was known for short, but stayed in the Treasury.

My new Division was called Overseas Finance General (OFG). The Assistant Secretary in charge of the division was Douglas Allen, who was eventually to succeed William Armstrong, first as Permanent Secretary of the Treasury and then as Head of the Civil Service. Both of them, fortunately, appear to have taken a rather better view of me than did most of the Treasury top brass of that time. The other Principal in OFG was Douglas Wass, who was in due course to succeed Douglas Allen as Permanent Secretary of the Treasury, so there was a lot of Permanent Secretary potential in that Division.

Our external financial policies in those days were dominated by two relationships – with the United States and with the Commonwealth, especially with those Commonwealth countries which were part of the sterling area. Sterling was still, after the dollar, the world's principal reserve currency and perhaps even more widely used than the dollar in international trade. But we did not now have the industrial and economic strength, after the war-time depletion of our resources, or the gold and foreign currency reserves to go with this role. The management and defence of sterling, honouring the accumulated claims against it out of inadequate resources, the avoidance of a massive running down of sterling holdings or a sudden switch out of sterling into gold or other currencies – these were the constant and overriding preoccupations of the Treasury at top level. We relied heavily on the help and cooperation of the United States to enable us to cope at all with this besetting problem.

The work of OFG was concerned largely with the two new international bodies set up as a result of the Bretton Woods conference: the International Monetary Fund, otherwise known as the IMF or simply the Fund, and the International Bank for Reconstruction and Development, also known as the IBRD or the World Bank or simply the Bank. The two Bretton Woods institutions together were always referred to as the Bank and the Fund, though in other contexts the Bank, *tout court,* meant the Bank of England, with which, like the rest of the Finance side of the Treasury, OFG was very much involved. Our other concerns included the General Agreement on Tariffs and Trade; in this case, since the United States had not ratified the proposal to establish an International Trade Organisation, the GATT was used as a term to denote not merely the international agreement on trade but also the *de facto* international organisation which came into being to operate it. Finally, OFG was the Division concerned with relations with the United States and Canada.

Since the war had not been fought on American soil, the United States and Canada had emerged from it with expanded industries and undepleted resources. Canada, like the United States, though on a much smaller scale, was in a position to extend help to others, and for a time it loomed larger on our economic horizons, and played a somewhat bigger role in international affairs, than it does now. At the end of the war, when American war-time lend-lease was abruptly cut off, along with the American loan of over $4 billion which we negotiated to tide us over, we secured an interest-free loan from Canada – now, incidentally, long since paid off.

The American loan to the United Kingdom was used up more quickly than had been intended, but Western Europe as a whole got relief from the dollar shortage through Marshall Aid. The Organisation for European Economic Cooperation (OEEC) was set up with its headquarters at the Chateau de la Muette in Paris to administer the Marshall Plan. During this period the role of the IMF was largely in abeyance so far as concerns short-term balance of payments support to member countries, since the United States, which would have had to put the IMF in funds for this purpose, had been providing dollars to the rest of the world by direct aid. But by the time I went on to the Overseas Finance side this situation was changing and the IMF was becoming of increasing importance as a medium for balance of payments support.

The United Kingdom had the second biggest quota in the IMF and the second biggest subscription to the International Bank, the United States having by far the leading position in both. The UK therefore had the second largest voting power in the Bank and the Fund. This reflected our historical position in world trade and finance, not our current economic and financial strength. We were potential drawers of dollars and other currencies from the Fund, rather than potential suppliers of sterling to other member countries needing to draw it. In the International Bank, whose task, now that the reconstruction phase in Europe was over, was to channel long-term development capital to member countries, we had paid in 2 per cent of our subscription in gold or dollars, as all member countries were required to do, but were releasing our 18 per cent 'national currency subscription' for use by the Bank only in dribs and drabs, and only for lending to sterling Commonwealth countries who spent our contribution largely on purchases from the United Kingdom. Only the United States, Canada and Venezuela had paid over this 18 per cent of their subscription at the beginning. Nobody was actually required to pay up the remaining 80 per cent of subscriptions, which constituted uncalled capital, on the strength of which the Bank could make bond issues to raise capital from world markets to finance its operations.

It was against this financial background that the Anglo-French invasion of Egypt burst upon a shocked world. This was designed finally to resolve the crisis which had existed for some months after Egypt nationalised the Suez Canal, owned by British and French interests. While still in TI Division I had been very peripherally involved in that situation. Since the Ministry of Transport was one of my spending Departments, I had to give Treasury clearance for their scheme for war risk insurance to enable British shipping to go on operating in areas which might be affected if the Suez crisis went wrong. But this in itself implied only that hostilities of some kind were feared as a possibility, not that they were being actively planned. It was only by accident, at an inter-Divisional meeting which I attended, that I learned, through an indiscreet reference by a certain Assistant Secretary to some other contingency plans, that an occupation of the Canal Zone was among the possibilities contemplated. Seeing my shocked reaction, the Under Secretary who was chairing the meeting hastily stifled that part of the discussion.

On the day that the news of the Suez operation broke, I was

involved with a team of International Bank people who were in London to negotiate a Bank loan to one of our colonies. Even though this territory was on its way to becoming independent, the United Kingdom had to guarantee the loan and was responsible for the negotiations. The shocked disbelief of the Bank people was typical of the general reaction to the invasion. Everyone I knew of in Whitehall, even those who had been upset by Egypt's seizure of the canal, was against the Anglo-French action – not necessarily or not solely on grounds of political morality, but because of the damage done to our relationships with America, the damage to the Commonwealth and the damage to sterling. At the extreme, if the Suez policy had not been reversed, it seemed to us that the Commonwealth and the sterling area could have broken up. There were many, however, who thought the military action in Suez wrong in terms other than of expediency. The deceit involved in the pretence that the Anglo-French intervention was meant to keep the Israelis and the Egyptians apart, when there had obviously been collusion with Israel to bring about a situation in which this excuse could be used, was particularly hard to stomach.

If you are a career civil servant in a system such as ours, it is in the nature of the work that you will be involved in policies or measures which you do not necessarily support. But the Suez policy was, I think, quite exceptional in British post-war administration in terms not merely of the differences of views and of value judgments involved, which are to be expected in the management of affairs, but of the problems of conscience which it raised. This was the only occasion in my time in the government service when I had to reflect how the British civil service, with its commitment to work for the government of the day, irrespective of its policies, differed from officials in Hitler's Germany who had helped to carry out the Nazi atrocities.

The developments which followed demonstrated the differences between the two situations. One of these events was the resignation of Edward Boyle from his post as a Treasury Minister, because of his disapproval of the Suez invasion. Though opposition to the policy within the Conservative ranks was limited, the hostility to it from the other parties and from informed opinion generally was intense. That is to say, even the Suez situation did not invalidate the concept of a civil service working for the government of the day on the basis that, if its policies were wrong, it was for the democratic process to change either the government or its policies.

It was perhaps not so much this domestic process as the external pressures which caused the Suez policy to be reversed. When Sir

Anthony Eden resigned as Prime Minister because of ill health, his colleagues chose Harold Macmillan, a hawk on the Suez issue, for the succession, rather than the dove-ish Butler. In the event, it was Macmillan who led the camouflaged retreat from Suez while professing not to do so.

As part of the process of restoring normal relations with Egypt, Sir Denis Rickett, a Third Secretary on the Overseas Finance side, flew back and forth negotiating terms for the unblocking of Egypt's sterling balances which had been blocked in response to the nationalisation of the canal. So we had the rather unusual phenomenon of a Treasury knight recurrently in the news. After the dust had settled, Edward Boyle was restored to office as Parliamentary Secretary at the Ministry of Education.

The term 'U-turn' was not yet in vogue at that time, but this was a reversal of external policy *par excellence* deserving of that tag. It was a turning point in the recognition of the passing of Britain's ability to play independently – or even, in this case, in conjunction with the French – the role of an imperial power on the world stage. Like all major U-turns, this volte-face was forced on the government by the pressures of the real world and not by some civil service conspiracy of the kind that current mythology holds responsible for more recent U-turns. Whether officials liked the Suez policy or not, it was not they who frustrated it; and when the policy had to be abandoned, they worked to make good the damage.

As soon as the British government had agreed to pull out of Suez, the Americans were ready to give their help, previously withheld, in putting together a package of financial measures to support sterling. For one thing, they did not want to see the collapse of sterling as a reserve currency, leaving the dollar to bear the whole weight of the reserve currency role. Support through the IMF was the centrepiece of the package. It also included a dollar line of credit from Eximbank to be drawn down on the strength of dollar securities which we still held in the government's portfolio. These were the balance of the much larger quantity of foreign securities once held by private individuals in Britain, but requisitioned by the government during the war and mostly sold off in America so as to obtain dollars to pay for essential supplies. We did not draw on the line of credit immediately, but did so later and pledged securities *pro rata* from the portfolio.

At some stage Eugene Black, the American President of the International Bank, held out the possibility of a further dollar loan which, though its attraction for us would be the further support for our balance of payments, would be linked by the Bank to the financing of our nuclear power programme, in which at that time we led the world, and from which the Bank hoped to get experience of value to them in making loans to nuclear power projects in other countries. These negotiations failed, as was the case with an earlier attempt to negotiate a Bank loan for the Colonial Development Corporation and a subsequent negotiation on a proposed International Bank line of credit for the Colonial Development Corporation and the Commonwealth Development Finance Company together. In all these cases one of the stumbling blocks arose from the Bank's adherence to very strict conditions and formal rules, which they were not prepared to bend at all in our favour as had been done for some other countries; as the second most important member country, we were expected to set a shining example.

A rather different point of difficulty on our side was our unwillingness to give an official exchange guarantee to the electricity board concerned or the CDC or CDFC. Even to admit, by giving an exchange guarantee, that a change of parity was conceivable would have offended against the sanctity of the sterling rate. Recalling those events one is struck by the impermanence of our international preeminence and of our nuclear lead, and of the fixed exchange rate and the taboo on exchange guarantees, all of which were part of the order of things at that time.

But let me now pick up the threads of my public expenditure theme because, although I stayed on the Overseas Finance side for some years after the Suez business, important developments were taking place meanwhile on the expenditure side.

THE POLITICAL DIMENSION: A LITTLE LOCAL DIFFICULTY

Decision-making on public expenditure in Britain is a curious amalgam of the technocratic and the political. What I have described so far is the old technology, so to speak – that is, the annual budgetary system coupled with day-to-day case work. Before the 1960s Treasury planning and control of public expenditure consisted of these procedures and of nothing else.

My account is a worm's eye view of the system as it then was, but it clearly did not look any different from the top, as we can see from the posthumously published book on *Public Expenditure, Management and Control*[1] by Sir Richard Clarke, who was made Deputy Secretary

[1] The Macmillan Press Ltd, 1968. The draft of the book was edited and prepared for publication after Clarke's death by Sir Alec Cairncross.

on the public expenditure side of the Treasury in 1960, and Second
Permanent Secretary in 1962. A mathematician by background,
before becoming a civil servant Clarke had at one time been a
financial journalist writing under the pseudonym Otto, the forename
by which he was generally known. In his book Otto Clarke writes as
follows:

In retrospect, the main characteristic of the system was its diffuseness and
decentralisation. The management and control of government expenditure
was seen as the examination of a mass of spending proposals from departments, each to be considered 'on its merits', with a Judgment Day in January
when the Estimates (over 2000 sub-heads) were added up and a view taken
whether the Budget prospect called for special 'economy' action and if so (as
in 1958), how much, and emergency action initiated accordingly. The responsibility for the work on the Departments' proposals was carried by the
Principals in the Supply (and mixed Supply/Establishment) divisions of the
Treasury, normally one Principal responsible for the work arising from each
department, and the problem was referred to the Head of the Division or
higher when it was particularly difficult and controversial or if agreement
could not be reached. (p. 3)

The functioning of the system relied heavily on the Principals and
others in the Treasury divisions dealing with Supply expenditure and
on their relationships with their spending Departments. I should add
that, in spite of the dichotomy between Supply Divisions and
Establishment Divisions, the staff expenditure dealt with by the latter
is a particular category of Supply expenditure – a category which was,
however, subject to much more detailed Treasury control than other
Supply expenditure, because of the Treasury's ultimate responsibility
for the size and management of the civil service. In general, the
management and execution of expenditure programmes and projects
– in contrast to policy-making, which is highly collectivised in Cabinet
and Cabinet committees – was and is decentralised to the spending
Departments. The Permanent Secretary of each Department, who is
the Department's official head, is also normally Accounting Officer
for the Departmental Votes, advised by his own Principal Finance
Officer, and personally answerable to the Public Accounts Committee of the House of Commons. The Department's accounts are
audited by Exchequer and Audit Department, whose head, the
Comptroller and Accountant General, reports to the Public Accounts
Committee and not to the Treasury, with which, however, he does
have a special relationship.

This is in sharp contrast to the French system of control, at any rate as it was when I used to deal with the French Ministry of Finance and Economic Affairs. The Ministry had an Inspecteur des Finances outposted in every spending Department and local authority. It carried out the audit function for public expenditure. One of its Directorates, which had a large staff for the purpose, vetted and approved every public sector contract, whereas our Treasury has only a loose coordinating role in public purchasing policy.

Given the differences between the two systems, the Treasury's ability to bring an informed judgment to bear on a Department's spending proposals, and to play any role beyond the crudest arithmetical allocation of available funds, depends a good deal on the 'desk officer's' mastery of the subject matter in his field and his contacts with his opposite numbers in the spending Departments. The ground-clearing carried out on this network is an important stage in the collective framing of policies which have a major financial dimension.

The two Americans, Hugh Heclo and Aaron Wildavsky, who are joint authors of a widely read book called *The Private Government of Public Money* (Macmillan, 1974), were struck by this phenomenon of what they term a 'private' political administrative community at the centre of British government. Hence their concept that 'governing public money is a private affair'. Although they were writing of the system as it had developed by the 1960s, their description of what they call the 'village life' of Whitehall would have fitted the 1950s equally well. It is an accurate description so far as it goes, but the notion which they developed from it of government by this little Whitehall community seems to me misguided, because their analysis is solely in terms of what I call the technocratic dimension and, in its original version at any rate, misses the political dimension, which is ultimately decisive.

The opening sections of this book discussed briefly the developments such as industrial or demographic change, or the growth of popular expectations, which create pressure for state services and benefits, and which cannot always be suppressed – though they often are – even in non-democratic societies. In our system of parliamentary democracy the pressures feed up in one way or another until decisions to spend or not to spend are reached through the processes of collective Ministerial government, and this is what I mean by the political dimension.

General elections provide the occasion *par excellence* for political pressures to be transmitted directly into the policy-making process.

As an election approaches, policy-making is taken out of the hands of the government machine which has been making and carrying out policy, and is transferred to the party machine where policy for the next Parliament, in the form of the election manifesto, is drafted by party officials, working parties of Members of Parliament, and so on, and approved through the party hierarchy. Ministers of the party in power before the election become involved in the manifesto, but their officials do not. Manifesto commitments are undertaken in a way which bypasses the hurdles of Whitehall analysis and scrutiny. Programmes and policies for at least the initial period of a government's life are determined by these extra-governmental processes.

During the thirteen years of Tory rule, from 1951 to 1964, with which I am still dealing in this part of the book, general elections and manifestos had a less disruptive effect on policy than later became the case. But from then up to the 1979 election there took place with regularity a change in the political complexion of the government in power, and a reversal of the previous government's policies, every five years, give or take a year. Moreover the sanctity of the manifesto developed over this period.

The pressures do not, of course, work only in one direction. When government expenditure leads to high taxation, or to a high level of borrowing which pushes up interest rates and which may involve inflationary methods of financing, there are counter-pressures to cut expenditure and reduce taxation and government borrowing. This is especially so if public services are believed to be over-staffed and inefficient and not giving value for money. Thus Conservative governments came to power in 1970 and again in 1979 committed to cut taxation and expenditure in general, while giving priority to defence.

But in either case, once a government is in power, manifesto commitments have to be legitimised and translated from party policy into government policy by the collective decision-making process. At this stage the political dimension is re-connected with the technocratic dimension.

The doctrine of collective Cabinet responsibility applies in principle to the whole spectrum of government policy, but in practice the multiplicity of policy decisions, large and small, which require inter-Departmental clearance is vastly greater than could be handled in actual Cabinet meetings or even in the endless series of meetings of Ministerial Cabinet committees which help to create an intolerable timetable for the more senior and busier Ministers. A great deal of business is therefore carried out by inter-Ministerial correspondence; it is in fact rather exceptional for one individual Minister to write to another individual Minister and almost always his letter is copied to, say, half a dozen other Ministers, or to the rather larger number of Ministers who make up a Cabinet committee, or to all the members of Cabinet. The photo-copier is nowadays an essential element in the machinery of government.

Even so the system could not work without the technocratic back-up, whether working through official committees run by the Cabinet Office or other inter-Departmental committees or the network of informal contacts between officials. If Heclo and Wildavsky were to take a look at the way Whitehall handles almost any major subject, say international trade or the European Economic Community, they would find a 'village community', similar to that on the public ex-penditure front but in this case consisting of old hands conversant with the GATT and the Treaty of Rome and the common agricultural policy and the problems of the textile industry, putting their heads together to try to reconcile conflicting interests and clear the ground for Ministerial agreement. Within the EEC, something of the same process now takes place between as well as within capitals in order to settle collective Community policy, with the Council of Ministers playing a role roughly similar to that of the Cabinet.

The translation of the manifesto into government policy, and the re-connection of the political and the technocratic dimensions, begins within hours of the election, with the drafting of the Queen's Speech setting out the new administration's programme and priorities for the coming session of Parliament, and its approval by Cabinet committee and by full Cabinet. This is a crucial stage at which the shape of things to come is worked out at short notice, and to secure or to avoid a particular form of words, or even a particular nuance, can be of great importance. It is the stage at which the illusions of the hustings first start to come to terms with reality, in the shape of the constraints of the Parliamentary timetable, the technical problems of translating highly generalised aspirations into specific legislation and workable schemes, the existence of international commitments, and so on. Later on, reality makes itself felt in other forms, such as the economic situation, the behaviour of industry, actions of foreign powers and by-election results. As a result, if a particular item from the manifesto is left out of the first Queen's Speech, as many of them must be, the situation can change so much that it will never get into the programme later on.

But we should not be misled by this into elevating the technocratic element above the political element in our view of things. Officials do not create the realities which I have described. It may fall to officials to advise of their existence and how to cope with them, but at the end of the day the decisions that matter are taken not in the Whitehall village but in the castle of No. 10 Downing Street and the Cabinet room. A particular demonstration of this was given early in 1958 by the fate of the policies of the Chancellor at the time, Mr Peter Thorneycroft, as he then was, which were designed to control the money supply and public expenditure. Mr Thorneycroft spoke publicly about the need to attack inflation at its source by controlling the amount of money – a point of view which was to become familiar in 1980 but which was not much heard either in the Treasury or elsewhere in the 1950s. In the late summer of 1957 – summer being the regular time of year for economic packages in the stop–go era – he introduced a package of measures which included raising bank rate to the then sensationally high level of 7 per cent.

Although I was a member of Mr Thorneycroft's supporting delegation at the annual meeting of the Bank and Fund in Washington in September that year, being on the Overseas side I knew nothing of what might be going on elsewhere in the Treasury on the monetary and fiscal front or of the Chancellor's attempt to secure cuts of £50 million in the Supply Estimates submitted by spending Departments; his aim was to bring the Main Estimates for the coming year back to the level, not of the corresponding Main Estimates for the prior year, but to the out-turn for that year, that is, Main Estimates plus Supplementaries. It was not therefore a terribly draconian proposal since, if accepted, it would still have meant starting the new financial year with Main Estimates above those a year earlier to the extent of the Supplementaries introduced in the meanwhile. Since, as I have said, I was not in the picture about these developments, it was as much of a surprise to me as the Suez invasion had been when, in January 1958, both the Chancellor and the two junior Treasury ministers – Enoch Powell the Financial Secretary and Nigel Birch the Economic Secretary – resigned over their failure to secure these reductions.

As I now know, the Chancellor was not put up to this fight by Treasury officials; nor on the other hand was he restrained from it by them. Sir Roger Makins, whom Macmillan had brought into the Treasury as its Permanent Secretary after a successful diplomatic career, was not in his natural element in this affair. The impetus had therefore to come from within the Ministerial Treasury team. In the end, after a series of inter-Ministerial discussions both inside Cabinet and outside it, Cabinet overruled the Chancellor in the knowledge that he would treat defeat on this issue as a resigning matter.

The collective nature of decision-making on the expenditure side of our financial affairs is in sharp contrast to the tradition that, on the taxation side, the Chancellor is largely master in his own house. The Prime Minister, who is titular First Lord of the Treasury, also tends to play a major role in taxation policy, but the rest of Cabinet – notwithstanding the doctrine of collective responsibility – have a purely passive role. The Chancellor may, nowadays, go somewhat beyond the tradition of informing Cabinet of his Budget proposals immediately before the Budget itself. Cabinet Ministers generally may be given an opportunity to air their views on Budget strategy. But for practical purposes they are not put in a position to approve or disapprove the specific tax proposals in the Budget. As a result, neither individual spending Ministers who sponsor expenditure proposals, nor Cabinet who collectively have the ultimate right of approval over them, have a similar responsibility for raising the money to finance these measures. Even in a Conservative government which in principle believes in low taxation, and all the more so in a government without any such belief, spending Ministers are generally not inhibited by the financial implications of their proposals. Treasury Ministers therefore tend to occupy a lonely position in Cabinet on expenditure matters. Much depends on the standing and force of character of the Chancellor of the Exchequer and also on the Chief Secretary, the Treasury Minister who, since this post was created in 1961, has had particular responsibility for public expenditure. As much or more depends on the support which they get from the Prime Minister. Without that, the Treasury Ministers cannot have much hope of prevailing over spending Ministers.

Macmillan's blithe acceptance of the resignation of all three Treasury Ministers (there could not be a fourth at that time because the post of Chief Secretary had not yet been created) did not cause too many ripples at the time. Macmillan himself did not even delay his planned departure on an overseas visit, but went off, dismissing the issue as 'a little local difficulty'. But in retrospect it came to be seen as a traumatic incident in modern Conservative history and one which seriously undermined the authority of the Treasury in controlling public expenditure.

OVERSEAS FINANCE: EUROPE

The year after these dramatic developments – that is, in 1959 – I was made an Assistant Secretary, which is a crucial promotion in a civil service career, and became Head of an Overseas Finance Division called OFT4. I was 40 and had been a Principal for twelve whole years. Some years and some two or three promotions later, the letters of congratulations on my appearance in the Honours List included one from an Under Secretary under whom I had worked in OFT4, and who remarked in his letter that there had once been serious doubt whether I could ever be promoted above Principal. However, whatever the reasons for my own slow promotion, there was a promotion block in the senior grades, which made advancement slow for most people. Douglas Wass, for instance, about whom there were no such doubts, was 39 when he became an Assistant Secretary in 1962.

OFT4 was one of a number of 'territorial' divisions on the Overseas Finance side, and was concerned mainly with the Commonwealth, but I was given an additional role on overseas aid to the under-developed countries. This was a field of policy in which Britain was entering a new phase following the 1958 meeting of Commonwealth Finance Ministers – who adjourned to Montreal to have their own customary meeting after the annual meeting of the International Bank in Washington – and as a result also of initiatives by the new Kennedy administration in the United States. Until then our bilateral aid had normally been confined to our own dependent territories under the Attlee government's Colonial Development and Welfare Act. Our governmental assistance to other countries – as distinct from the large private capital flows for which we always sought to take credit – was generally provided under a multilateral umbrella such as the International Bank or the Colombo Plan for technical assistance to countries in South and South East Asia. But in 1958 our balance of payments had enjoyed an unusually favourable year – a state of affairs which did not in the event last very long – and conversely countries such as India had run down their sterling balances and were becoming increasingly short of foreign exchange. Britain therefore announced at Montreal a new policy of Commonwealth Assistance Loans for independent Commonwealth countries which were in need.

This assistance took the form of Section 3 loans, that is, loans by Export Credit Guarantees Department under Section 3 of the Export Guarantees Act. The loans were tied to purchases of United Kingdom exports, and initially had to be repaid over three to five years, so they were more like an extension of export credit than of development assistance. However, in the course of time the terms were progressively brought more into line with the circumstances of the underdeveloped countries.

There was still no such thing as an aid programme embracing these

Section 3 loans together with the money channelled through other Departments, including the Foreign Office, the Commonwealth Relations Office and the Colonial Office (all of which have now been rolled up into the Foreign and Commonwealth Office). There was not even a readily available set of figures bringing together the various aid items. Even within the Treasury, while the Section 3 loans were a below-the-line item and were dealt with on the Overseas Finance side, grants such as those to the colonies were provided through Votes and were dealt with by IF (a mixed Supply/Establishment Division) which came under a different chain of command.

However, during my time on this work we constructed the first aid programme in which, though the various items of aid expenditure were still channelled through the different Departments concerned, they were brought together, for the purpose of policy-making, in a single functional programme. Leaving aside the defence budget, this was the first functional public expenditure programme, that is, one in which the expenditure was considered primarily in terms of the function to which it was directed – in this case, the function of aid to the underdeveloped countries – rather than in terms of the 'spending authority' concerned, that is, the particular Department or financial institution, or in terms of the particular Vote or below-the-line account. Later on, after William Armstrong had become Permanent Secretary of the Treasury, this increasingly functional approach to policy was reflected in a Treasury reorganisation under which OFT4 became FD1, standing for Development Finance One. However, we had still not reached the stage of determining the aid programme within the framework of an overall public expenditure total, for which no framework existed yet.

There was at that time no separate Overseas Development Administration (ODA). The coordination of aid policy and the aid programme was carried out by the Treasury, under the aegis of Denis Rickett at Third Secretary level and with myself as prime mover at my level. Notwithstanding the great differences in background and personality between us, once we got to know each other we worked well together, and it seemed to me that we discharged the coordinating and policy-making functions with a fraction of the manpower later brought to the task by the ODA and at least as well. Within the constraints of the economy and the balance of payments, the United Kingdom played a creditable enough role in a number of new developments, such as the international consortium to help India's second five-year plan, the setting up of the International Development Association as an affiliate of the World Bank to provide aid on softer terms than the Bank could do, and the creation of the Development Assistance Group (DAG).

A UK initiative which came to nothing was a proposal, in the early days of the DAG, that all aid should be untied – that is, the recipient country should be able to use it to pay for goods from any supplier and not solely for exports from the donor country. This would of course have been helpful to the underdeveloped countries, but a main reason for the proposal was the belief that it would also help British exports, since we would be able to win export orders financed by aid from other donor countries. I always thought the idea unrealistic, like some others from the fertile brain of the Bank of England adviser who took part in our counsels, and predictably it got no support from the other main donors. I also before long came to look back on the initiative as misguided, since it relied almost exclusively on our experience with untied International Bank loans to sterling area countries such as India, out of which we picked up a disproportionate amount of export business. But that was an unrepresentative situation, and as time passed it became increasingly clear that we were losing market share in export markets. Moreover, the tying of aid was useful in creating a lobby in favour of aid not solely among do-gooders but also among industrialists who wanted the contracts which it would finance.

The DAG itself was an initiative of the Kennedy administration, as part of their drive to raise the total aid effort and to get a better sharing of the burden among the industrialised countries, principally the countries of Western Europe, which had now emerged from the phase of post-war reconstruction, and Japan, which had also rebuilt in a manner even more dramatic but even less well realised in Britain at that time. George Ball, Kennedy's Under Secretary of State, visited the capitals of Europe to propose the transformation of the OEEC into the OECD (the Organisation for Economic Cooperation and Development), with the United States and Canada as full members instead of affiliates as before.

Although the membership of the OECD, unlike that of the OEEC, was not to be confined to the Europeans, it was still not thought that it would be acceptable for Japan to become a member of the OEEC or its successor body. The Americans proposed that there should be a separate body of donor countries, which was first informally known as the Group of Eight and then was set up as the Development Assistance Group, operating from the OEEC headquarters at the Chateau de la Muette but not formally part of the OEEC. Japan became a member of the DAG, remained a member of it when the DAG subsequently became the Development Assistance Committee of the

OECD, and finally became a member of the OECD. In this way the Japanese worked their passage back into the international community.

Along with the proposals which led to these developments, George Ball suggested that the time had come for the United Kingdom, which had provided the chairman of the OEEC ever since its inception, to pass the chairmanship over to a European; Mr Heathcoat Amory, who had succeeded Mr Thorneycroft as Chancellor, agreed to this without fuss. In this way, at an undramatic meeting in a Treasury conference room, with the Ministers and top officials seated on either side of the conference table, and the lesser lights ranged on their seats round the outskirts of the room, Britain's post-war leadership of Europe quietly passed from us.

Or rather, this was an act of recognition of the passing of our leading role, not merely on the world stage, for that had gone by the time of Suez, but even in Europe, though I do not think that Whitehall had taken the significance of what was happening in Europe. The European Economic Community had come into being without us, since we had not sought to become involved in the negotiations between the six founding members which led to the Treaty of Rome in March 1957. We then tried to negotiate a wider free trade area of Western European countries, including the Six, which the French torpedoed in November 1958. As a salvage operation, we led the formation of a less ambitious European Free Trade Area, in which none of the other members – Norway, Sweden, Denmark, Austria, Switzerland and Portugal – was of comparable weight to the United Kingdom.

Even then I do not think that Whitehall at either Ministerial or official level grasped the political and economic implications of the Community. Normally it is the function of officials to bring illusion into relation with reality, but some officials can be as capable of illusion as most politicians are, and there seemed to me even at the time a lack of realism about many of our external economic policies. This consisted of a failure to distinguish between what we should like to happen and what was going to happen, between what would suit us and what would suit other countries, between the views we hoped that they would take and the views that they did take.

It could be argued that this reflected the same refusal to accept what everyone else regarded as the inevitable that had got us through the war and that may have been a necessary part of the motivation of the people in Whitehall – in some cases the same people who had carried the war-time burden – in coping with our problems after the war.

Moreover, in some of these matters, Whitehall may not have had much real option anyway. Nevertheless, especially in the matter of our various negotiations with Europe, I remain a little astonished at such blind spots as the failure to appreciate the antipathy which extended to Britain so long as we appeared to be identified with the Americans. French pride could more easily come to terms with the Germans, who had occupied France but who had in the end been defeated, than accept the hegemony of the Americans who, together with Britain, had liberated France. In the DAG I got my first glimpse of the contempt felt by our French opposite numbers for the way in which the British lined up with the Americans.

The shift of power and influence which was taking place was economic as well as political, but this was not apparent until about the end of the 1950s. As late as 1956, in his book *The Future of Socialism* (Jonathan Cape), Tony Crosland took the problem of economic growth as solved: 'I no longer regard questions of growth and efficiency as being, on a long view, of primary importance to social-ism. We stand, in Britain, on the threshold of mass abundance . . .' Surprising as it now seems, Crosland was able to compare Britain's industrial performance favourably with that of other countries:

From 1948 to 1954 the British national income rose, in real terms, by 20% – a figure only slightly below that (22%) achieved in the USA, conventionally saluted as the world's most productive economy. Output per man-year has risen by about 2¼% per annum since 1948, and by 3% per annum in manufacturing industry . . . The British post-war performance also compares favourably with that of other countries. The Sixth Report of the OEEC shows that with the possible exception of Sweden, industrial pro-ductivity has risen by more in Britain since before the war than in any other European country; while the rise since the war has been almost exactly the same as in the United States.

But within a few years France was achieving a much faster growth rate than this, which in turn was outstripped by the German economic miracle, while industrial growth in Japan exceeded anything in Europe. The complacency epitomised in Macmillan's slogan 'you have never had it so good' was replaced by dissatisfaction with our rate of growth which, though higher than anyone would have predicted,[2] compared poorly with the rising prosperity across the

[2] Cf. Nicki Kaldor's cautious assumption, in an appendix to Beveridge's *Full Employ-ment in a Free Society* (Allen and Unwin, 1944), of a minimum 13 per cent increase in productivity by 1948 as compared with 1938, averaging the greater productivity gains in manufacturing industry with the slower rate of change in distribution and service.

Channel, and was punctuated by recurring sterling crises. This sea change in the national mood led to two historic statements in the summer of 1961: Mr Selwyn Lloyd – yet another new face in the office of Chancellor of the Exchequer – announced a proposal to set up a National Economic Development Council, which came into being the following year and which in 1963 approved a 4 per cent growth rate for the economy; and Mr Macmillan announced that Britain would open negotiations to join the EEC.

Among people who were close to these events at the time, a good deal of credit for the shift of policy on Europe is given to Sir Frank Lee, who was at that time Permanent Secretary at the Board of Trade and was later to succeed Makins as Permanent Secretary to the Treasury. The Community was still generally referred to as the Common Market and was thought of as primarily a trade arrangement. It was only at a late stage in the negotiations that I heard one of my official masters in the Treasury comment that the Common Market had developed from being an economic issue with political aspects to a political issue with economic aspects. But I share the view that Macmillan's motivation was primarily political from the outset, and that a crucial factor in his conversion to Europe was the failure of his attempt to gain a niche in history by acting as a bridge between the American and Russian superpowers. The breakdown of this policy took a dramatic turn in 1960 with the shooting down of an American U.2 spy-plane over Russia. I had an eye-witness description of the Prime Minister sitting in No. 10 with his foreign policy in ruins around him and asking himself what he was going to do for a foreign policy now.

Later in 1962 I was moved sideways off overseas aid to be Assistant Secretary in charge of another Overseas Finance Division called FWE (Finance Western Europe), where my work would cover the financial arrangements for our entry into the EEC. In the event I did no more than dip my toes into the subject, but my recollection is that this task was viewed in the Division as largely technical and that no one was conscious of the major public expenditure problem which was later to emerge. Re-reading fairly recently all the White Papers issued over the years in connection with our various negotiations to join the EEC, I was confirmed in my view that the cost of entry was seen primarily in balance of payments terms rather than in expenditure terms; it was not generally appreciated that a large part, though not the whole, of the balance of payments cost was *ipso facto* a public expenditure cost.

However, in January 1963 I was relieved of the need to master this subject when, at a very advanced stage in the EEC negotiations,

General de Gaulle reacted to Macmillan's deal with President Kennedy on nuclear weapons, which was agreed at their meeting in Nassau, by saying no to British membership. (The phrase is from Nora Beloff's 1963 Penguin Special called *The General Says No*.)

Without the EEC work the FWE job was not particularly heavy. However, for some time in 1953 I continued as chairman of a DAC working party in Paris on the terms of aid, though I no longer dealt with aid policy in Whitehall. The Americans had proposed me for this assignment some months earlier, and Denis Rickett – after initial reluctance because he knew, though I did not, that I was about to be moved to FWE – had finally agreed. For my part I was glad to have reasons for frequent visits to Paris at that time. My report was, I think, fairly prophetic in anticipating that there would be a debt service crisis in the underdeveloped world if the donor countries went on providing so-called aid in the form of hard loans with high interest rates and short repayment periods. The report had a little effect, I believe, in influencing the UK and some other donor countries, though not all, to soften the terms of their aid. I was also, during my time in FWE, a member of Edward Heath's team when, as Minister of State at the Foreign Office, he made a round of visits to the capitals of the EFTA countries, as part of our effort to rebuild EFTA since our hopes of joining the more important EEC had been dashed. Other assignments entailed going with Reginald Maudling to OECD and NATO meetings in Paris, and with John Boyd-Carpenter, who had returned to the Treasury as Chief Secretary, to Bonn for rather unrewarding negotiations with the Germans on a fresh 'offset agreement' to redress the balance of payments cost of our troops in Germany.

In October 1964, after eight years on Overseas Finance, I was moved back to the public expenditure side. I was not overjoyed at this, especially as it involved no promotion, but I was assured that I would not improve my promotion prospects by staying too long in OF and the move would be better for my career in the longer term. I viewed this with scepticism, but in the event there proved to be some truth in it. On rejoining the public expenditure side I found that great things had been happening and that a new system had been introduced, generally known as the PESC system or simply as PESC. Let me explain this system and how it had come about.

THE TECHNOCRATIC DIMENSION

Various individuals and committees played a part in the run-up to the new system, but one man, Otto Clarke, stands out as its architect and master builder. He was a large man, both physically – at any rate he had a large dome of a head – and in the scale of his ideas, in which he believed with a force and a passion which was sometimes a little surprising in relation to the nature of the issue or the facts of the situation. The creation of the new system was a great conceptual achievement. To secure its acceptance by Whitehall was a feat of will and organisation. I say this as someone who – to understate the point somewhat – owed nothing to patronage from that quarter. Whether the new system was something *sensible,* and whether our last state was better or worse than our first, are questions on which judgment has to be deferred for the moment.

In earlier sections I have described the fragmented and *ad hoc* character of the handling of public expenditure in the 1950s, and I have quoted Otto Clarke on the 'diffuseness and decentralisation' of the old system. He went on as follows:

The merits of this degree of decentralisation can be argued at length; but the crucial point in relation to what came later is that even in Supply expenditure ('public expenditure as a whole', about twice as much as Supply, was not yet a working concept) there was no process of reasoned judgment of the scale of aggregate acceptable expenditure, or its indications for taxes, or its allocation between the departments and services . . . The point at issue, easier to see now than it was at the time, was whether the Treasury and then the Government could develop a rational public expenditure policy (in this most 'political' of all the fields of government). If they were going to do this, a new system would clearly be required that treated 'public expenditure' as one subject and not as thousands of individual spending decisions. (p. 3)

In effect, the die was cast for a change of system from the time of a report in 1958 from the Select Committee on Estimates (H.C. 254 1957–58), which Clarke takes as the starting point for his book, and which considered 'whether the present "system" of Treasury control is as effective as modern conditions demand'. The Committee came to the following conclusion:

The system appears to work reasonably well. But it would be idle to pretend that your Committee is left entirely without disquiet . . . Accordingly they recommend that a small independent committee, which should have access to Cabinet papers, be appointed to report upon the theory and practice of Treasury control of expenditure.

The following year the Chancellor of the Exchequer, Mr Heathcoat Amory, set up a committee under the chairmanship of Sir Edwin

Plowden, as he then was, to report on the subject. The committee had a mixed composition of outsiders and civil servants; Otto Clarke himself was one of the civil service members of the committee from 1960. The Plowden Committee reported to the Chancellor of the Exchequer in 1961 and an edited version was presented to Parliament (Cmnd. 1432).

The Plowden Report contained a crucial recommendation that arrangements should be introduced for making surveys of public expenditure for a period of years ahead, and that all major individual decisions involving future expenditure should be taken against the background of such a survey and in relation to prospective resources. This recommendation was accepted, and the new public expenditure survey system was introduced under Otto Clarke's direction. So from then on we had a new technology interacting with the political process, and there is no avoiding a short description of the new system if we are to understand the framework for the passionate political debates of the following decade.

Two key features of the system were that it was constructed in terms of functional programmes, not in terms of spending authorities, and that the programmes, up to 1980, were costed, not at current prices, but in constant prices – or funny money, as this price basis has come to be called by its critics. As regards functional programmes, the discussion of the aid programme in the previous section has illustrated what is meant by this concept. Or to take education as another example, the totals for the education programme brought together all the expenditure devoted to the function of educating people, broken down into spending on young children, on primary schools, on secondary schools, on universities and so on – not broken down according to the spending authorities who provide or disburse the money, such as the Department of Education and Science and the local authorities. In 1981, there were fourteen separate functional programmes, but there were also three territorial programmes for Scotland, Wales and Northern Ireland, and to that extent the functional approach has been diluted.

These functional programmes are drawn up for the whole period of years covered by the public expenditure survey. Up to 1979 this was a five-year period. In each successive survey all the programmes are brought up to date and rolled forward; one year from the old survey period drops out and normally one fresh year is brought in. In the 1980 survey the period covered was reduced to four years; this effect was secured by not bringing in a fresh year on this occasion. However, provided that the period is not reduced further, the process of rolling forward should in future work in the same way with a four-year period as it did with a five-year period, with one old year dropping out and one fresh year coming in. The little chart in figure 2.1 illustrates how public expenditure is rolled forward from one survey to the next, and how Year 2 in the earlier survey becomes Year 1 in the next, and so on – with the important difference that, in the course of being rolled forward, all programmes have to reflect changes in prices and in policies.

1980 survey	1981 survey
Year 1 1980–81	
Year 2 1981–82	Year 1 1981–82
Year 3 1982–83	Year 2 1982–83
Year 4 1983–84	Year 3 1983–84
	Year 4 1984–85

Figure 2.1

An exercise of this magnitude, accounting for over 40 per cent of the national income, is bound to be complex, but even so the amount of work involved in these public expenditure surveys, and the number of forms to be filled in, is staggering. The functional breakdown is accompanied by a variety of supplementary pieces of analysis which have proliferated over the years – partly to meet the demands of the House of Commons Expenditure Committee. The supplementary data include a breakdown of programmes in terms of spending authorities – central government, local government and public corporations – and a further breakdown in terms of economic category, that is, into current expenditure on goods and services, current expenditure on subsidies and grants, and capital expenditure of various kinds. These figures are all compiled in such a way as to dovetail into the classifications used by the Central Statistical Office in the national income and expenditure accounts; this is a further achievement to the credit of the mathematically minded founding fathers of the system, but it adds to the complexities and pitfalls of the operation, and can be a great tribulation to those who have to prepare the figures for the individual programmes.

But these complexities are almost as nothing compared to the mysteries of the constant price system. The principle is straightforward enough. When we are looking back at the past, we need a way of measuring changes which have taken place – increases or reductions in GDP, for instance, or in the standard of living – in real terms and not simply in terms of the money of the day. Unless these money figures are adjusted to take account of inflation, they give no idea of what really happened. So we have indices of output, consumption, and so on, covering a series of years but expressed in the prices of a particular year – that is, in constant prices. In this context nobody derides constant prices as funny money.

In the same way, the architects of the new public expenditure surveys looked for a means of planning programmes ahead in volume terms, or in terms of the real resources involved, and not in terms of the money of the day which, in an inflationary era, would lose a greater or lesser part of its value each year. They therefore applied the constant price technique to the future as to the past. In other words, programmes for a series of years ahead were expressed in the prices of a particular year – which, in public expenditure parlance, means 'in survey prices' – with the intention that, when the time came, each programme would be converted from constant prices to prices of the day.

But though the principle of constant prices may be relatively simple, in practice the business of rolling programmes forward, taking account of price changes as well as policy changes and other new developments, has been fiendishly complicated. The little chart in figure 2.1 showed how Year 2 from one survey becomes Year 1 in the next, and so on. Figure 2.2 takes the operation a stage further and shows in simplified form how each Year 2 programme from the 1979 survey emerged from the process of change as the corresponding Year 1 programme in the 1980 survey, etc. However, it is in one respect of purely historical interest, since 1980 was the last year in which the constant price system was used. The switch in 1981 to carrying out the survey on the basis of assumptions about cash prices in future years, which will no doubt throw up a different set of complications, is discussed in chapter 6.

If we are talking about the more 'controllable' programmes, any changes between one survey and another, apart from price changes, ought to be the result of a deliberate policy decision to increase or to

1979 survey[a]			1980 survey[b]
Year 1 programme			
Year 2 programme	+ revaluation + additions − reductions	=	Year 1 programme
Year 3 programme	+ revaluation + additions − reductions	=	Year 2 programme
Year 4 programme	+ revaluation + additions − reductions	=	Year 3 programme
Year 5 programme	+ revaluation + additions − reductions	=	Year 4 programme

[a] All programmes in this survey were at 1979 survey prices.
[b] All programmes in this survey were at 1980 survey prices.
Note: There are no Year 5 programmes in the 1980 survey because of shortening of the survey period.

Figure 2.2

cut the programme – I shall discuss later how this has worked in practice. The projected public expenditure totals include a contingency reserve to provide for additional items which may have to be approved between surveys; conversely, a deduction is made from the projected totals to allow for shortfall, that is, the tendency for some programmes to be underspent. A programme which has been increased during the year by a decision to allocate more resources to it will go into the new survey fatter than it came out of the last one, and vice versa.

But there are other programmes which are demand-responsive or open-ended, and which the Americans call 'uncontrollable'. The amount spent on unemployment benefit, for instance, will depend not only on the rate of benefit, which is controllable, but on the number of people out of work, which is not. As another example, there are various schemes involving grants or subsidies which are payable to anyone who satisfies the conditions and applies for money; in this case the amount spent will depend not only on the rate of grant, which is fixed, but also on the number of applicants, which can vary. The figures for this kind of programme will change from one survey to another according to how things have gone and how they are expected to go. One of the biggest uncontrollable items is debt interest, which is not a 'programme' but forms part of total public expenditure.

PESC

I must now explain the use of the term PESC. This is an acronym for the inter-Departmental committee called the Public Expenditure Survey Committee under whose aegis the annual survey takes place. The chairman is a Treasury Deputy Secretary and the committee is run by the Treasury, not by the Cabinet Office. Each spending Department is represented on the committee by its Principal Finance Officer, who is usually an Under Secretary, but some big spenders like the Ministry of Defence have a Deputy Secretary as PFO, while in a small Department the post may be held by an Assistant Secretary.

The committee which oversees the survey, and the survey itself, have for a long time been so identified with each other that the Whitehall village community generally speaks of the PESC system rather than of the survey system, or simply of PESC, meaning the whole paraphernalia and not merely the committee. If you are a Department wanting money for an expenditure proposal, and if you have got provision for your proposal 'in PESC' – that is, somewhere in the survey tables, possibly subsumed as a small component item in a much larger aggregate – you are on the way to success. If your proposal is 'not in PESC', you have a hard time ahead of you.

Now, before this whole process can be put in hand, guidelines for the exercise have to be approved by Cabinet, and even at this stage there can be a good deal of infighting about the survey rules because, though spending Ministers are assured that they are not being asked to take any decisions at this stage, they know the rules of the game can go a long way towards determining who wins. Once the guidelines have been settled, the chores of working out all the figures and putting the tables together on the basis of the guidelines, and the preparation of the PESC report to go with the programme figures, between them take several months. The report is discussed in the inter-Departmental committee but, though the aim is to produce an agreed document so far as it is a statement of fact, the PESC report as a whole is a Treasury piece of work and Departments are not necessarily committed to it in other respects. As Edward Boyle commented a good many years ago in the *Political Quarterly*, the success of a Departmental Minister depends on how much money he can get out of the Treasury for his policies, and neither he nor his officials will readily agree to anything which might prejudice their case in advance of the final decisions in Cabinet.

The PESC report as such is not circulated to the Cabinet, though it can be made available to each Cabinet Minister by his own officials, and it provides essential background for the Cabinet discussion of public expenditure; the document which goes to Cabinet is a paper by the Chancellor or the Chief Secretary, reporting on the findings of the survey and putting forward the recommendations of Treasury Ministers on future expenditure. In previous years this went round in the late spring or early summer, but in 1981 the date for circulating the paper was shifted to the autumn. Although the Plowden Report recommended a public expenditure committee of senior Ministers to give the Chancellor support, this led only to the use of *ad hoc* groups of Ministers on two or three occasions at particular stages in the public expenditure exercise, and not to the creation of a standing Ministerial committee in this field. The annual battle is therefore fought out in full Cabinet from the outset.

It would be unheard of for Treasury Ministers to get full and detailed agreement to their proposals at the first encounter. With luck they may get a general endorsement in principle, after one or two discussions in Cabinet, for their proposals for the totality of expenditure, with or without some modifications, leaving the implications for individual programmes still to be settled. This stage would then typically be followed by a round of bilateral discussions between Treasury Ministers and spending Ministers, usually supported by officials on both sides. Officials may also do a certain amount of ground-clearing or tidying up before or after the Ministerial bilaterals. Treasury Ministers then report back to Cabinet the agreements or compromises reached bilaterally or the disagreements on particular programmes which now have to be resolved in Cabinet. At this stage the expenditure totals which Cabinet approved earlier on may have to be reopened because of the impossibility of fitting into them the claims which spending Ministers are unwilling to withdraw and which Cabinet are not prepared to overrule.

From beginning to end these Ministerial discussions tend to spread themselves over a period of months, with something of a respite in the middle during the summer Parliamentary recess. As the months pass, it becomes operationally necessary to take firm decisions on programmes for the financial year immediately ahead; spending authorities cannot wait until the last minute to learn what money they are going to have, though sometimes it is a very close run thing. Programme figures for the later years can generally be settled on a more provisional basis, but they must contain enough hard core to enable Departments to commit themselves ahead to a greater or lesser degree, according to the nature of the projects involved. There have been some cliffhangers, but for the past decade or so this difficult gestation period has resulted each year, by the time of the Budget or earlier, in the publication of the results of the exercise in a public expenditure White Paper. Up to 1981 the White Paper figures were expressed in survey prices. Programmes for one year ahead only were converted into cash figures in the Budget, in the way I have just described. The White Paper figures for two or more years ahead do not enter into the Budget.

So from 1961 onwards the old, *ad hoc,* year-at-a-time technology was displaced – or rather supplemented, because all the old Budget procedures still continued – by the new, comprehensive, medium-term planning apparatus. The new system was admired by foreign observers, especially visitors from the United States, which had still to develop its own initiatives aiming at improved budgetary control, and which eventually took the different route of strengthening the apparatus for Congressional oversight. Heclo and Wildavsky, while not uncritical of some aspects of the British system, especially the subordination of micro-analysis of policies to macro-analysis of the economy, found it a sophisticated system and one well adapted to the talents of the 'private political administrative community' – a concept I have discussed in an earlier section.

And yet, in spite of the sophistication of the system, by 1975 it was coming under criticism on the grounds that public expenditure was out of control and that this profligacy was a major factor in the country's economic ills. An influential report by the Expenditure Committee of the House of Commons – itself considerably influenced by a memorandum from Wynne Godley, a former economic adviser to the Treasury who had played his part in the development of the survey system and contributed to its increasing complexity, but by now Director of the Department of Applied Economics at Cambridge and disillusioned with his own former handiwork – was exceptionally critical of the system and appeared to hold its shortcomings responsible for the excesses which had taken place. The charge was not simply that expenditure had escalated year by year above the levels previously planned, but also that decisions on public expenditure programmes had been taken without regard to the means of financing them, so that the end result was inflation of the money supply.

What had gone wrong?

WHAT WENT WRONG

Planners and would-be planners of public expenditure, from
Beveridge onwards, have thought in terms of a year-by-year increase
in the national output, available for division between public
expenditure and the rest of the economy – that is, private investment,
private consumption and exports. Tony Crosland's book, from which
I have already quoted, developed the idea of higher public
expenditure rather than nationalisation as a central feature of
socialism. The thesis of his book was that socialist policies need no
longer be concerned primarily with the ownership of the means of
production or with a programme for economic growth, though that
remained important, but should apply the gains from economic
growth to greater equality, especially through educational reform,
and to programmes of social welfare. Though Crosland has become
more of a cult figure among the moderate left since his death than he
was at that time, when he was still on the lower rungs of his political
career, his book played a part in the development of the policies of the
Labour Party while it was in opposition and awaiting a return to
power.

Meanwhile the Macmillan era had some years to run, and Labour
had some years to wait, at the time when the PESC system was
introduced. It was a system which lent itself very well to the concept of
allocating the projected growth of GDP between public and private
expenditure. The normal pattern was for the public expenditure
exercise to be linked with a medium-term assessment of the outlook
for the economy. In each of the first two exercises under the new
system (that is, the 1961 exercise and the 1962 exercise) the
prospective increase in resources for the five-year period covered by
the survey was put at 3 per cent a year. This proved to correspond very
well to the average rate of growth in GDP over the period 1960–66, so
in this respect these early exercises went better than those which were
to come.

In Otto Clarke's eyes the essence of the PESC approach was to limit
the growth of public expenditure to the growth in resources; this
would have the effect of maintaining at a constant figure the
proportion of the national output allocated to public expenditure. If
there is a theme to his book, it is the story of his unsuccessful efforts to
attain this result. For the start of the 1961 exercise he did in fact secure
a remit to the Treasury to work out a plan under which public
expenditure over the survey period would take an unchanged share of

GNP, a share which, on the definitions then in use, was reckoned at the time to be 42½ per cent. On the revised definitions which were adopted in 1976, public expenditure in 1961 would have been put at a little under 34 per cent of GDP. However, the way in which public expenditure is measured statistically at any time does not make any difference to the actual amount which is being financed out of taxation and public borrowing, and Clarke's concern was to avoid an increase in the burden of taxation.

Now, if that result was to be achieved, programmes had to be worked out within the constraint of a 3 per cent overall limit. But on Clarke's account, though a quantitative limit was applied to some programmes, in others 'policies were framed in qualitative terms' and spending Departments tabled their 'estimates of what would be involved in 1965–66 under existing policies' (p. 53). As a result, the PESC report 'proved beyond any reasonable doubt that unless the Government (and any other Government in sight) were prepared to make fundamental changes in their policies, it would be impossible in the long run to contain public expenditure at around 42½ per cent of GNP' (p. 55).

So this was the first thing which went wrong. In spite of the remit to work out a plan for keeping public expenditure as a constant percentage of GNP, the working rules adopted for the exercise were such that it was bound to produce a different result. Clarke writes that this could not have been avoided at the time, but at least the working rules could have been framed in such a way as to put the onus on spending Departments to bid for anything in excess of an objectively determined quantitative limit, instead of putting it on the Treasury to argue for a reduction in subjective Departmental estimates of the cost, as they saw it, of carrying out existing policies.

It may well be that in the short run the outcome would have been the same irrespective of the way in which that particular exercise was set up. This can be judged from the fate of the package of measures announced by the Chancellor, Selwyn Lloyd, in July 1961 as yet one more summer package in response to one more sterling crisis – which included among other items a public sector pay pause and a commitment to keep the following year's Estimates within 2½ per cent, in real terms, of the original 1961–62 Estimates (i.e. the Main Estimates, not including Supplementaries). At the time it seemed that at last the moment of truth had arrived for Britain, but the moment soon passed and the package did not hold together long. The Chancellor's initiative on the Estimates, which was rather reminiscent of Peter Thorneycroft's in 1957, met a similar fate, and the eventual increase in Main Estimates from year to year was 4½ per cent. Selwyn Lloyd himself was one of the casualties of the shift back from stop to go, and he was replaced by Reginald Maudling, who embarked on his 'dash for freedom' from the stop–go cycle.

In the short run the extent to which the growth of expenditure outstripped the growth of the economy was not as great at that stage as has sometimes been supposed. But the method of approach adopted in the 1961 expenditure exercise proved costly in the long run, as it set a precedent for basing Departmental claims on 'the costing of existing policy', which was a feature of the 1962 exercise also and of subsequent exercises. As a result, when programmes were rolled forward in successive surveys, they went into the new survey fatter than they had emerged from the previous survey, not because of any new Ministerial policy decisions in the meanwhile, but simply because of a rather subjective reassessment of the cost of the old policy in terms of real resources, over and above revaluation to take account of inflation. There is nothing sacrosanct about the percentage of GDP which public expenditure represents at a particular time; but what went wrong from the Treasury's point of view was that the Treasury's own survey system, as it was operated in practice, imparted a bias from the outset in favour of a constantly rising percentage.

But at any rate the planning of expenditure was still being related to a realistic appraisal of the economic growth rate. In 1963 this too went wrong, after the recently created National Economic Development Council approved the adoption of a growth rate of 4 per cent a year for the economy. As a consequence, Clarke writes that 'it was impracticable to conduct long-term public expenditure planning on any other estimated rate of growth of resources than 4 per cent p.a.' (p. 71). The 1963 exercise was conducted on this basis. The public expenditure plans for the period 1963–64 to 1967–68, published in a White Paper towards the end of the year (Cmnd. 2235), showed aggregate expenditure increasing by 4.1 per cent a year.

So we entered a period in which the growth of public expenditure was planned on the basis of an economic growth rate which had not been achieved in previous years and was to be achieved only in a few of the years which followed, and only at the expense of balance of payments deficits.

Theoretically [Clarke writes], the Government could have said reasonably and legitimately that it would continue to plan expenditure on a 3 per cent growth rate for resources until the various obstacles listed in the NEDC report had been sufficiently overcome to make it reasonably assured that the 4 per cent objective would be achieved.

But the overriding consideration was that the 4 per cent had become a fundamental ingredient of the Government's (and indeed Mr. Maudling's) policy, both to refute the political charges that the Government was restrictive and hostile to growth, and to provide a basis for a possible bargain with the trade unions linking together economic growth and incomes policy . . . (p. 71)

Now it is true, of course, that the government could not disown the NEDC target, since the Chancellor himself took the chair at the meetings of the Council, which was made up, as it still is, of members of the government and representatives of both sides of industry, plus some independent members. Nevertheless, it remains astonishing that the Treasury as a Department were prepared to accept with such fatalism the elevation of what was no more than an aspiration for economic growth into a firm commitment to the growth of expenditure. Or rather, it would be astonishing if we did not have so many other illustrations of the way in which plans can take over from reality.

The government had only a year or so to go after the 4 per cent commitment, and the expansion of programmes usually takes time to acquire momentum. A table showing the development of public expenditure from 1959 onwards appears in Appendix I at the back of this book (table A.1) and it can be seen that, between 1959 and 1964, the year in which the Conservative government lost office, public expenditure (on the 1976 definitions) rose as a percentage of GDP by less than a single percentage point over the five years, which were a period of relatively good economic growth.

But by the last year of the period, the momentum had grown. Public expenditure went up by 5.7 per cent in the calendar year 1964, and was now growing at a faster rate than the economy. A number of symptoms of excess pressure on resources were present. Although inflation was moderate by later standards, the figures in Appendix I show that GDP in current prices was rising at more than twice the trend 3 per cent rate of increase of GDP in real terms, the difference being accounted for by inflation. There was a mounting tide of imports and the trade deficit rose in 1964 to the highest figures since the Korean war. These indicators pointed to the need for a change in the exchange rate (we were in those years still on a fixed rate) or in fiscal policy, or both, and a shift of resources into the balance of payments. However, the long summer of 1964 wore on and autumn came without a change of policy. Sir Alec Douglas-Home had succeeded to the premiership when Macmillan gave it up because of ill health and R. A. Butler was manoeuvred out of the great prize for the second time. It was generally believed that new decisions on economic policy would not be taken before the coming general election, but the election was put off, and meanwhile the current account deficit escalated.

The election was finally held in October 1964 and was lost by the Conservatives after they had been in power for thirteen years, the longest continuous period of office enjoyed by a single party in Britain in modern times. It was also a period of economic growth, punctuated by sterling crises and the stop–go cycle. The early years of this period had the benefit of the world recovery from the effects of the second world war, the disappearance of shortages of supply and an improvement in the terms of trade. The phasing out of food rationing and subsidies, the unwinding of the Korean war rearmament programme, together with economic growth, enabled the country to move out of austerity into an era of rising public and private consumption. On the overseas front it was a period, apart from the Suez aberration, of continued decolonisation and of withdrawal, though only slowly, from the pretensions of great power status. The major new feature was the reorientation – but too late and unsuccessfully – towards Europe, though even then it was hard to cut the umbilical cord with the Commonwealth and to downgrade the American relationship.

Critics on the left dubbed this period thirteen years of Tory misrule. Yet, on the public expenditure front, if it was misrule it was of an opposite kind to traditional right-wing parsimony. There was a fair amount of expenditure which failed to pay off on nuclear and aerospace projects – fields in which, because of our war-time role, we had at one time the only capability outside the United States – and there was a school of thought in the Treasury that the country's industrial performance generally suffered through the diversion of too many resources to defence and high technology. But a good deal of the emphasis in public expenditure was on social programmes and measures to help the areas of high unemployment. For all his patrician leanings and his preference for aristocratic connections in those he appointed to high office, Harold Macmillan retained a genuine and deep-seated revulsion against the kind of mass unemployment that the country had experienced in the 1930s. Now, in the 1960s, an upward kink in national unemployment, which led to a disproportionate increase in the regional employment figures and to charges of a division of Britain into two nations, the North and the South, was sufficient to trigger off contracyclical programmes and special measures for the worst affected areas. And yet the unemployment of 1962 which preceded Maudling's reflationary budgets did not exceed half a million, and it had fallen well below that by 1964.

So the failures of those thirteen years were in a sense relative – a failure to retain our pre-eminence of the immediate post-war years or to match the phenomenal economic growth of other industrialised countries. Underlying this, however, were basic weaknesses in our industrial performance and our capacity to adapt to a changing world. From the left there was mounting criticism of the Establishment, including the civil service, which was held responsible for resistance to innovation and planning – though the National Economic Development Council and the National Incomes Commission (Neddy and Nicky) were two quite important initiatives in economic planning. Douglas-Home, to an even greater extent than Macmillan, appeared to personify the perpetuation of privilege and the class system. Harold Wilson's Labour government came into power committed more to the white hot technological revolution than to the extension of public ownership. But the most pressing failure which it inherited was represented by the unmanageable deficit on the balance of payments.

3

The Wilson Years

THE NATIONAL PLAN, ETCETERA

At the end of September 1964, I went to my last international meeting in Paris in my Overseas Finance capacity, then flew back to London to take over an Assistant Secretary post in a Treasury division called AT, which stood for Agriculture, Trade, Transport and Towns. Over part of this field it was a successor to the now defunct TI, in which I had worked earlier as a Principal. The Under Secretary in charge of AT was a former Board of Trade man called Russell Bretherton, noted for his peppery manner but underneath it a rather kind man, who had briefly represented the UK in the talks with the Six in 1955 about the proposed European Community until we ceased to attend.

I had two or three weeks to settle in before we were hit by the full impact of the new Labour government's 'first 100 days', a phrase much in vogue at the time. Nationalisation did not feature prominently in the new government's approach. Apart from the re-nationalisation of steel, the emphasis was on intervention in the economy rather than on extending public ownership. AT, because it covered that sector of the expenditure front, was much involved in most of the new initiatives for intervening in industry. The private sector reacted with hostility to these policies, in spite of the fact that they involved a good deal of government largesse for their benefit.

The Treasury, under James Callaghan as Chancellor, had to share responsibility in the economic field with the newly created Department of Economic Affairs under George Brown, an arrangement designed to produce 'creative tension'. We also shared the same building with them. A concordat was hastily drawn up setting out the respective responsibilities of the Treasury and the DEA. Harold Wilson has written of the division of labour in terms of the Treasury having responsibility in the monetary field and the DEA being concerned with real resources. Another way of putting it was that the Treasury kept responsibility for short-term management of the economy while the DEA were in the lead on longer-term policies. George Brown was number two in the government and the DEA took the chair in various committees dealing with economic matters such as regional policy and external economic policy. The Chancellor still had hold of the actual levers of economic and financial policy, including taxation and public expenditure – subject always to the collective process of decision-making on this matter – but in practice this freedom of action was constrained by the triangular relationship involving the Prime Minister, George Brown and himself.

With the creation of the DEA, the planning function which had previously been performed outside government proper by the NEDC was now brought within Whitehall itself, though the NEDC continued its separate existence as a tripartite body on which the government and both sides of industry were represented. The new Department was put together quite rapidly. Assembling new Departments and dismembering them according to the prevailing vogue and the penchant of Ministers of the day is something at which Whitehall has of necessity become very practised. (The Ministry of Technology was another new creation which took place at the same time.) Sir Eric Roll, who had been Economic Minister in the British Embassy in Washington, became the new Department's first Permanent Secretary, and for a time held both posts, commuting between Washington and London. Douglas Allen came in as Deputy Secretary dealing mainly with policy on pay and prices, and Sir Donald MacDougall came over from NEDO to take charge of economic planning. Some of the other DEA people came over from the Treasury, more from other Departments, and a fair number from the outside world. Critics of the civil service as unreceptive to new ideas cannot have witnessed the missionary spirit, sometimes spilling over into an uncritical enthusiasm for practically any fresh initiative, which the new Department generated among its recruits. There was also a certain amount of promotion going there, which is generally good for morale.

The DEA promptly fell to work compiling the National Plan, which in due course appeared as a White Paper (Cmnd. 2764) in September 1965. Much of this document struck me at the time of its preparation as a sort of What's On In Whitehall. That is to say, various Departments tabled statements of what they were doing and would in any case have been doing in their respective fields, which now became contributions to the National Plan. However, the centrepiece of the Plan was the growth target of 'a 25 per cent increase in national output between 1964 and 1970'. This objective had been chosen 'in the light of past trends . . . and a realistic view of the scope for improving upon these trends. It involves achieving a 4 per cent annual growth rate of output well before 1970 and an annual average of 3.8 per cent between 1964 and 1970'.

The Plan also stated that 'The Government have made a careful review of all the major programmes of public expenditure. These have been made consistent with the Government's decision to limit the growth of total public expenditure to an average of 4½ per cent a year at constant prices between 1964/65 and 1969/70'. There is a certain irony about the use of the word 'limit', as though the decision involved an act of austere self-denial, when in fact the government were planning to go beyond their predecessors' decision to increase public expenditure in line with an unrealised rate of economic growth and to increase it in excess of an unsustainable rate of growth. Yet the term had some validity in the sense that, if one took the projections of 'the cost of existing policies' which the new government inherited, then added on the additional cost of improving social security benefits and abolishing the prescription charge for medicine on which the government had decided during the first 100 days, some scaling down was required even to keep within the planned 4½ per cent growth rate for public expenditure.

One area in which there was real retrenchment was the defence budget, which was to be stabilised at the 1964–65 level, that is, at £2000 million at constant 1964 prices, instead of rising to £2400 million on the same price basis by 1969–70, as had previously been planned. This required the abandonment of a good many commitments, starting with a number of expensive military aircraft projects, of which the TSR2 was the most publicised. There was also a review of items of 'low economic priority such as prestige projects' outside the defence field, but this did not lead to any savings, unless one counts under that head a decision against a project for a nuclear-powered merchant ship which would never have been approved anyway. The Anglo-French Concorde supersonic passenger aircraft, which was the prestige project *par excellence*, survived the review intact because the French, who regard prestige as a benefit worth paying for, refused to consider termination of the project.

Jim Callaghan, unlike his Labour predecessors in the Treasury, who had been middle-class intellectuals, was the first and the only Chancellor of the Exchequer in the period covered by this narrative to have spent his early life in a household which knew shortage of money. He had therefore more than a purely intellectual commitment to the role of public expenditure as an instrument for welfare and equality of opportunity. He was also, as Member for a South Wales constituency, sympathetic to measures for promoting industrial development and employment. The same comment might be made of Callaghan's attitude as of Hugh Gaitskell's support for the Korean war rearmament programme – that it is a mistake for a Chancellor of the Exchequer to be in favour of expenditure. Jack Diamond on the other hand, later Lord Diamond, who was Chief Secretary at the Treasury throughout the Labour administration, cast himself in a habitually critical role in relation to particular expenditure measures, but this did not extend to criticism of the overall expenditure strategy which featured in the National Plan.

The intellectual climate in which Labour came to office was of course favourable both to economic growth targets, which had been supported from all sides in the NEDC, and to planned growth of public expenditure, which had been adopted by their predecessors, and they had no reason to question the strategy. On my own recollection William Armstrong, as Callaghan's Permanent Secretary, did not seek to dissuade him from the view that there was nothing sacrosanct about the existing public expenditure/GDP ratio and that there was no specific figure within which that ratio must be contained.

The fatalism with which the Treasury seems to have accepted the National Plan commitment is borne out by Otto Clarke's account of the matter in his book on public expenditure. Clarke goes so far in fact as to commend (on p. 120) the acceptance of the 4½ per cent growth limit for public expenditure as 'a remarkable achievement' and 'good statesmanship'. In an editorial footnote on this, Alec Cairncross remarks that 'It is not clear why, after the lengthy discussion of the previous government's commitment in 1963 to the objective of 4 per cent growth and the risks that this entailed in the planning of public expenditure, no comment is made on the still greater risk entailed in the commitment in 1965 to an even faster growth in public expenditure'. It is true that a little later on (p. 132) Clarke writes as follows: '. . . the 4½ per cent growth rate was too high . . . The National Plan growth figures were also too high.' However, he goes on to say: 'But after the all party acceptance of "Neddy" in 1963, Mr. Wilson, Mr. Callaghan and Mr. Brown could not in practical terms have worked on lower figures . . . For my part, I never thought that a lower figure than 4½ per cent could be acceptable, and I cannot recall that there were others in responsible positions who disagreed.'

No doubt that is true, so far as it goes, but it fits in better with the criticism of civil servants as too disposed to tell Ministers what they want to hear, or at any rate not to tell them what they do not want to hear, than the latter-day myth of the obstructionist civil service. The period immediately after an election is of course a tricky one in relationships between new Ministers and old officials. Nevertheless, in my experience Ministers for whom I have worked, including James Callaghan, have been prepared to give a hearing to frank advice, even if they do not accept it, provided that they believe in the adviser's competence and good faith and that the dialogue stays within the four walls of the Department.

Not that, in any event, there is anything necessarily wrong in principle in a policy of letting public expenditure rise at a faster rate than output, thus increasing the public expenditure/GDP ratio, provided that it can be financed in a non-inflationary way and that there are systems for getting value for money out of the expenditure. Moreover the ratio was not as big then as it was to become in the 1970s or as it still is in the 1980s. But, as Cairncross's editorial comment suggests, there were great risks in anticipating a growth of output which still had to be achieved. Moreover the inherited current account deficit indicated a need to shift resources into the balance of payments rather than into public expenditure. So, if we are resuming our tally of what went wrong with the great new public expenditure planning system, we notch up the fact that the target rate of growth in GDP to which the 1964 expenditure strategy was geared was one which put great strain both on the economy (for instance, as early as 1965 a typical summer package of measures became necessary, including a messy six-month postponement of new capital projects in the public sector) and also, in conjunction with prevailing cost levels and a fixed exchange rate, on the balance of payments.

In that situation the most fateful decision taken during the first 100 days, taken in fact in the first few days after the 1964 election, was one which did not feature in the National Plan at all, that is, the rejection of devaluation. The decision against devaluing the pound, which was either supported by most Establishment opinion at the time or at any rate not opposed by it, was taken at a meeting of a small group of Ministers after an earlier meeting with an equally small number of officials. Among Whitehall economists generally there was a division of opinion on this issue, but the pro-devaluation school of thought was either not represented or was not vocal at these particular discussions, in which political rather than purely economic considerations were uppermost. This was the first Labour government for thirteen years. If, following the Cripps devaluation of 1949, the new Labour government were to do the same as one of its first acts, it would be easy for its opponents to identify Labour administrations with devaluation of the currency. The mere prospect of a Labour government might be enough to trigger off a run against the pound. Moreover, working-class people would suffer from a devaluation which increased import costs in terms of sterling and so raised the cost of living.

Some who took this view then still take it, so far as concerns the situation in 1964, even if they came round later, at varying dates, to believing that the time had come to devalue. However, whatever the case for seeking to defend the existing parity in 1964, it was inevitable that from then on the government would be contending with unrelieved balance of payments difficulties and pressure on sterling, with repeated recourse to the IMF and central banks for balance of payments support. By way of mitigation of the trade effects of the exchange rate, a temporary import surcharge was imposed on imported goods, which caused a great storm internationally and especially in EFTA, and a 2 per cent rebate of indirect taxes was introduced for exports. In addition, those economic advisers who would have liked to see us devalue hoped instead to get a 'devaluation effect' through various schemes of assistance to manufacturing industry, which would as a result be better able to compete with foreign manufacturers in spite of the high exchange rate for sterling.

Initially, the new team of Ministers and advisers found themselves rather short of instruments and powers – meaning legislative powers – to match their interventionist ambitions. The purposes for which governments in this country can spend money are limited not by law but by understandings which have been agreed over the years between the Treasury and the Public Accounts Committee of the House of Commons. Under these conventions it is acceptable to spend money within reason on a once-for-all basis on some new item of expenditure without passing specific legislation for the purpose, provided that Parliament approves Estimate provision for the expenditure, which then, under the procedures governing Vote Estimates, derives its ultimate legislative sanction from the Appropriation Act. But the convention is that specific power should be taken for any major continuing new service. Whichever of these two procedures is relied upon, it is possible in cases of urgency to proceed in advance of either Estimates or legislation by drawing the money from the Contingencies Fund (formerly known as the Civil Contingencies Fund) and notifying Parliament that this is being done;

the normal method of informing Parliament in this kind of case is either through an oral statement by the Minister concerned or by means of a written answer to an arranged Parliamentary Question, for which purposes Ministers have friendly Members of Parliament prepared to table such questions whenever asked. The money drawn from the Contingencies Fund in these circumstances is repaid to it after the Estimate has gone through; no final charge remains with the Contingencies Fund. It fell to me to give this advice to Ministers and spending Departments so often that it is still, some years later, fresh in my mind.

The position in 1964 as regards financial powers for intervention was that the government had traditionally supported industrial research and development in a number of ways, but assistance to industrial production had been much less systematic. Various Acts of Parliament over the years had authorised schemes of assistance to particular industries, notably launching aid for aircraft projects, but also such cases as rationalisation of the cotton industry and a certain amount of finance for film production. There were also general powers under the Local Employment Acts to help enterprises that provided jobs in the development areas, but there were no general powers, of the kind which some of the new team wished to see, to spend money on intervention in the whole range of industry throughout the country.

The nearest thing to that was a little known and little used provision in the Borrowing Control and Guarantees Act 1946. This piece of legislation was mainly concerned with the control which used to be exercised in Britain over the raising of loans, but there was also a clause enabling the Treasury to guarantee loans for the benefit of UK industries. Early in the government's life, when the Chancellor was approached about the problems of a Clydeside shipyard called Fairfields, and brains were being racked about ways and means of doing something for them, I reminded Bretherton of the existence of this provision, which was in the event used to guarantee a loan of £1 million from the Bank of England to the shipyard. We did not know, of course, that this was to be the forerunner of a flood of legislation and money for the Clydeside shipyards and the shipbuilding industry generally.

One of the initiatives designed to provide new powers and instruments of intervention was the creation of the Industrial Reorganisation Corporation (IRC), with funds for investing in the private sector of industry. This body was financed partly by government loans and partly by so-called public dividend capital

(PDC) from a DEA Vote. This is a quasi-equity type of government financing which, unlike issues from the National Loans Fund, does not carry fixed terms for repayment or interest, and which in practice, more often than not, ends up as an outright grant. The IRC was modelled to some extent on the Italian IRI, but its special role was to promote mergers in industry, since there was at that time a belief in the advantage of large-scale organisation. The biggest merger which it helped to promote was the ill-fated creation of British Leyland. One of its more successful operations was of the opposite kind – the de-merger of the failed Cammell-Laird group, through which the potentially profitable engineering side was split off and became the Laird Group, unencumbered by the continuing losses of the Cammell-Laird shipyard on Merseyside.

But the IRC did not altogether provide the desired capability for intervention, partly because it was not always as pliable as Whitehall might have liked, and partly because – even though its public dividend capital gave it a good deal of flexibility in the terms of its operations – it could not dissipate its resources on projects with little or no prospect of a financial return, even if there were political reasons for wanting to intervene. Powers for the government itself to put money directly into industry were taken at a later stage in the Industrial Expansion Act. This gave Departments wide powers to finance industrial investment schemes without having to introduce further primary legislation (that is, without a fresh Act of Parliament each time), but on the basis that each scheme would be embodied in subordinate legislation in the form of a Statutory Instrument laid before Parliament. At the same time the Treasury's guarantee powers under the 1946 Act were repealed as being unnecessary under the new arrangements. The Industrial Expansion Act, and in particular the involvement of Parliament through the Statutory Instrument procedure, were largely the conception of Anthony Wedgwood Benn after he succeeded Frank Cousins as Minister of Technology, but this legislation did not take place until a relatively late stage, and in the event hardly any use was made of these enabling powers.

There were other new developments on the Ministry of Labour front, which also came within AT's sphere of interest, especially the first ever national redundancy payments scheme, including a National Redundancy Fund financed out of a supplement to national insurance contributions. I saw this as having the social objective of giving workers something of the same kind as golden handshakes received by industrialists. Enthusiasts in the DEA saw it as a measure to promote mobility of labour. Nobody at the time foresaw the role of this scheme as a palliative to take some of the sting out of mass unemployment. The Labour government also decided to go ahead with plans prepared under their predecessors, but not yet implemented, to set up Industrial Training Boards financed by levies on employers.

Meanwhile a profusion of unorthodox schemes for stimulating economic growth flowed from the fertile minds of the new men in Whitehall. Generally speaking these schemes were selective in the sense of involving subsidies for whole categories of production or whole parts of the country (possibly at the expense of other categories of industry or other regions) rather than selective action related to particular projects of the kind with which the IRC was concerned. Ideas of this kind, such as a scheme for a subsidy from the South to the North, had been publicly aired as part of the great debate before the election about how to get Britain out of its rut. A number of schemes, listed – if I remember correctly – Plan A, Plan B and so on, down to Plan F, were remitted for study. Out of these only one was adopted and the others were put aside, though not, as it transpired later, forever.

The plan which found favour was the scheme for investment grants, which were to replace certain tax allowances for capital expenditure, that is, investment allowances and, in the Development Areas, free depreciation The scheme was announced in a White Paper on *Investment Incentives* in January 1966 (Cmnd. 2874) and given legal effect by the Industrial Development Act of 1966. The new capital grants were focused essentially on plant or machinery in private sector manufacturing industry, but it is always difficult to draw the line in selective schemes, and so the grants also applied to some other parts of the private sector – extraction and construction, and to scientific research related to all these industries. The grant scheme also covered computers – irrespective of the industries using them – ships, hovercraft and mining works. The standard rate of grant was 20 per cent, with a higher rate of 40 per cent for the Development Areas. However, quite early on, when it was thought that a stimulus was needed in order to bring forward investment, it was announced that these rates would be increased, as a temporary measure, to 25 per cent and 45 per cent respectively in 1967 and 1968.

Several strands of thought came together in this scheme. The prime object was to promote higher economic growth, since Whitehall economists (both the resident kind and the new men) found a close correlation between investment and growth in other industrialised countries, though I myself attached as much or more importance in our circumstances to better industrial relations and use of manpower. At the same time the scheme was designed as a further instrument for steering investment to the Development Areas and, side by side with the new grant scheme, a new and wider concept of these areas was introduced, with strong support from the DEA. Almost the whole of Scotland became a Development Area, and the Development Areas in Wales, the North and the South West and on Merseyside were substantially extended. Northern Ireland, which is administered separately, has never been a Development Area as such but has always had equivalent or better treatment in subsidy schemes. (A note on the financial arrangements for Northern Ireland appears in Appendix II.) Thirdly, the scheme was designed to favour science and technology, and it is interesting that in 1966 hovercraft were seen as having a great future. (A hovertrain for use on land was scotched only with some difficulty.)

Finally there was the objective, unavowed publicly, of providing a 'devaluation substitute' by means of a subsidy for manufacturing industries that had to compete in home and export markets, since an overt export subsidy was ruled out. There is no great administrative problem about export subsidies. At that time, for instance, one could have increased the value of the export rebate so that it did more than rebate indirect taxes, or later on, after the introduction of VAT, one could have had a negative rate of VAT for exports, but it would not have been possible to get away with these devices. British governments tend to believe that they are the only ones to observe the provisions on export subsidies and such like in the GATT, which is the least favourite of the international institutions in their eyes. In fact the EFTA provisions on state aids and export subsidies were much more binding at that time, as are the EEC rules today, being designed in both cases to ensure that the removal of tariffs and import quotas is not negated by other measures which prevent the operation of a free market; but though the GATT does not have the same legal force as the EFTA agreement or the Treaty of Rome, it gets its force from the right of retaliation. Investment grants and such like were the nearest that could be found to a way round these difficulties, but inevitably, whatever their merits in other respects, they were a very poor fall-back as devaluation substitutes.

A principal advantage claimed for investment grants – though devotees of the profit motive would see this as an argument against the whole idea – was that companies would get them irrespective of the profits which they were making, whereas they get the benefit of tax allowances only if they are making profits against which to set the allowances. This change was seen as particularly favourable to the setting up of new enterprises, especially in the Development Areas. It was also planned that companies should get the benefit of the grant payments with a much shorter time-lag than in the case of tax allowances. Initially the grants were not to be payable until eighteen months after the capital expenditure had been incurred, so as to avoid a double cost to the government while the old tax allowances were being worked off, but later on the time-lag was to be progressively reduced to an interval of only six months.

After the main policy decisions had been taken, responsibility for working out the administrative arrangements and preparing the legislation was handed over to the Board of Trade, which was still the leading Department in this field, as the Ministry of Technology's functions were still relatively limited. We had expected that the scheme would embody, for instance, schedules of the types of plant and machinery which would be eligible for grant, but, instead of framing the scheme in terms of objective criteria of that kind, the Board of Trade adopted, as a central concept, the criterion that grants would be payable on capital expenditure incurred for the purpose of making an article. There was no attempt to spell out which industries would be counted as manufacturing industries or what items would be treated as plant or machinery. Everything depended on a subjective judgment of the purpose for which capital expenditure was incurred, and the legislation gave the Board of Trade complete discretion in exercising this judgment.

Subsidy schemes tend to be open-ended to a certain extent, and the investment grant scheme was bound to be demand-responsive in the sense that the size of the grant bill would depend on the level of investment. The more successful it was as an incentive scheme, the more it would cost. But the investment grant scheme was gratuitously open-ended in these other respects also. We had no means of knowing how many companies would apply or for how much. However, the Board of Trade officials who were in charge of working out the scheme were rather strong-willed individuals and, since they would have the responsibility of running the scheme, they were given their head in devising it.

Investment grants for ships proved to be particularly disaster prone. It was not open to us to tie investment grants to equipment made in Britain, but in general it was a condition of the scheme that grants were payable only on plant and machinery installed for use in this country. However, ships were the only capital item to which, in the nature of the case, this condition could not be applied. Grant could therefore be claimed towards the cost of ships bought abroad and plying their trade between other countries. In the worst cases grants were being claimed by foreign-owned brass plate companies registered here for the sole purpose of getting these subsidies. But even in other cases where companies were registered in the UK in the normal way, there might be little or no benefit to this country to justify subsidising them at the taxpayer's expense. Moreover the bill for investment grants for ships began to get out of hand.

The Treasury therefore proposed that a balance of payments test should be introduced in these cases and that ships should not get grants unless it could be shown that there was a net benefit to our balance of payments. But the Board of Trade resisted this measure on the grounds that the EFTA countries would object to it as a piece of discrimination against ships bought from their shipyards. At one point I was deputed, on the Chief Secretary's behalf, to carry on a discussion of possible solutions to this problem with Edmund Dell, who was at that time Minister of State at the Board of Trade. Agreement was reached quite quickly on a compromise under which a balance of payments test would be introduced with an exemption for ships bought from EFTA countries, but this settlement was not accepted on my own side, and the issue continued unresolved, with more money running out, to my chagrin. Some time later, when the issue came before Ministers collectively, this compromise proposal was accepted after all as the solution to the problem, and the earlier objections to it appeared to have been completely forgotten.

I shall come back to the investment grant saga later on, but we need to digress briefly from the expenditure theme to note that meanwhile a great deal of effort had been exerted on the pay and prices front, initially in the form of a voluntary incomes policy, and then through the instrument of the National Board for Prices and Incomes, with statutory powers to vet increases in wages and prices. In this phase of policy the government had power to delay particular increases though not to veto them altogether. Although there are inevitably different assessments today of the effectiveness of these efforts, there is a case for regarding the Prices and Incomes Board as one of the more successful experiments in this field of policy.

REP – THE GREEN PAPER

In the event, investment grants were not the only scheme to emerge from the welter of plans for new taxes and subsidies. The Selective

Employment Tax (SET) and the regional employment premium (REP) followed in 1966 and 1967 respectively. The persistence of Nicki Kaldor had a lot to do with this. In the public mind he tended to be bracketed with another of the economic advisers imported into Whitehall, Thomas Balogh, because they both came from Hungary, but apart from that, and the fact that they both later became members of the House of Lords, they were quite unlike each other. Whereas Balogh's manner towards ordinary civil servants was dismissive, Kaldor was endlessly persuasive (though not himself readily open to persuasion) and would cultivate anyone, regardless of grade, who had a part to play in the schemes dear to his heart. He also had the great advantage of being located in the Treasury and having the ear of the Chancellor of the Exchequer.

Another point of interest in these events is that the proposal for the regional employment premium was published in the first ever Green Paper, which set a precedent for trying out new policy proposals in a consultative document instead of announcing cut and dried decisions in a White Paper. The Green Paper was William Armstrong's idea and I was the draftsman, but the neo-Keynesian economic theory, as distinct from the practical administrative side, was pure Kaldor. That Green Paper in fact represented the heyday of neo-Keynesian theory and a low point for monetarist doctrine.

My involvement in the story began when I was asked to call on William Armstrong, who told me that employers were to pay a new tax on each employee, but some industries were to have the tax refunded and others would get it back with a premium added. When I asked what was the point of this, he replied 'None at all'. This no doubt reflected his concern about getting a complicated new scheme of this kind to work in the short time allowed for its introduction, in contrast to Nicki Kaldor's tendency to disregard mere administrative difficulties. From the Chancellor's point of view, as I now know, the point of SET was that, contrary to previous advice, he was now being advised that there was a need to raise extra taxation, but he was unwilling to change tack and increase any of the traditional taxes; he therefore welcomed a proposal for broadening the tax base. From Nicki Kaldor's point of view, the scheme had the additional virtues of subsidising manufacturing industry, which had the greatest potential for increased productivity and made the greatest contribution to exports, at the expense of the service industries which, in his eyes, had less scope for increasing their productivity and which primarily served the home market; it would also act as a further devaluation substitute. The nationalised industries, local authorities and agriculture were to get neutral treatment and would receive the tax refund but not the premium.

As William Armstrong explained to me, it would not be possible simply to exempt this neutral category from paying SET in the first place, because the tax was to be collected as a supplement to national insurance contributions, and it would not be feasible administratively to introduce selectivity into the collection of insurance contributions-cum-SET. The desired effect would therefore have to be achieved in a roundabout way. All employers would have to pay the tax, and a suitable Department had to be found to pay the refunds and premiums to eligible employers out of a new Vote. Ned Dunnett – Sir James Dunnett, at that time Permanent Secretary of what was then the Ministry of Labour and is now the Department of Employment – had agreed that his Department would take this on, subject to two stipulations: that the scheme should be based on the Standard Industrial Classification (SIC), and that there should be tribunals to adjudicate on disputes about the application of the rules. I was to go over to the Ministry of Labour, which was promoting Kenneth Clucas to Under Secretary to take charge of the scheme, and work out with them arrangements that would meet the requirements of accountability and stand up to Parliamentary scrutiny.

The SIC, of which I had never heard until then, was explained in a Ministry of Labour booklet, which was used for various statistical purposes, and which listed every conceivable working activity under the appropriate classification – manufacturing of various kinds, construction, distribution and so on. The SIC embodied the useful concept of 'establishments', and from this starting point we worked out further rules to determine which were manufacturing establishments and which were not. Establishments which were eligible under the rules had to be registered at the outset of the scheme. At the end of each period the employer filled in a fairly simple form stating that he had paid Selective Employment Tax on a specified number of workers in the establishment and claiming the refund or the refund plus premium on each worker. The Selective Employment Payments scheme was the very opposite of the investment grants scheme in three important respects. First, the discretionary element was reduced to a minimum, and any disputes over the application of the rules were resolved by a tribunal and not by administrative fiat. Second, from the time of registration of establishments we knew how many applicants for SEP there would be and could make a fairly close estimate of the amount that would be involved. Finally, the scheme could be operated by the existing

Ministry of Labour offices without the need to set up a whole new administrative machine.

Nicki Kaldor was not pleased with me over the payment of the premium for everybody in a manufacturing establishment rather than for those workers in it who were actually engaged on the manufacturing process. Since statistics existed of the numbers of fitters, electricians and so on, he had envisaged that the subsidy would be paid only in respect of workers in such categories, to the exclusion of clerks and cleaners and so on. However, I was quite clear that, while it was possible to frame simple rules so that establishments where most of the staff were engaged in office work or transport would be excluded from subsidy, an establishment as a whole had to be in or out. Once there was money at stake, and if it became a matter of more than statistical interest how a worker was classified, cleaners would become craftsmen at the stroke of a pen in order to attract the premium.

Wynne Godley, one of the regular economic advisers and not a political appointee, was another who was not pleased with me because he believed that these rules would vitiate the theoretical estimates which he had worked out for the scheme. However, the Estimate which was put to Parliament for the first Selective Employment Payments Vote was reasonably in line with the theoretical estimates, and the out-turn for the first seven months of the scheme, that is up to the end of March 1977, fell short by only £10½ million of the Estimate provision of £312½ million, which was an exceptionally close result. The refunds of SET, though provided from Voted money, did not count as public expenditure, since they merely acted as a form of tax exemption, but the premium payments did count as additional expenditure.

Of course, using the SIC, which had been drawn up as a basis for statistics and not for subsidies, threw up a number of borderline problems, such as the treatment of a bakery (manufacturing) with a baker's shop attached (retailing), which constituted one establishment for SIC purposes. When Nicki Kaldor first sold the scheme to James Callaghan, I do not believe that the Chancellor had bargained for such contentious issues as the comparative treatment of publishers who did their own printing, and who would therefore get the refund and premium on all their staff, and non-printing publishers who would pay the tax without refund and who would thus be at a disadvantage as regards their publishing costs, unless a special dispensation were made in their favour – as, in the end, was done, on the urging of economic advisers while I was away from the office.

However, borderline problems are inevitable in any selective scheme. The initial rules, which were worked out under great pressure of time and without consultation with the industries affected because of the secrecy required, stood the test of time rather well, and purely from the point of view of good administration I got as much professional satisfaction from my part in that scheme as from practically anything else I had a hand in.

The administrative simplicity of the scheme for selective employment payments was one of the reasons why, with regional policies so much in vogue, it was only a matter of time before a proposal emerged for adding a regional dimension to the scheme. The proposal involved an extra premium of £1 to £2 a man per week, with smaller sums for women and young people, for employees in manufacturing establishments in the Development Areas. One of the troubles with inflation is that particular sums of money lose their significance; a weekly subsidy of a pound or two per head would not today seem very striking, but at that time it represented 5 to 10 per cent of labour costs. The figure of £1.50 a man which was eventually adopted involved total payments of £100 million a year. Although this was less than a twentieth of the defence budget, it can be compared with spending in 1967–68 of £15 million on the arts, £76 million on science through the Research Councils, or £205 million on Overseas Aid, and so it entailed a middling-sized additional expenditure programme.

The REP proposal was processed through an inter-Departmental group of Permanent Secretaries, with William Armstrong as Chairman and myself as scribe. William Armstrong took personal charge of the arrangements as the Second Permanent Secretary post on the expenditure side of the Treasury was vacant, since Otto Clarke had left to become Permanent Secretary of the Ministry of Aviation and then of the Ministry of Technology. Peter Vinter, the Deputy Secretary on the PESC side, who was a bright, friendly person, filled the breach for most purposes, without promotion.

Armstrong was objectivity personified. At the time of our first encounter some years earlier, when he was an Under Secretary and I a Principal, I was astonished to find myself talking to someone among my elders and betters on the Overseas Finance side who had an open mind on things and wanted to know the facts of the case and the arguments. After he became Permanent Secretary, if there was anything he wanted to talk about, he still always found all the time that was needed for it, no matter what else was happening. He seemed, in fact, incapable of having a view until he had gone through this process of weighing all the evidence and all the arguments. And yet, though this did not emerge clearly until a later stage, there coexisted with this intellectual detachment a curious messianic streak, deriving perhaps from his Salvation Army background, which could lead him to become committed to otherwise uncharacteristic emotional attitudes in particular situations.

After an exhaustive series of discussions, in which he allowed everyone to talk themselves out, he finally let me draft a report to Ministers, as I had been impatient to do, in order to get a decision on REP in time for the 1967 Budget. Even then the report did not come down for or against the scheme but recommended that, if the government wished to take it further, there should first be consultation with industry, after which the proposal should be tabled for public discussion. In due course it fell to me to draft a memorandum for publication. There was, however, some uncertainty as to whether the Chancellor was to accept paternity for the proposal, and at one stage responsibility for issuing the memorandum at Budget time was handed over to the Department of Economic Affairs, where Sir Donald MacDougall had all along been a strong supporter of the idea of a regional labour subsidy. It was at this juncture that the DEA chose a green cover for the publication in preference to the other colours available from Her Majesty's Stationery Office, since the document was to be something different from the traditional White Paper and there were already Blue Books, while there were objections of one kind or another to the other shades in HMSO's colour range. But as the Budget approached, with nothing else of major interest in it, there was some fear that the Chancellor's thunder would be stolen by the REP memorandum. Since it was now too late to claw it back from the DEA altogether, it was published in the names of the Department of Economic Affairs and HM Treasury jointly, but still in the green cover chosen by the DEA.

Speakers in the Budget debate which followed immediately applied the term Green Paper to this memorandum, and the phrase then passed into Whitehall usage to denote a consultative document, even though so-called 'Green Papers' came to be issued as what were formally White Papers. The phrase 'White Paper with green edges' tended to be used to denote a semi-consultative document setting out proposals which were fairly firm, but not quite so. But although there was quite a lot of interest in the modest innovation which that first Green Paper represented, it was a disappointment in the sense that it stimulated hardly any informed discussion or comment on the substance of the document, and the reactions to it added nothing to the argumentation for and against the proposal. After taking views round the table in his office, the Chancellor decided in favour of the regional employment premium. I myself, while having no belief in the slide-rule calculations of economic advisers such as Nicki Kaldor and Robert Neild, took the view – a little to their relief, I think – that putting £100 million a year into the Development Areas was bound to have some effect.

The Green Paper began with an opening phrase which still seems to me to have quite a good ring: 'In the space of two generations there have been massive changes in the way that people in Britain earn their living.' It went on to show how these changes had produced a disparity between unemployment in the Development Areas and in the country as a whole, and to argue that the regional employment premium might reduce this disparity by something like a half over a period of years – an example of the kind of slide-rule calculation to which I have referred. It was ironic, writing in 1983 when the national unemployment rate had risen above 13 per cent, to look back and see how small total unemployment was and how limited the regional disparity. The figures quoted in the Green Paper showed that in the period 1959–1966 the worst year was 1963, when the unemployment rates for Great Britain and the Development Areas were 2.2 per cent and 4.4 per cent respectively. In 1966, the year of the Green Paper, the corresponding figures, which gave so much concern, were no more than 1.4 per cent and 2.7 per cent.

It is even more ironical, at a time when monetarist doctrine is in the ascendancy in government economic policy, even if only for the time being perhaps, to re-read the Green Paper argument that 'provided these payments are confined to manufacturing industry in the Development Areas – their effects on the pressure of demand and the balance of payments will not be such as to require offsetting taxation to release resources for the subsidy'. Nor would there be any need to cut other public expenditure. The underlying thesis, not made altogether explicit in the Green Paper, was that, with the uneven distribution of employment in the country, attempts to run the economy at a high level of activity led to over-heating in the areas of high employment while unemployment was still relatively high in the Development Areas. By producing a shift in demand and output from the former to the latter, the regional premium would make possible a higher but more evenly spread total demand, thus increasing net output and resources without the inflationary chain reaction which usually resulted from attempts to expand the economy. One assumption which was essential to this chain of argument was that 'the premium payments would not be swallowed up by extra wage increases' in Development Area companies. In this philosophy the function of taxation was expressed in terms not of providing the government with money, but of reducing the taxpayer's use of resources, so freeing resources for other uses. Since REP would increase net total resources, it did not create any need for taxation in order to free resources.

I did myself insert into the development of this theme a statement that 'The regional premium will, of course, have to be paid for in the sense that the Exchequer will have to provide funds for the scheme and account for them as it must do for all programmes of Government expenditure'. But the Green Paper did not say where in fact the funds were to come from – the word money did not appear anywhere in the text – and I for one should not have been able, in the state of my knowledge at the time, to explain how in fact they were to be provided. But, with one exception, nobody asked. Nobody, so far as I know, even raised the question of the implications for the money supply. In 1981, when this book was first being written, the country was being run in accordance with a medium-term plan to reduce the rate of growth of the money suply. In 1966 nobody talked, or cared, about the money supply.

The only person who, to my knowledge, asked where the cash for the £100 million was to come from was one of the reporters at William Armstrong's press conference on the publication of the Green Paper, to whom Armstrong replied that this 'came close to the creation of money'. About a dozen years later, when we had both left the Treasury, I reminded him of this and said that it now seemed to me that what was involved was in fact the creation of money – though, within the total growth in the money supply, it would hardly be possible to identify £100 million which was being created specifically to finance REP. Armstrong said that it was because of this last point that he had talked about 'coming close' to the creation of money, but he agreed that it was money creation which was involved.

Let me now try to set out how, after this lapse of time, I see the limits on public expenditure in terms of resources on the one hand and money on the other.

THE LIMITS OF PUBLIC EXPENDITURE

If resources are to be used by the state rather than by private individuals, the state must find a means of appropriating resources for its own use and denying their use to the individual. There was a time in history when this could be done without involving money. The Pharaohs could meet the labour cost of building the Pyramids through the use of slaves. Emperors and kings might find the resources for their wars by direct pre-emption of goods and services – by requiring vassal princes or feudal barons to provide men or materials, by exacting tribute in kind, by living off the land, or by expropriating their enemies. In Britain the nearest we have got in modern times to such means of commandeering resources for the use of the state without proper payment has been conscription, which, in the two world wars and for a period in peace-time, enabled manpower to be mobilised at much less than its cost in a free labour market.

But, generally speaking, in the money economies of today, the state has to pay with money for the resources it uses, and for the most part it has to raise the money in two ways: by taxation, in which for this purpose we can count national insurance contributions,[1] and by borrowing. Both taxation and government borrowing from the public are methods through which people and companies forgo spending part of their money incomes on consumption or private investment; their individual claims on resources are thus surrendered to the state. The function of taxation is not merely to 'release resources' but also (unless the government is running a budget surplus designed to reduce total demand and is therefore not spending all its tax revenue) to enable the government to pay for the use of resources. What is involved is not a direct transfer of resources like tribute in kind, but a transfer of money claims on resources, and this is equally true when private savings are transferred to the state through government borrowing. To the extent that the government spends the money on goods and services, it is not the same mixture of goods and services as the private citizen would have bought, and the prices which it pays for similar types of goods and services may also be different. To the extent that the government, having received the money, re-transfers it through 'transfer payments' such as subsidies and social security benefits, though a good deal of the money may go back to the people

[1] Beveridge drew the following distinction between taxation and insurance contributions: 'taxation is or should be related to assumed capacity to pay rather than to the value of what the payer may expect to receive, while insurance contributions are or should be related to the value of the benefits and not to capacity to pay' (The Beveridge Report on Social Insurance, 107). But both do in fact make demands on the taxable capacity of employed people and reduce take-home pay. In OECD statistics 'Social Security taxes' are treated, along with direct and indirect taxes, as making up total taxation.

who contributed it in the first instance, part will also go to different people, so that we get a redistribution of income which in its turn will be spent on a different mixture of goods and services.

If we ask what are, or should be, the limits of public expenditure, in one sense this involves value judgments about the kind of society we want; it raises issues about the role of the market and what functions should be taken out of the market into the public services. From another point of view the question can be framed in terms of the limits on taxation beyond which you get a taxpayers' revolt, either at the ballot box or through the growth of tax evasion and the black economy or in the form of a preference for tax-free social security benefits over taxed employment; and it can be framed in terms of the limits beyond which the government cannot borrow savings from the private non-bank sector without paying excessive interest rates and crowding out private industrial borrowers. I do not propose to take any of these issues further in this section, but to probe a little the question of whether and in what circumstances it is possible to circumvent the constraints of taxable capacity and of the supply of savings by the creation of money. For that was the issue, though it was not explicitly stated, which was raised in relation to REP by the Green Paper, and it was a central question in 1981 for the management of the economy as a whole.

Let me, at this stage, introduce one refinement. Governments with a budget problem tend to look at the scope for increased rents and charges (although these are generally treated statistically as reducing the public expenditure bill rather than as a means of financing it) and to resort to sales of government-owned assets as ways of easing these constraints. But in practice it is usually a great struggle to keep public sector rents and charges moving up in line with inflation, and it is only lately that it has been possible to look upon a few of the publicly owned monopolies, and especially the nationalised gas industry which has benefited from the world-wide escalation of oil and gas prices, as a source of net cash flow for the government. As for disposals of assets, the scope for raising money in this way tends to be less in practice than in theory, and each operation brings in only a once-for-all receipt. In any event, after allowance has been made for these possibilities, the typical problem for a contemporary government, faced with a given level of expenditure to finance and wanting to avoid tax increases so far as possible, is how much to borrow and from what sources.

In a situation of full employment, with productive capacity fully used and output growing as fast as the growth in productivity will allow, an analysis in neo-Keynesian resource terms or an analysis in monetary terms will produce the same answer. If you do not want inflation, the government can in principle borrow only as much as people in the non-bank sector are prepared to save and to lend to the government, thus 'releasing resources' or, more strictly speaking, transferring their money claims on resources. In some circumstances the government may borrow from abroad, which means that foreigners must lend their savings and thus make claims on resources available. Beyond that, any further government borrowing can come only from the banking system, which involves the creation of money, popularly though not accurately referred to as 'printing money'. This effect can be produced in two ways. On the one hand the government is putting into people's pockets, by means of public expenditure, more money than it is taking out through taxation and borrowing of savings. At the same time, the sale of government securities to the banks increases the reserve assets against which the banks can give credit; the specific effects on credit and the money supply will, however, depend on the system of monetary control in operation at the time and the role of reserve assets in the system. (In practice, under the various systems adopted in Britain for some time now, reserve assets have not been a limiting factor on bank lending.)

Additional bank borrowing by the private sector, whether companies or individuals, can equally be said to involve the creation or 'printing' of money. Some annual increase in the flow of money is necessary to accommodate growth in output and real incomes, and to that extent borrowing from the banking system by the government and private sector combined need not be inflationary. But, beyond that, the financing of government expenditure in this way, if resources are already fully stretched, must tend to be inflationary, whether one describes this in terms of the creation of money or the creation of excess demand on resources.

This has been demonstrated throughout history when the necessities of war, or of preparations for it, have driven governments to print money to finance the defence effort, because they have been unable, or have felt unable, to extract the required resources from the public by taxation or borrowing from the non-banking sector. This could be seen happening in, for instance, Israel in the 1970s and early 1980s when, in a fully stretched economy forced to operate on something like a permanent war footing, there has been increasingly massive government borrowing from the Bank of Israel. The result is an excess of money, and price inflation, which has the effect of imposing additional taxation by reducing the value of private incomes and savings. Outside the United States, and especially in France, the view is widely held that it was through inflationary government borrowing that the United States financed the Vietnam war. But because the dollar is a reserve currency, the effect was to pump out dollars through a current account deficit in the balance of payments, which had to be held in the reserves of other countries, thus obliging them to finance the Vietnam war.

We have a different situation if resources are under-utilised and there is a deficiency of effective demand. That was the situation *par excellence* in the great slump of the 1930s when men and machines languished in enforced idleness. This was the background to the Keynesian doctrine of the use of public expenditure, accompanied by an expansion of the money supply, to prime the pump, after which the multiplier effect progressively takes up the slack in the economy. Neo-Keynesians add to this the further proposition that the rising level of economic activity and income generates increased savings and tax revenue out of which to finance the higher level of government expenditure in a non-inflationary way.

However, we need to be clear about the kind of situation in which this policy will work. The existence of unemployment by itself is not a sufficient condition. All the factors of production have to be available and the situation has got to be such that an injection of extra demand will bring them into use and generate additional output, rather than merely push up wages and prices. The poverty of an underdeveloped country lacking capital equipment and essential materials and skills cannot be cured by printing money. Even in a more advanced economy attempts to stimulate demand will misfire and generate inflation if the reason why resources are unused is not a lack of money in the economy but a structural disequilibrium or a friction in the working of the market, such as shortages of skilled labour or of essential supplies or equipment. 'Keynes never intended that his demand management techniques should be used to cope with such Frictional and Structural Unemployment', to quote from Professor James Meade's Snow Lecture on Stagflation delivered in Cambridge in 1978, 'but only with what we may call General Unemployment; namely a widespread unemployment of labour and capital equipment of all kinds, due to a general deficiency of demand for the products of industry' (reprinted in the *Listener* on 14 December 1978).

It is debatable, I suppose, whether Nicki Kaldor was going against the true faith of Keynesianism in proposing to apply techniques that were meant for dealing with general unemployment to the problem of regional unemployment. We need to distinguish between on the one hand the fairly straightforward issue of a regional labour subsidy, for which a reasonable case on merits could be made out, and on the other hand the case for financing it without tears. It is a fairly recurrent experience to find Ministers and Departments arguing for special treatment of particular expenditure schemes on the grounds that the definitions of public expenditure are wrong and that the sums involved in their schemes should not count as public expenditure at all, or should be counted net and not gross; the Green Paper argument was an unusually sophisticated version of this approach. But in principle, if you want to control public expenditure within quantitative limits, it is necessary to be very tough in dealing with this kind of special pleading. However, consideration of the REP proposal was never linked with a reappraisal of the general public expenditure scene. If that had been done, I find it hard to believe that a plausible case could have been made out for isolating £100 million of additional expenditure to be financed by means of an increase in the money supply at a time when the total of public expenditure was getting increasingly out of hand and the hour was near when it would have to be cut back.

THE WAR OF JENKINS' CUTS

The bubble burst later that year. The figures in table 3.1, taken from the longer series of figures in Appendix I, show how rapidly public expenditure had been pumped up since the Labour government had come to office, while the growth of GDP had fallen short of the National Plan target. These figures are based on the definitions which were adopted in 1976 and which were then used for the 1977 public expenditure White Paper. The changes as compared with the old definitions, including a revised treatment of the figures for debt interest and the nationalised industries, are explained in a section in

Table 3.1

	Public expenditure % increase over previous year	GDP % increase over previous year	Public expenditure as % of GDP
1964–65	+3.8	+4.1	33.9
1965–66	+5.9	+2.2	35.1
1966–67	+5.7	+2.1	36.3
1967–68	+13.1	+2.9	39.9

chapter 5 headed 'What is Public Expenditure?' But in case it should be thought that the record on public expenditure in the years in question might be shown in a more favourable light if we stuck to the old definitions, let me quote a variety of figures (though they can be skipped by anyone who is not particularly concerned with the detailed evidence) put together by Samuel Goldman for a work on *The developing system of public expenditure management and control*, which was published by HMSO in 1973 as the second in a series of Civil Service College studies. According to figures in his text, public spending rose by 9 per cent in real terms in 1967–68, a post-war record, after rising by 6.7 per cent and 6.6 per cent in the two previous years. A statistical appendix to his study shows public expenditure rising from 45.9 per cent of GNP at factor cost in 1965 to 51.8 per cent in 1968, on the definition then in use. (The table on p. 148 of Otto Clarke's book shows a very similar increase in the public expenditure/GDP ratio.) Another table in the appendix to Goldman's work, which differs in excluding selective employment premiums, REP and investment grants, shows public expenditure going up by 5.2 per cent a year in real terms, even without these items, from 43.8 per cent of GNP in 1964–65 to 49.8 per cent in 1968–69.

So, on any definition, public expenditure had been growing in excess of the rate projected in the National Plan and much in excess of the growth in the economy, so that there was a large and rapid shift of resources into public expenditure at a time when the case for a shift of resources into the balance of payments was becoming increasingly clear and the exchange rate increasingly untenable. A number of the advisers and officials who had been against devaluation in 1964 had come round in the meanwhile to accepting the need for it. In November 1967, after mounting pressure on sterling and a massive loss of reserves, devaluation was announced.

James Callaghan has made no secret of the fact that, though in later years he could come to view a change in parity as primarily a technical operation, at that time he regarded devaluation as a political and moral defeat in the battle to maintain the value of the pound through containing costs and increasing productivity. It is curious how different our situation looked in Paris, where I was taking part in a European committee on space policies just before our devaluation, and where the prospect of a change in our parity was seen as eroding somewhat the increased competitiveness which the French had enjoyed since their own successful devaluation in 1958. This played an important part in enabling them to take advantage of membership of the Common Market; and the fact that the Wilson government, shedding their illusions about Commonwealth trade, had in May 1967 made the UK's second application to join the EEC (though negotiations did not actually begin until after they lost office) was yet one more factor in making devaluation seem inevitable. I myself practically prayed that we would not put it off, but that we would go on from this to work our way out of the cycle of current account deficits and the recurrent need to go round the world's capitals and financial institutions with the begging bowl.

For Callaghan it was psychologically impossible to stay at the Treasury after what seemed to him at the time as a failure to maintain the external value of the sterling holdings. He took over at the Home Office from Roy Jenkins who, in a straight exchange, became Chancellor of the Exchequer. Roy Jenkins, as I knew, had been convinced for some time of the need for devaluation, though he played no part in the decision to devalue. However, in order to 'make devaluation work', two things were necessary on top of the change of parity itself: restraint in domestic consumption, public and private, so as to release resources to improve the balance of payments, and – since we had moved on to a lower fixed rate, not on to a floating exchange rate – restraint in wage and price increases. This had been the 'devaluation strategy' under the previous Labour government, which was frustrated by the Korean war rearmament programme. The measures of restraint announced at the time of the devaluation included only limited cuts in the public expenditure field, affecting investment by the nationalised industries and defence expenditure for the year ahead. One of the new Chancellor's first tasks, therefore, was to initiate an across-the-board scaling down of existing expenditure plans for the next two financial years, 1968–69 and 1969–70. This exercise involved the use of the 'PESC system' and the forward projections of expenditure for the first time to secure deceleration to a lower growth of public expenditure. It also involved Roy Jenkins in a series of Cabinet meetings, unprecedented in number and duration for meetings devoted to public expenditure, in which he carried the burden of securing the policy decisions which were needed for this. (I find that the number of Cabinet hours taken up by these meetings was even longer than I was aware of at the time – 32¼ hours spread over eight meetings, which took place in less than a fortnight, as compared with the normal pattern of one or two Cabinet meetings a week to deal with the whole range of government business.) These came on top of bilaterals with various key colleagues and Ministerial meetings of less than the full Cabinet.

These decisions were relayed to us in the Treasury from the Cabinet

Office in the form of terse summaries on slips of paper in locked green despatch boxes. As each batch of decisions was taken, the slips of paper were put in one of these stout green boxes and sent over to Peter Vinter, who was holding the fort in the absence of a successor to Otto Clarke. On a number of occasions Heads of Divisions – including myself, as I had been promoted to Under Secretary in the course of 1967 to become Head of AT Division when Russell Bretherton retired – gathered in Peter Vinter's room to witness the unlocking of the green box and the reading of the Cabinet decisions. It was rather like the gatherings of party workers which take place at the headquarters of the political parties on general election nights to receive the election results as they come in from the constituencies. On one occasion nobody could locate the key to the green box, which had to be opened by brute force. Attempts to prise it open with paper knives and such like were hopeless, and I cannot remember on my own account how it was forced open in the end, but I am told that it was done by dropping the box from a considerable height down one of the stairwells in the Treasury building. (This information comes from Peter Baldwin, at that time the Chancellor's Principal Private Secretary.)

The results were announced in a statement by the Prime Minister, Harold Wilson, to the House of Commons on 16 January 1968, the text of which, with a single supporting table, was issued as a White Paper (Cmnd. 3515). Compared with today's elaborate public expenditure White Papers, it was a slim document with only a dozen pages of text, of which three and a half pages dealt with changes in defence plans. The White Paper announced an acceleration of the withdrawal of our forces from the Far East, and also a withdrawal from the Persian Gulf – the famous East of Suez policy – both to be accomplished by the end of 1971. The economies on the civil side included a postponement of the next general increase in social security benefits (expenditure on which had increased by 48 per cent at current prices from 1963–64 to 1967–68), deferment by two years of the raising of the school leaving age, and the re-introduction of prescription charges.

These were difficult political decisions, as were some of the other policy changes, of a kind which a Chancellor cannot expect to secure without a good deal of in-fighting. Yet the table showed planned expenditure in 1968–69 as being reduced through these measures by no more than £300 million (at 1967 survey prices) from a total of well over £15,000 million at which the plans had stood just before the exercise – a reduction of less than 2 per cent, which would still leave planned expenditure rising by 4¾ per cent over the previous year. This was in line with the theology which persisted for some time that the 'focus year' in public expenditure planning should be Year 3, that is, the second financial year ahead, and that relatively little can be done to affect the year immediately ahead. The capital expenditure of the nationalised industries was shown separately from the main public expenditure totals and was not subject to any further reduction beyond the saving already announced at the time of devaluation.

For 1969–70 the reduction in planned expenditure was £416 million or 2.6 per cent. Moreover, these savings did not take credit for the forgoing of any general uprating in social security benefits, presumably because index-linking of benefits was not automatic in those days (it was not made automatic until the next Labour government) and so provision for an annual uprating would not have been built into the baseline figures. The year-on-year increase projected for 1969–70 was no more than 1 per cent in real terms. This would represent a really sharp deceleration in the growth of public expenditure, but the financial markets were unimpressed at the time of the Prime Minister's announcement – perhaps because of the delayed-action nature of the policy changes, perhaps because they were announced in isolation from the tax increases which were to follow in Roy Jenkins' first Budget. He had been advised against digging a hole in the economy before he was ready to fill it; the measures to make devaluation work therefore came by instalments, and sterling remained under pressure for some time until the situation had clearly been turned round.

The public expenditure survey system is like painting the Firth of Forth bridge, in the sense that hardly have you got to the end of one operation than you have to start on the next. After his gruelling experience in that first marathon series of public expenditure Cabinets, the Chancellor naturally looked for some better way of handling the next public expenditure round, and proceeded by way of a series of bilateral meetings with spending Ministers, with official support on both sides. In the statement which he made in February 1969 following this exercise, and which was published as a further slim White Paper (Cmnd. 3936), he confirmed that the growth in expenditure in the two years covered by the previous White Paper would be within the limits which it had set – 4.6 per cent in 1968–69 and 1 per cent in 1969–70 – and announced that programmes in the year beyond that, 1970–71, would be kept within a growth of 2 per cent with a further 1 per cent for contingencies. On this basis, public expenditure would be allowed to resume its upward trend but at a pace within the economic growth rate of which the country had shown itself capable.

In the event, the deceleration in the growth of public expenditure in Roy Jenkins' time as Chancellor, measured on the same basis as in the opening paragraph of this section, was even greater than he took credit for in the 1969 White Paper, perhaps because the rate of increase before his cuts was underestimated at the time. The figures for the years after his measures are shown in table 3.2.

Table 3.2

	Public expenditure % change over previous year	GDP % increase over previous year	Public expenditure as % of GDP
1968–69	−1.1	+3.3	38.2
1969–70	−0.1	+1.8	37.5
1970–71	+2.7	+2.2	37.7

Roy Jenkins had a number of assets in dealing with the public expenditure side of his portfolio. He had an instinct for the requirements of his various Ministerial posts, and as Chancellor pursued a campaign for economy without exempting expenditure proposals for which personally he might have a soft spot. His hand was strengthened by the general feeling that, after James Callaghan's departure from the Treasury, another change of Chancellor was unthinkable. On the DEA front he did not have to contend with George Brown, who had by now moved on to become Foreign and Commonwealth Secretary, and who, soon after the expenditure cuts, resigned from the government in a huff precipitated by a failure to consult him on the handling of a crisis concerning the price of gold. He had been replaced at the DEA by Michael Stewart, who in turn had been succeeded by Peter Shore. In 1969 the DEA itself was wound up. Its dismantlement was carried out with the same administrative smoothness as had gone into its creation. It was mourned for years afterwards by some of the younger enthusiasts who had served in it, but according to well-qualified opinions the Department's role had been vitiated from the outset by the concept of creative tension, which required a great deal of top-level time to be constantly applied to the matter of Ministerial relationships.

The Chancellor was also relieved of the distraction of having to turn his mind from time to time, as those before him had been obliged to do, to civil service pay negotiations, and such like, when responsibility for these matters was hived off in 1968 to a new Civil Service Department, one of the changes recommended in the Fulton Committee on the civil service. I thought the Fulton Report a loaded piece of work in many respects, but I approved of this measure since, like many other Treasury people, I was relieved not to be at risk any longer of being shifted back on to Establishments work as my next posting in the Treasury. William Armstrong became the first Permanent Secretary of the new Department and Head of the Civil Service. He was succeeded at the Treasury by Douglas Allen, who was by that time Permanent Secretary of the DEA, and who thus left that Department before it was wound up.

Meanwhile the investment grants saga had continued to unfold. The original Estimate for grant payments in 1967–68 had been £166 million, which had to be topped up by a Supplementary Estimate of £60 million. Later a second Supplementary of £50 million was tabled, but this too was found to be an underestimate, and it was replaced by a Revised Supplementary Estimate for £89 million – a rather unusual procedure. (The total bill for investment grants in 1967–68 is shown in table 3.3.) The amount of these supplementaries was, for those days, rather staggering. Though part of the extra requirement came from a planned acceleration of payments, much of it arose because of an inability either to estimate in advance how much would be applied for or to do anything to cut applications down when they were put in. And the full horror of investment grants for ships, which I anticipated in an earlier section, was still to emerge.

Table 3.3: Investment grants, 1967–68

	£m
Original Estimate	166
Supplementary Estimate	60
Second Supplementary Estimate (Revised)	89
Total	315

A remit was therefore handed down to officials of the Treasury and the spending Departments to examine ways of bringing this expenditure under control. By this time, responsibility for investment grants had passed from the Board of Trade to the Ministry of Technology, which was expanded into a giant Department by swallowing up other

Departments or, as in this case, part of their functions. The negotiation with Mintech on the investment grants remit turned out to be even more protracted and difficult than might have been expected. Although it was conducted at top official level on both sides, I know that, on the Mintech side, I was cast, unjustly, in the role of *bête noire*.

One gambit tried on the Mintech side was to propose that investment grants should be treated as 'negative taxation' and therefore excluded from the public expenditure figures altogether. Whatever the case for excluding them for the purpose of the kind of statistical comparison which appears at the beginning of this section, investment grants were undoubtedly government expenditure which had to be financed like other expenditure, and to have accepted this proposal would have been fatal to any hope of keeping the grant payments within bounds. So the negotiation reached a state of stalemate. Meanwhile the Chancellor's public statements were now tending to place a new emphasis on the need for investment, which seemed to me to introduce a new factor into the situation and to make some sort of détente rather desirable, though I do not imagine that I was ever given any credit for these sentiments. This led in due course to a formula which enabled the Treasury to disengage with a modest degree of honour, but the fact is that 'capital grants to the private sector', which in 1964–65 were no more than £16 million, can be seen from the tables in Samuel Goldman's study to have shot up to £573 million in 1968–69 at 1971–72 out-turn prices (the actual expenditure figure at 1968–69 prices would of course have been less) and to have risen still further to £677 million (on the same price basis) in 1969–70; so evidently, if the Treasury saved any honour in that exercise, we did not save any money.

AFTER PESC, PERC

Notwithstanding the investment grant saga, the period after the Jenkins' cuts was the heyday of the PESC system. The section of Samuel Goldman's study dealing with this phase is headed 'The public expenditure system comes into its own, 1969–70; the Green and White Papers'. It was a period when the system underwent a good many refinements (mostly as a result of an in-house review to which Goldman refers) and acquired its high reputation with scholars overseas.

The Second Permanent Secretary post on the expenditure side which had been vacated by Otto Clarke was filled in 1968 by Sir David

Serpell. It was not long before he too moved on when he in turn 'got his own Department' and was succeeded by Goldman, but he stayed long enough to preside over the group or committee (which surely could only be dubbed PERC) carrying out the public expenditure review. The only public manifestation of this re-thinking was a Green Paper – an illustration of how this little innovation had caught on – called *Public Expenditure: A new presentation* (Cmnd. 4017, April 1969) which led to the introduction of a regular series of annual public expenditure White Papers setting out the government's programme and policies for a period of years ahead. The first of these appeared in December 1969.

This internal Treasury re-thinking went on *pari passu* with some re-thinking by the Select Committee on Procedure about the role of Parliament in this field. This led, though not immediately, to the replacement of the Select Committee on Estimates by a Select Committee on Expenditure. One feature of this, which I favoured, was that the new committee was given enhanced rights of scrutiny which covered the whole field of public expenditure, reflecting the burial of the old rigid demarcation between Supply expenditure and below-the-line expenditure.

Though the Green Paper was a landmark of a sort, it may seem odd that the review should have led to the issue of a document about presentation without a word on the crucial question of control. However, two things need to be said in extenuation. First, a preoccupation with the statistical treatment of public expenditure was to some extent forced on the Treasury as a result of recurrent attempts to circumvent expenditure limits by changing the statistical conventions. I came frequently to reflect that challenging the definitions is the last refuge of a spending Minister up against the spending limits. Otto Clarke writes, on p. 130 of his book, that 'Mr. Crossman had attacked these [the definitions] in the 1965 operation because they limited his freedom of manoeuvre on housing subsidies (and this of course happened again when he became responsible for social security later, and claimed that "transfers didn't count".)' He refers on the same page, rather charitably, to 'a valuable but time-consuming discussion with Dr. Balogh about some of our definitions' and observes that Dr Balogh's criticisms were much more sophisticated than Crossman's. But the statistical presentation contemplated by the Treasury for resolving these issues was perhaps in its turn too over-sophisticated to be put into effect. The situation was, in my view, made worse rather than better by bringing the whole of the capital expenditure of the nationalised industries into the public expenditure figures without the sophistication of setting off depreciation funds and trading surpluses against the gross investment figures.

Secondly, the Green Paper was only the tip of the iceberg. On control, Goldman writes that 'All the apparatus which had been developed so far, including medium term assessments, monthly Running Tallies of expenditure, and management of the Contingency Reserve, was brought into play to this end' (p. 11). This was something of a change from Otto Clarke's philosophy that 'trying to police allocations by statistical measurements . . . would not be effective' (p. 129 of his book) and that 'the implementation has to be done by departments' (p. 132).

It is also clear from what Goldman writes (e.g. on pp. 39–40 of his study) that there was a good deal of internal soul-searching in the Treasury, which continued after he had taken over from Serpell, about the constant price convention. As 'survey prices' were always overtaken by inflation by the time that the annual public expenditure survey began, let alone by the time that it was concluded, Ministers were taking their decisions in terms of figures which understated the current cash requirement by an enormous amount. However, nothing came of ideas for carrying out the surveys in terms of something nearer to current cash prices.

A good deal of attention was given about that time to the 'relative price effect', that is, the extent to which pay and prices affecting public expenditure programmes rise at a faster or slower rate than pay and prices in the economy as a whole, and to methods of accounting for and controlling differential cost increases in the public services. But in spite of this concern with *relative* inflation in the public sector, the PESC system remained accommodative of the *general* rate of inflation. Goldman refers to 'the allegation that working in constant prices encourages inflation by provoking disregard of price changes and hence of the additional money costs of inflationary wage increases'. But he goes on to say: 'I doubt whether this is or has been a significant result of constant price measurement' (p. 34).

There were people in the Treasury who were bothered about this aspect of the system. I recollect that, some time earlier, Peter Vinter had organised a certain amount of discussion on the subject, in which I advanced the idea, purely as a *jeu d'esprit*, of a Cash Contingency Reserve. Under this notional system, once Estimates for the year ahead had been worked out at existing price levels, a total cash sum would be fixed in advance to cover all Supplementary Estimates for cost increases, and all proposals for such Supplementaries would be treated as claims against this CCR. My recollection is that Peter

Vinter was quite attracted by the idea, but it was of course much ahead of its time, and Otto Clarke did not take it further. Samuel Goldman in his turn saw no case for that kind of change in the system:

One cannot discourage inflation by forcing those who have to plan the orderly use of major national resources in public programmes to cut back or accelerate because prices and incomes have deviated from what had been expected, whether upwards or downwards. It would be illogical for example to reduce the hospital building programme because the wages of nurses had risen more than had originally been estimated; though there would have been a case for looking at the whole of the health programme (or anything else) if incomes here were to move as a permanent matter to a higher level compared with incomes in other parts of the public sector. (p. 39)

His views must of course have been greatly influenced by the success of Roy Jenkins' measures in bringing the growth of public expenditure back on to a reasonable course. Both on the definitions then in use, and on the changed definitions later adopted, by 1970 these measures reduced public expenditure as a percentage of GNP or GDP by above 2 percentage points from the peak 1968 figures which I gave at the beginning of the last section. A marginal change of that order in that space of time is a considerable shift. 'After many vicissitudes,' wrote Goldman, 'we have evolved a system for managing the public sector which despite many deficiencies is probably superior to that found anywhere else in the world.' He recognised that the performance of the system would depend on the government's objectives but thought that 'short of a major revolution in the attitude of governments to the relation between public and private sectors we are not likely to see the former expand at a rate as violently out of line with growth of the economy as in some of the phases of the past two decades . . .' (p. 53).

Goldman was of course too prudent a man to record a wholly unqualified appraisal of the outlook, but the fact that someone of his ability and good judgment could write in this vein at all, on what was very nearly the eve of Waterloo for the PESC system, is liable to discourage even qualified predictions about anything which depends on human behaviour. For there were developments in the pipeline in the post-devaluation years which were to build up great pressures on the system.

THE SEEDS OF STAGFLATION

The post-devaluation strategy was a spectacular success in turning the balance of payments round from deficit on current account in 1967 and 1968 into a growing surplus in each of the next three years, while the large outflow on capital account was turned into an inflow by 1970. But a price had to be paid for our increased competitiveness in world markets in the shape of higher sterling prices for our imports, including food prices, something which always generates pressure for compensating wage increases. Observers of the international scene at that time have remarked that an upsurge in wage demands and a hardening of trade union bargaining attitudes developed more or less simultaneously in other industrialised countries also, and it would be an oversimplification of what happened in Britain to put it down to devaluation and the squeeze which followed. However, for whatever reasons, in the post-devaluation years the rate of increase in the retail price index and in unit wage costs started to move up, and unemployment, for the first time since the war, fluctuated above the half million mark instead of below it.

This trend became much more pronounced in the period of office of the subsequent Conservative government (to which we shall come in the next chapter) when in 1971 prices and wage costs both showed a year-on-year increase of 9 per cent or more and unemployment passed 700,000, and far worse figures were still in store. However, if we look at the figures in table 3.4, which have been worked out from data in *Economic Trends*, it is not fanciful to see in the final phase of that Labour administration the emergence of stagflation, with price increases, wage increases and unemployment interacting with one

Table 3.4: The birth of stagflation

	Retail price index	Wages and salaries per unit of output	Unemployed including school leavers: UK	
	% increase over previous year	% increase over previous year	'000s	% change over previous year
1964	+3.3	+3.2	349	−29.4
1965	+4.7	+4.1	299	−14.3
1966	+3.9	+4.9	281	−6.0
1967	+2.6	+1.9	503	+79.0
1968	+4.7	+2.0	542	+7.8
1969	+5.4	+3.4	518	−4.4
1970	+6.4	+9.4	555	+7.1
1971	+9.4	+9.0	724	+30.4
1972	+7.1	+8.8	804	+11.0

another – though GDP continued to rise and stagflation had not yet turned into slumpflation.

In this final phase the Labour government switched its strategy, and abated the battle to contain wages by incomes policy but mounted a new campaign to impose the rule of law on the prevailing anarchy in industrial relations. However, it is clear from the revelations which have occurred since then that not everyone in the government supported the proposals which were set out in the White Paper called *In Place of Strife*. In the end the Prime Minister had to settle for a 'solemn and binding' undertaking on behalf of the TUC, personified forever in the mythical character of Solomon Binding, that they would themselves deal with unofficial strikes and inter-union disputes.

Some of the principal actors in that drama would hold to this day that it was this dissension on industrial relations within the Labour movement which cost the Wilson government the 1970 general election, and the notion that the Labour Party must never again quarrel with the trade unions had a lot to do with the way Labour Party policy developed between the first and second Wilson governments. For the first Wilson administration, including Mr Wedgwood Benn in his less populist phase, remained to the end a government seeking to make the mixed economy work and to energise British industry rather than to take it over or run it.

On another view, which I find more plausible, a principal reason – over and above the pendulum character of British politics – why the Labour government was not re-elected in 1970 was that public opinion was not yet convinced of the government's success in getting the balance of payments right and overcoming the series of crises which had been a feature of its earlier years. A poor result in the trade figures for one particular month helped the hostile propaganda campaign which was waged against the government on this score. But in fact the new Conservative government, though it inherited the incipient problem of stagflation, also inherited a balance of payments situation which was more favourable on both current and capital account than at any time since the war.

4

The Heath Years

AFTER PERC, PARC

The Conservative administration formed by Edward Heath in 1970 was the only government since the war to take office without either a balance of payments problem or an industrial relations crisis on its hands. It did not therefore have to take crash action to carry out the changes in which it believed, but had an initial period of calm in which to sort them out. In a good many respects its philosophy anticipated the brand of politics which later came to be associated with Margaret Thatcher. There was the same commitment to restore a market economy, the same aspiration to roll back the frontiers of the public sector and to restore at least some parts of the nationalised industries to private ownership, and the same intention to bring the trade unions within the rule of law. This was the philosophy of Selsdon Man – the persona which had emerged from the policy conference which Heath had held at Selsdon Park while still in opposition – but not of monetarist man, nor was there the explicit rejection of Keynesian economics which was to come with Margaret Thatcher's government.

The first Chancellor of the Exchequer in the Heath government was Iain Macleod, who was something of a hero to his circle of supporters, but very soon a lost hero, for – after years of ill-health – he died very soon after becoming Chancellor, before he could make any lasting mark on the Treasury. I had no direct contact with him in this short time. His successor as Chancellor was Anthony Barber, who had been at the Treasury as Economic Secretary in the previous Conservative administration, and who no doubt would have preferred to return in rather different circumstances. Maurice Macmillan was Chief Secretary, and Patrick Jenkin and Terence Higgins were Financial Secretary and Minister of State respectively. Later on, in 1972, Maurice Macmillan was made Secretary of State for Employment and Patrick Jenkin moved up to the Chief Secretary post.

The new government had their predecessors' expenditure plan available to them, in the form of the latest public expenditure White Paper. The Treasury, under the new Ministerial team, immediately embarked on negotiations with spending Departments in order to scale their programmes down. The extent of the scaling down, as reflected in the new government's first public expenditure White Paper – and to use figures taken from Goldman's study – was £300 million in programmes for 1971–72, rising to reductions of over £1500 million in programmes for 1975–76.

Charges for public services were to be introduced or increased wherever possible and subsidies were to be reduced. At the Department of Education and Science, Margaret Thatcher came to prominence in connection with the withdrawal of free school milk, an economy which one local council was for some time unwilling to introduce, thus creating a crisis in the relationship between central and local government. A Housing Finance Bill was introduced to enable council house rents to be increased, a measure which in the event proved quite inadequate to contain the rising cost of housing subsidies, but which encountered wide opposition and moved some otherwise moderate Labour members to fury. The Clay Cross councillors became heroes with the Labour Party, to its discredit, for refusing to implement the Act. A move to introduce charges at local libraries, about which I felt rather sad, failed because of legal complications.

My Division, AT, which under the Labour government had been so heavily involved with new expenditure schemes on the industrial front, was now equally heavily involved with retrenchment on that same front, where the giant Ministry of Technology was soon merged with the new mammoth Department of Trade and Industry, which also swallowed up the old Board of Trade. Investment grants and SET were ended and the Prices and Incomes Board was wound up. John Davies, the Secretary of State for Trade and Industry, in spite of a speech in which he had announced the government's determination not to rescue lame ducks, nevertheless had some sympathy for the idea of retaining an institution, such as the Industrial Reorganization Corporation, for helping companies in temporary trouble over stiles; but that, too, was wound up. A more surprising casualty, when we were on the verge of a great wave of consumerism, was the Consumer Council, whose abolition did not save much money. The enabling powers in the Industrial Expansion Act were repealed, thus leaving the government without even the limited powers to give Treasury guarantees for particular industries which had existed before the

Industrial Expansion Act. My own view was that, although the new government were against intervention in industry, they would find themselves obliged to intervene in some situations, and there would be advantage in having instruments of intervention available; however, the Ministerial team, while recognising that there might be such situations, believed that the right course would be to have specific legislation to deal with each case as it arose.

On the regional front, the new government meant to rely principally on measures to improve the environment of the older industrial areas, thus making them more attractive places for good managers, which was seen as a key feature in locating industry there. As a result of the abolition of investment grants, with their large regional differential, industry in the Development Areas lost perhaps the most important benefit which it had enjoyed; it was given partial compensation on the taxation front in the form of free depreciation on plant and machinery. REP was to be phased out, but before the election Conservative spokesmen had said that they would honour the Labour government's undertaking to maintain this subsidy for a period of years, and Anthony Barber was scrupulously concerned to fulfil this pledge. No immediate action was taken, therefore, to withdraw the subsidy beyond the opening of consultations with the TUC Secretariat about the method eventually to be adopted for phasing out REP.

As regards the machinery of government, the Prime Minister – who had promised in the Conservative election manifesto a new style of government – introduced two innovations designed to improve policy-making. One was the creation of the Central Policy Review Staff within the Cabinet Office, where it was to provide briefing for Cabinet as a whole and for Cabinet committees on the full range of government business, in contradistinction to the briefs which individual Ministers got from their own Departments on subjects in which they were directly involved. Lord Rothschild, a member of the famous merchant banking family and a scientist by training, was brought in as the first head of the CPRS. Its compact body of staff were recruited in part from outside and in part through borrowing civil servants, including some bright young people, on secondment from their Departments. Another of the functions of the CPRS was to prepare wide-ranging papers as a basis for periodical across-the-board reviews by Ministers collectively of the progress of their policies. Later on the CPRS came to be treated as an in-house research or consultancy capability and was commissioned from time to time to carry out exercises or studies on particular topics and problems, making use of outside experts and consultants as required.

But the feature of the CPRS which most directly affected the handling of the public expenditure exercises was that it was given a remit to prepare a joint paper with the Treasury on priorities in public expenditure, which Ministers would consider at an initial stage in the annual PESC review. This was designed to enable them to give a steer to the Treasury and spending Departments on the carrying out of the exercise.

In principle, given the highly decentralised character of our system of administration by Departments, it seems to me that there was a reasonable case for some strengthening of the centre through the kind of capability which the CPRS was designed to provide. Victor Rothschild achieved something of a success in putting his 'thinktank', as the press liked to describe it, on the map, and until 1983 it survived the continual chopping and changing in Whitehall organisation – which I have not set out to chronicle exhaustively in this book, although the rise and fall of new Departments crops up regularly in the narrative. It must therefore be deemed to have justified its existence. In particular, it has probably been useful from time to time to the Prime Ministers who have had it available to them. Although the Prime Minister is titular overlord of the Treasury and of the Civil Service, there is no 'Prime Minister's Department', and Prime Ministers, for all their great power in some respects, may in some other senses feel at a disadvantage, with only the handful of dedicated people in No. 10 serving them directly, vis-à-vis the Ministerial barons each with the resources of a great Department of state at his disposal. To some extent the Cabinet secretariat helps to fill the gap and the Secretary of the Cabinet himself, while in one of his aspects the servant of Cabinet as a whole, also has a special position in relation to the Prime Minister. A strengthening of the resources available in the Cabinet Office could potentially enhance this function.

Nevertheless, I doubt very much whether the CPRS made a significant difference in my time to the functioning of the Cabinet machine. It is true that Cabinet Ministers, on subjects in which their Departments are not directly involved, may feel dissatisfied with getting no Departmental brief or one which merely advises that there is no Departmental interest (signifying that the Minister is free on these occasions to take whatever line he likes); and it is not unknown for a Minister in this position to get, through his personal secretary, a pirated brief from a Department with more expertise. But though individuals in the CPRS were assigned to particular areas of policy, their 'open briefs' to Cabinet committees were generally less expert than the Departmental papers on the subject under discussion. Though

Victor Rothschild himself was liable to take a strong line on subjects dear to his heart, such as the administration of scientific research, his people seemed frequently to be in a position to do no more than try to identify pros and cons in a rather elementary way and list intelligent questions to be answered.

Of the published studies carried out by the CPRS over the years, some seemed to me reasonably useful in focusing attention on such things as the energy problem or the state of the motor car industry, without in any direct way greatly advancing solutions in these fields. When it came to their *magnum opus* of recent years – the CPRS report on overseas representation – though it may have served a political requirement at the time to assign this remit to the CPRS, in my view it took them out of their depth; certainly the more important of their long list of policy recommendations were stillborn. We did not see similar publications from the CPRS after Margaret Thatcher took office.

As regards the collaboration of the CPRS with the Treasury in the public expenditure field, up to a point it was sometimes useful to have a second non-spending-Department voice, as had been the case with the DEA; but if the object had been to give priority to control of total public expenditure, diluting the Treasury's role would not have been the most natural way of going about it. From what I know of the arrangements in other countries, I should say that the industrialised countries with a relatively low proportion of GDP going to public expenditure, in particular Japan and France, were those where there was least challenge to the authority of the Ministry of Finance. No one actually spoke, in the CPRS context, of the 'creative tension' which had been supposed to exist between the DEA and the Treasury but, as Goldman put it, there was 'much overlap with Treasury responsibilities and scope for friction and misunderstanding' (p. 43). The style of management which had helped to put the CPRS on the map was liable also to involve a rather idiosyncratic concept of collaboration. Unlike the DEA, the CPRS did not have a separate Departmental Minister; therefore, given its position at the centre, much would depend on the Prime Minister's attitude to public expenditure and the Treasury.

The new government also brought a number of executives from business and industry into Whitehall, who were given assignments in various areas of administration. Two of them were assigned to look into the public expenditure arrangements, which they duly found wanting. 'PESC is purely incremental' was a phrase used by one of them which stuck in my mind. By this he meant that the annual surveys merely re-costed programmes and policies without radically reviewing them to see whether they should go on at all. He contrasted this unfavourably with the system operated in the company where he had been employed, under which a schedule of issues requiring attention over the period ahead was regularly brought before the Chairman. Following this assignment, there came a decision to supplement the PESC system with a new system of Programme Analysis and Reviews (PAR).

The new system was coordinated by an inter-Departmental committee under Treasury chairmanship called, inevitably, PARC, which in turn was to report to a new ministerial committee. The CPRS also had a leading role. Within this framework a schedule was worked out of PAR reviews to be carried out by spending Departments over the period ahead. Of necessity the list was selective rather than comprehensive. Individual reviews were carried out by staff assigned to them in the Departments concerned, but the Treasury and CPRS were represented at their meetings and from time to time joined with the Department in taking stock of progress in their reviews. Different Departments went about their reviews in different ways, but a common theme was the attempt to measure outputs or results in relation to costs.

There was a case in principle for some new capability or system which would be concerned with the quality rather than the quantity of public spending, and with the micro-economics of particular programmes rather than the macro-economic decisions on the total of expenditure and its allocation between one programme and another, or quite simply with efficiency and value for money. Other countries also have from time to time become concerned with these facets of public expenditure. In the United States, in particular, a number of ideas have had their vogue. One was PPB, or Programme Planning and Budgeting; another was Management by Objectives (MBO), and yet another was known as Zero Sum Accounting or, alternatively, under the Carter administration, Zero Base Budgeting (ZBB).

Writing after one year's experience of the PAR system in action, Samuel Goldman stressed its limitations as an aid to decision-making but nevertheless described it as 'the most important and hopeful field for development of the present system' (p. 51). In the event the PAR system ran into the sand and did not long outlast the Heath government. In my view this was inherent in the fact that the system was conceived out of a misunderstanding of the way in which government and government spending work, and of the differences between running a country and running a company. In spite of an ambiguity as to how far PAR was meant to be concerned with the determination of policy and how far with methods of carrying it out, the PAR approach, if taken seriously, was bound to concern itself with policy implications. But policies on public expenditure cannot be divorced from the political process. To criticise the PESC system as 'purely incremental' was to ignore the fact that policy reviews were regularly being carried out in response to political and economic pressures, and decisions on them were being taken on the political plane, either in parallel with or outside the technological PESC progress – outside the Whitehall system altogether in the case of manifesto policies, as I have shown. The figures resulting from the political decisions were then assimilated into the PESC machine.

To the extent that the PAR system was designed to take a radical look at policies and not merely at methods of carrying them out, there was a lack of reality about the idea that the whole organic process of policy formation could somehow be subordinated to a mechanical review procedure. Spending Ministers and their Departments simply did not put the crucial policy issues in their fields on the PAR list. The only exception to this was the subject of higher education, which the Department of Education and Science wanted to look at anyway, and which it suited them to offer up as their PAR contribution. In the defence field, on the other hand, though there were major issues which would have to be resolved sooner or later, only peripheral aspects of the defence budget were offered as PAR subjects.

Defence is a good illustration of the way in which – manifesto commitments apart – programmes and policies are reviewed and changed when the pressure of events makes itself felt, rather than at the behest of some theory of administration. The prevailing Conservative ethos in 1970 was favourable to defence (as in 1979 also) and Lord Carrington, who was Defence Secretary in the Heath government, carried a lot of weight in Cabinet. The broad approach of the Ministry of Defence was to maintain the existing size and structure of the armed forces but even this, because of the continuously increasing sophistication and cost of weapons systems, required a growing defence budget. In addition, every time that the forces had to undertake a task, such as keeping the peace in Northern Ireland, or buy a particular piece of equipment from British rather than American industry, for reasons which they regarded as extraneous to their defence role proper, they would argue – usually with success because of Lord Carrington's political muscle – that the cost of these items should be treated as special additions to the defence budget.

Defence is also a good illustration of the fact that there is a great temptation for people to believe what it suits them to believe. Traditionally, those concerned about footing the bill have tended to argue that the need for a large defence budget is exaggerated, sometimes contending that there is nothing much that Britain can do about Russian aggression anyway and that only the United States can provide the counterweight, while those concerned about the country's defence have tended to play down the problem of financing it, and if ever a choice had to be made between a more and a less optimistic assumption about the growth of resources, naturally they would support the high growth assumption. Both of these lines of argument are of course wishful thinking. There is a problem about defence, and there is a problem about paying for it.

The problem of an accommodation between the defence viewpoint and the Treasury viewpoint was bound to present recurring difficulty in the public expenditure exercises under the Heath government, as it has continued to do since. Recurrently, too, there was the prospect of an impasse which could not be resolved by minor adjustments but only by a more radical look at defence options, which was eventually put in hand, paving the way for the full-scale defence review later announced by the Labour government. The CPRS as well as the Treasury were represented in these exercises, but there was never any question of treating defence strategy as a fit subject for the PAR programme.

Nevertheless, we did now have PAR as well as PESC, the CPRS and businessmen as well as the Treasury. The apparatus for a new style of government, designed to promote more rational choices, was in place. If things went wrong under the Heath government it was not for lack of new systems.

THE GREAT U-TURN

The policy on lame ducks underwent trial by ordeal early in the government's life because of the threatened closure of the shipyards on the Upper Clyde and of Rolls Royce, the great aero-engine company. In both cases the government's initial intention was to let market forces prevail, in the belief that some more viable enterprise would emerge as a result. In both cases concern developed when it appeared that the market would not after all pick up the pieces and reassemble them.

The anxiety over the shipyards arose from the prospective worsening of the already high level of unemployment on Clydeside which, it was thought, might lead to social unrest of some sort. The Prime Minister appointed three wise men to advise on the outlook for ship-building on the upper Clyde. Funds were provided to keep the yard going pending their report; when it was presented, and held out some hope that a viable shipbuilding operation might not be impossible on the upper Clyde, a full-scale rescue operation was mounted and a new shipbuilding company was set up with government money to take over from the failed company.

The Rolls Royce affair was more complex and the potential con-sequences of the company's failure more far-reaching. In the days of the Labour government the company had made what was hailed at the time as a major breakthrough by developing the technologically advanced RB211–22 engine – the first in the RB211 family of engines, which in 1981 still remained crucial to the company's existence – and by securing orders to supply the engine to the Lockheed Corporation in the United States for its new TriStar wide-bodied passenger aircraft. But from the first there were problems about financing the development and production of the engine. The IRC put some money into the company, but its affairs were still giving concern when the Conservative government took over. A failure to go through with the RB211 project would have been a great blow for Lockheed, which was in any case in financial trouble itself. In addition, the possibility of a closure of Rolls Royce put at risk the supply of replacement engines and spare parts to the Royal Air Force and the air forces of a number of other countries, as well as for civil aircraft powered by various Rolls Royce engines. Finally, if Rolls Royce collapsed, it was feared that a large number of its sub-contractors up and down the country would also go out of business, causing widespread unemployment.

A Whitehall committee, mainly composed of officials but chaired by Lord Carrington, the Defence Secretary, met daily over a con-siderable period. The Treasury were represented by Raymond Ged-ling, the Deputy Secretary under whom I now worked and who had come to us from the Department of Health and Social Security to find himself caught up in a hectic series of exercises and operations rather unlike the home life of the DHSS. The amount of top-level time which I have seen taken up in Whitehall over the years by this and other situations involving individual large companies in trouble is something which seemed to me to give at least some force to the case for an expert instrument to handle as much of the detailed work as possible. In the end, as in the Upper Clyde case, a new government-owned company, Rolls Royce (1971) Ltd, was set up to acquire the assets from the liquidator of the failed company, and continuing funds were provided from the Department of Trade and Industry to meet losses on the development and production of the RB211 series. So, within a year the Conservative government had carried out the first new programme of nationalisation since the Attlee government.

Though these disasters were averted, at a cost, unemployment rose throughout 1971, from over 700,000 in the first half year to more than 800,000 in the next quarter and over 900,000 by the end of the year, and the government's anxiety rose with it. The Chancellor's tax reductions in his 1971 Budget did not seem to be having the required reflationary effect, or at any rate not quickly enough, and so contracyclical public expenditure measures were resorted to as well. Having been made a Deputy Secretary that summer, so that I now covered a wider range of programmes than before, with Douglas Allen's blessing I coordinated a Whitehall exercise to bring forward selected investment projects in the nationalised industries field. We would have done this in any event, but the Treasury's hand was in fact forced by indications that otherwise the CPRS would have made a bid to take the lead. The biggest and most concrete item in this package was a power station which the Generating Board had planned to start in a year's time, but which they were happy to bring forward by a year in return for reimbursement of the resulting additional interest costs on the capital expenditure. Apart from that it is difficult to judge what this package actually achieved. In spite of it the total investment programmes of the nationalised industries in real terms fell below the previously planned level, but perhaps they would otherwise have fallen still further.

With Peter Baldwin, who was the Under Secretary and later the Deputy Secretary on the PESC side, I also coordinated a contra-cyclical package to bring forward a defined amount of capital expenditure by the local authorities. We wanted to plan something more worthwhile than the traditional short-term 'winter works' programmes, which had been very expensive in 'cost per job' terms. On the other hand we wanted to put in hand reasonably quick-acting projects which, after allowing for the inevitable time-lags before anything actually started, would come to fruition in time to relieve the effects of the down-swing of the cycle, and not be so delayed as merely to reinforce the subsequent upswing. I was coming increasingly to realise what a bugbear time-lags are in economic management. We could not get a useful lead from the economic side on the probable duration of the recession. We therefore framed a plan for additional local authority expenditure on schemes which would not take longer than six months to get going, which would after that largely involve expenditure in the following twelve months, and which would be completed in a further six months after that – in other words, a two-year programme from beginning to end. I hoped that Departments would be able to monitor the progress of these schemes, so that we could form a judgment on how the plan had turned out for future reference, but in general the role of the Departments concerned was confined to sanctioning the raising of loans by the local authorities and did not involve the provision of central government finance. In the event, the expenditure under this contracyclical programme was simply merged with the general flow of local authority capital expenditure.

So a number of practical difficulties were involved in contracyclical programmes of public works. There was also the political or psychological problem that, at the first signs of a more relaxed attitude to public expenditure, spending Departments were not slow to climb on the bandwagon and put forward further proposals, some less relevant than others if viewed as 'contracyclical' measures, ranging from Operation Eyesore (a programme of work to improve the appearance of unlovely sites in selected areas) and special housing improvement grants to accelerated purchases of naval vessels and other defence equipment.

Still more was to come. The Treasury was out of favour, as was its tendency to believe that we were more likely to maintain our actual growth rate of around 3 per cent rather than to emulate the much higher economic growth achieved in the EEC, which we were now about to join. Edward Heath's achievement as Prime Minister was to convince the President of France, M. Pompidou, who had inherited the Gaullist mantle, that Britain was no longer tied to the United States, thus removing the block to our entry into the Community – though by now there was little room for manoeuvre on the terms of entry, which more or less came down to questions of the transitional period for adjusting to the full Community régime. The Prime Minister saw a need to prepare the country for entry into the Community by expanding and modernising our industrial capacity and strengthening the infrastructure, especially in the outlying regions.

The task of framing the response to this need was assigned to William Armstrong, in spite of the fact that, since leaving the Treasury for the Civil Service Department, he had had no responsibility for economic and financial matters, and still had no such responsibility on a day-to-day basis outside this special remit. However, though he had taken a positive line on the Fulton Committee's report on the civil service – partly, perhaps, to remove any grounds for criticising the service as negative in its response – and had applied himself with quiet enthusiasm to building up the new Civil Service Department, after the initial round of activity it was not an exciting post. Although the Civil Service Department had acquired a number of new functions – dealing with computers in the service, for instance – its bread and butter work on pay and complements and such like remained as humdrum as I have described it near the beginning of this book. So William now hankered to be involved in economic policy again, and evidently he had established a rapport with the Prime Minister.

His second in command in this exercise was Bill Nield, who had ceased to have a Departmental portfolio when the DEA, where he was Permanent Secretary at the time in succession to Douglas Allen, was wound up – a measure which he himself, I believe, had recommended. Since then he had been an additional Permanent Secretary in the Cabinet Office available for special duties. The CPRS also contributed to the work. Since neither was tied down by Departmental responsibilities or routine day-to-day functions, they were able to take part without the constraints which otherwise might have produced, in the one case, the need for a limit to be placed on the number and length of meetings, or in the other case some inhibition on unorthodox and expensive ideas.

Only a handful of people from a limited number of Departments were involved initially. Under Douglas Allen and Samuel Goldman, I carried the ball for the Treasury though, on my suggestion, Alan Lord, who was Deputy Chairman of Inland Revenue at an unusually early age, was also brought in. When so few people know what is going on, naturally misunderstandings and contretemps are liable to happen until the mystery can be cleared up.

Because of my previous involvement from the Treasury end with infrastructure programmes and schemes of support for industry, I think it fair to say that I was better placed than the generality of those taking part to give concrete shape to some of the ideas which were being floated. It was rather difficult, however, to prevent excessively large numbers from being attached to every proposal through a sort of bidding-up process, and it was hard work resisting the piling of Ossa on Pelion. The PAR approach, which was supposed to involve the costing of options and a comparison of inputs with outputs, had no place in this numbers game.

It became clear that two main features of the proposed package would have to be a new scheme of investment incentives, including a substantial regional differential, and some new machinery for dealing with selective assistance to industry. By way of a general investment incentive, on Alan Lord's initiative and with my support, agreement was reached, first at official and then at Ministerial level, on a nation-wide scheme of free depreciation, or more strictly speaking 100 per cent first-year capital allowances, for plant and machinery. The regional differential was to be provided by the restoration, in effect, of investment grants, but on a regional basis only and with some administrative improvements, including use of the Standard Industrial Classification in determining eligibility.

It took much longer to settle the rates for these regional development grants (which ended up pretty high – 20 per cent in Development Areas and 22 per cent in the Special Development Areas which had been created at some earlier stage) and their geographical coverage. After many combinations and permutations had been debated, it was eventually agreed that the grants should be paid on both plant and machinery and industrial buildings in the Development Areas and Special Development Areas and on industrial buildings only in the Intermediate Areas – a new category of 'assisted areas' which had been introduced in the latter part of Harold Wilson's government, primarily to give some help to the cotton towns. It was also decided to create additional assisted areas and to pay regional development grants for a limited period only on buildings in what were termed the Derelict Land Clearance Areas. Thus we now had four tiers of 'assisted areas' – Special Development Areas, Development Areas, Intermediate Areas and Derelict Land Clearance Areas – and there was something in the package for nearly everyone outside the prosperous South and South East and Midlands. Another decision was to continue REP at its full rate until September 1974 and phase it out after that.

As for a chosen instrument for selective assistance to industry, there was about that time a good deal of talk about 'City initiatives', and William Armstrong hoped that these might lead to a new private sector institution, possibly taking the existing Finance Corporation for Industry as its nucleus. However, nothing came of this, at any rate at that stage, and attention turned to the possibility of a new government-financed body. Given the remit to which we were working, I saw something to be said for a body which, like the IRC, would be provided with a certain amount of investment capital on which it would have to make a return, but which could also act as an agency for channelling outright government assistance in particular cases. Although William Armstrong's exercise was a well-kept secret, the idea of a new institution was in the air, and I remember a session of the

Trade and Industry Sub-Committee of the Expenditure Committee
when Antony Part, who was Permanent Secretary of the Department
of Trade and Industry, and Samuel Goldman were pressed hard by
the Members of Parliament on the Committee to give their views on
the case for a new agency as compared with direct government
support for industry. Since they did not know what the government
would eventually decide, they were obliged to take the line that there
were advantages in either course, without coming down in favour of
one or the other.

In the end, the Ministers concerned, a smaller circle than full
Cabinet, formed a clear preference for administering any new
schemes of assistance through a government Department, rather than
a non-Departmental institution. At this point Antony Part was quick
to come forward with a proposal, which was accepted, to create a new
so-called Industrial Development Executive within his own Department, in which people recruited from the world of finance and
industry would work side by side with regular civil servants in
administering selective assistance schemes; at the same time the
Department's regional offices would be reinforced and the top post in
a number of the regions would be upgraded, so once again a certain
amount of promotion was going for those in the right places for
selection. With the passage of time, however, the Industrial
Development Executive gave way in due course to a somewhat less
high powered Industrial Development Unit of the Department.

There was a certain amount of concern, at least among those who
cared about such things, about the relationship between any new
government funds for industry and existing sources of finance – in
case, for instance, soft money should drive out private investment
capital. My own approach was that the government should provide
selective assistance, in cases where there was an economic or social
return not reflected in the short-term financial return, only where
finance was not available from other sources on reasonable terms; this
latter stipulation was in due course written into the legislation, though
it was subsequently written out by the next Labour government.

It was at times something of a cliffhanger whether these decisions
would be taken in time for the Budget, but in the event they were
announced in the Budget on 21 March 1972 and in more detail in the
White Paper on *Industry and Regional Development* (Cmnd. 4942)
on the following day. The new powers required were taken later in the
Industry Act 1972. Even in Departments closely concerned, some
members of the Ministerial team did not know of the decisions until a
short time before they were announced, and when they were already a

fait accompli. While some who were in the old Macmillanite Tory tradition took the new measures in their stride, others who were more committed to the new Conservative market-orientated philosophy found it harder to reconcile themselves to this drastic reversal of policy. The existence today of two sharply distinguished strands of philosophy in the Conservative Party owes something perhaps to that divide. Certainly, that volte-face made a sharp imprint on the party's consciousness, and made the next Conservative government under Margaret Thatcher particularly resistant to any overt policy change which would seem like a repeat performance of Edward Heath's great U-turn.

END OF AN ERA

Traumatic though it proved to be, the U-turn did not lead to any immediate crisis in the country or the Conservative Party. In place of a restoration of market forces, we were now set for a period of big government. At the Department of Health and Social Security, Sir Keith Joseph presided over an expensive reorganisation of the National Health Service and a great expansion of the personal social services. Mr Peter Walker, having launched a reorganisation of local government in his time at the Department of the Environment, also at great cost, moved on to the DTI to back an ambitious and costly expansion plan for the British Steel Corporation. The Manpower Services Commission and the Health and Safety Executive were hived off from the Department of Employment with greatly increased budgets. The reorganisation of the water and sewerage services under regional water authorities was put in hand. The trio of Gaullist-style jumbo projects went on their way to the chagrin of the Treasury – Concorde which was under production, together with the third London airport at Maplin and the Channel Tunnel, which were both at the planning stage.

Meanwhile, concern about unemployment was matched by concern over rising inflation. In July 1971 the Confederation of British Industry took an initiative to restrain price increases by their member companies on the basis that the government would ensure that the nationalised industries did the same. The Chancellor had no alternative but reluctantly to accept the financial implications of this policy, which bore more heavily on the public sector than on private sector companies because nationalised industry prices had always been constrained. It was a policy decision which was not costed at the time, and on which it would now be difficult to put a true figure because the cost of price increases forgone was met only in exceptional cases, such as British Railways, by overt subsidies in the form of grants out of Votes. Generally speaking, the nationalised industries simply drew more money from the National Loans Fund. The public expenditure White Paper of December 1972 (Cmnd. 5178) described this situation in the following words:

Since July 1971 the nationalized industries have matched the CBI initiative on price restraint. Although this decision has worsened their financial position it has not affected investment programmes since . . . the industries have been able to borrow from the National Loans Fund to finance investment which, in the absence of price restraint, would have been financed from internal resources. (p. 44)

As I explain in Appendix III on 'The Mechanics of Public Expenditure', drawings from the National Loans Fund in a particular year do not, unlike Voted money, require Parliamentary approval; nor, at that time, were they subject to the administrative limits which have since been introduced. Under the definition of public expenditure then in use, it was the capital investment of the nationalised industries which scored as public expenditure, and not the government finance provided towards it. Thus these price subsidies, which escalated later on as price restraint was intensified, went largely unrecorded in the public expenditure figures. If the result was that a particular industry could not service its increased debt to the National Loans Fund out of its depressed revenue, the traditional way of clearing this situation up was to write off part of its debt to the Fund, with a corresponding increase in the national debt which the Treasury had to service; but a transaction of this kind did not surface at all in the public expenditure figures. The case for price subsidies is usually a matter for argument, but the case for identifying the subsidy and accounting for it seems to me overwhelming, and we did eventually secure acceptance of the principle that any subsidies to the nationalised industries should be financed by grants which would score as public expenditure.

During the Conservative government's first two years, public expenditure as a whole had grown at more or less the same rate as GDP. In the next two years it raced ahead. The 1972 White Paper treated this as a temporary phenomenon, to be followed by a period of retrenchment, and projected the percentage increases in expenditure over the preceding year at constant prices that are shown in table 4.1.

Table 4.1

	1972–73	1973–74	1974–75	1975–76	1976–77
Projected % increase (constant prices)	+6.2	+5.3	+1.7	+1.8	+1.4

The White Paper of December 1973 again projected a slowing down from 1974–75 onwards, to the distress of spending Departments and their Ministers for whom a rising expenditure projection was a sort of virility symbol. We can only speculate how far that improbable profile for the later years would have corresponded to reality if the Conservative government had stayed in power. For the first two years the actual increases in real terms turned out to be as shown in table 4.2.

Table 4.2

	% increase in public expenditure	% increase in GDP
1972–73	+6.6	+4.1
1973–74	+7.9	+4.0

In earlier sections, when describing the rate of increase in public expenditure, I have given figures based not only on the revised definitions adopted in 1976, which in my view are to be preferred, but also figures compiled on the old basis and taken from tables in the works by Otto Clarke and Samuel Goldman. However, the narrative has now moved on beyond the period when they were involved and about which they wrote. (Samuel Goldman left the Treasury for the banking world in 1972 and was succeeded by Douglas Henley.) I can therefore now quote only from the new series of figures, which forms Appendix I, but I do not think that the increases in the years after the U-turn would look any less startling on any other set of definitions.

The tax reductions of the 1971 Budget seem finally to have produced their effect at about the same time as the increased government spending, and in 1972 and 1973 there were record increases in personal disposable income. There was also a rapid growth in the money supply following the change in the system of monetary control known as Competition and Credit Control – a change relying heavily on movements in interest rates which, however, ministers were reluctant to accept when it came to the point. Inevitably, the balance of payments suffered. The inherited surplus was squandered and we moved back into deficit and pressure on sterling. The traditional response of deflating the economy was, of course, ruled out and Anthony Barber was unwilling to have his Chancellorship associated with a devaluation involving a straightforward downward change of parity. In June 1972, therefore, he adopted a floating rate for the pound. So from then on the Treasury no longer had to fight more of the losing battles to defend a fixed exchange rate which had absorbed much of their energies since the war, but now had the option – though one which involved another set of agonising decisions – of letting the rate float down rather than expend reserves to keep it up.

These policies did succeed for the time being in breaking out of the stagflationary phase in which both unemployment and inflation had been rising. The rate of economic growth was pushed up and unemployment was brought down in 1973 and 1974 (though it was never again to fall below the half million mark), but at the cost of higher inflation and a balance of payments deficit. Table 4.3 continues the

Table 4.3: Inflation takes off

	Retail price index	Wages and salaries per unit of output	Unemployed including school school leavers: UK	
	% increase over previous year	% increase over previous year	'000s	% change over previous year
1970	+6.4	+9.4	555	+7.1
1971	+9.4	+9.0	724	+30.4
1972	+7.1	+8.8	804	+11.0
1973	+9.2	+6.4	575	−28.5
1974	+16.0	+23.9	542	−5.7

series of figures from table 3.4 showing the trade-off between employment and inflation. Throughout the life of the Conservative government, the constant price system for planning public expenditure meant that programmes were maintained intact in volume terms no matter how much the amount of money required went up.

Faced with continuing wage and price inflation and the fear of worse to come, and failing to get trade union cooperation in voluntary wage restraint, by November 1972 the government saw no alternative but to introduce statutory control of prices and incomes, starting with a six-months' freeze. From then on, life in the Treasury was dominated by the attempt to make this policy work, punctuated by periodical distractions on the European front, another field of policy where the Treasury was out of favour for their scepticism about the possibility of immediately transforming the EEC from a common market into an economic and monetary union (EMU).

In prices and incomes policy William Armstrong once again played a central role behind the scenes – and less anonymously later on, as the Prime Minister's right hand man in meetings with the trade unions. In 1973 Douglas Wass was made an extra Second Permanent Secretary with oversight of this field of work. As it later transpired, this move was not made solely for organisational reasons but also to make it possible later on to appoint Douglas as Permanent Secretary of the Treasury without having to promote him from Deputy Secretary over the heads of the existing Second Permanent Secretaries, as had happened when William Armstrong had been promoted from Third Secretary to Permanent Secretary of the Treasury and his seniors were traumatically passed over.

Inevitably, there was a problem for the Treasury over reconciling their responsibility for price restraint with their financial responsibilities. This was a recurring issue whenever the counter-inflationary side of the Department wanted to put together a package of price restraint measures under which increases in such things as nationalised industry prices or rates would be wholly or partially forgone. Depressing nationalised industry prices even below the level permitted by the legislation on prices meant that demand for, say, power or transport was stimulated while investment to meet the demand was not allowed to rise correspondingly; though the financing of their investment from the National Loans Fund was allowed to go up, the investment itself was pegged within the public expenditure limits under the definitions then in force. Another damaging effect, it seemed to me, was that there was no link between wage increases and price increases in the minds of the people working in the nationalised industries. Their wage demands were therefore unaffected by whatever inhibition might have resulted if they and the public had seen wage increases as the immediate cause of price increases. Even when the miners were conducting their campaign to break through the government's incomes policy, the coal industry was cushioned from the full effects of wage and cost inflation by subsidies on coal prices.

As regards local authority rates, I should explain at this point, since there has not been a convenient stage for doing so before, that a distinction must always be kept in mind between the capital expenditure of the local authorities and their revenue expenditure. Although there was no direct control of their capital expenditure at that time, there was an indirect control because loan sanctions had to be approved for money borrowed for capital purposes: although this system did not regulate very tightly the amount spent in a particular year, and moreover borrowed funds could be topped up out of revenue, nevertheless it was possible to exert a degree of restraint on local authority capital expenditure over time. In fact, a frequent complaint was that the loan sanction system did not give locally elected councils any real discretion as to the choice of capital projects – a complaint partially met by the introduction of a 'locally determined' pool of projects, which was initiated in conjunction with myself by Douglas Janes when he was the Under Secretary at the Department of the Environment dealing with local government finance.

But there was not even an indirect control on the revenue expenditure of local authorities. In the early days of the PESC system there was in fact no effective link between the planning of current expenditure that went on locally and the figures for local government current expenditure that the Whitehall planners wrote into the public expenditure survey. When I first became familiar with this scene it struck me that the local authorities were in PESC but did not know it. Douglas Janes took the view that there were too many of them to establish direct consultation between Whitehall and individual local authorities, but a consultative council was initiated in which the various representative bodies of the local authorities took part. This produced a great improvement in communications, but the only instrument which the central government had for influencing the scale of revenue expenditure by local authorities was the rate support grant which it provided to complement their revenue from local rates. From a counter-inflationary point of view it was a natural approach to favour a generous rate support grant settlement so that the local authorities could moderate their rate increases, which, unlike national taxes, affected the retail price index. But this reduced the only inhibition on their mounting revenue expenditure, that is, the need to raise more rate revenue from the local electorate.

It was also a continuing struggle to keep the Milk Marketing Boards out of the red. The accounting arrangements were such that, if the price of milk was held down below the level needed to cover payments to the farmer plus distribution costs, the gap could be financed initially simply by letting the accounts of the Marketing Boards with the Ministry of Agriculture, and the agricultural Departments for the rest of the United Kingdom, go into deficit without an overt subsidy. But apart from this the government stopped short of food subsidies, to which Anthony Barber would have been strongly opposed.

Mustering support from Cabinet colleagues who were not themselves big spenders, the Chancellor launched an initiative to offset the growing excess over the expenditure levels which had been projected in the 1972 White Paper. On 21 May 1973 he announced a package of expenditure cuts designed to reduce programmes by £100 million in 1973–74 and about £500 million in 1974–75 compared with what they would otherwise have been. There was also an exercise to rephase building contracts, designed to save another £100 million or so in 1973–74. But the net result was still an increase in total expenditure planned for 1973–74, which was the current year, and it was only in the following year that a net economy was projected. This familiar prayer to be made good, but not yet, was greeted with some cynicism, and an Expenditure Committee report on the cuts in July 1973 commented that 'the succession of policy changes (first cutting 1974–75 by £911 million, then adding £1524 million, then cutting again by £535 million) departs drastically from what we have understood to be a central principle of public sector planning . . .'.

The point of the various counter-inflationary packages was only partly their real effect on price inflation; it was also the demonstration effect to show that the government was not asking trade union members to make all the sacrifices. As a further gesture, provision for threshold payments was introduced in Stage 3 of incomes policy, under which there would be automatic wage increases for every point by which the retail price index rose above a certain level. It was not anticipated that threshold payments would in practice be triggered off, but in the event costs rose unexpectedly because of higher world commodity prices, and then came the Middle East war, the oil crisis and the quadrupling of oil prices. The provisions of Stage 3 now fuelled inflation instead of containing it, as the RPI triggered off the threshold increases in wages.

The war of attrition on the incomes policy front moved into pitched battle when the miners began industrial action, starting with a ban on overtime, in support of a wage claim beyond the limits which were acceptable under incomes policy. The oil crisis hardened their attitude, since their hand was strengthened not merely by the jump in energy prices but by moves in the oil-producing countries to withhold supplies for particular destinations and fear of total interruption of supplies. There were queues at the petrol pumps; a rationing scheme for petrol was prepared and ration coupons were issued to motorists, though they were never in fact used. At times it seemed that a whole civilisation and way of life based on cheap and plentiful oil was under threat.

Electricity supplies were reduced in November at an early stage in the dispute. The following month industry was put on a three-day week. The miners were now not merely restricting output at the collieries but had mobilised their forces elsewhere to prevent distribution of coal stocks. There was apparently a new philosophy of industrial action to the effect that there was no point in a simple withdrawal of labour against which contingency measures might be effective, but that it must be backed up by whatever secondary action was necessary to ensure success. The government were unwilling or felt unable to make law and order prevail against these moves.

The public expenditure White Paper which appeared in December 1973 opened with the words, 'This White Paper is presented at a time of much uncertainty . . . In particular the future prospects for the supply and prices of oil to the Western world cannot yet be adequately assessed . . .' The Treasury had to consider whether in these circumstances the White Paper should be published at all, since it was impossible at short notice to re-open the forward programmes which had just emerged from the long drawn out survey process and carry out a radical fresh review. Douglas Henley took the view, rightly I believe, that it would be best to publish the programme figures, stressing their more than usually provisional character, as a point of departure for the changes which the new situation seemed to make inevitable. This view was accepted, but in the same month it was announced that programmes for 1974–75 would be cut by £1000 million; no figures were given about the implications of these cuts for the later years of the survey period. This was almost the last major economic decision of the Heath–Barber government, and its ability to carry out the cuts was never put to the test.

The traditional Christmas parties held by Treasury divisions, if they took place in parts of the building not served by the standby generator, were held by candlelight that year. In the New Year the Department of Energy was split off from the Department of Trade and Industry – the first crumbling of that great Whitehall empire – and

Patrick Jenkin moved there as Minister for Energy. Tom Boardman came from the DTI, where he had been Minister for Industry, to be Chief Secretary in the Treasury where he experienced, I believe, a rapid readjustment of perspectives.

To be part of the government machine coping with this situation and striving to keep things going gave a sense of awful but impotent responsibility. Housman's epitaph on an army of mercenaries who saved the sum of things for pay came recurrently to mind. To compare this situation with the hour when earth's foundations fled may now seem rather overdramatic. A little while afterwards, talking to one of my opposite numbers at the top of the Ministry of Finance in Paris, when I said that I felt that we had just pulled back from the brink, he said scornfully, 'Brink? What brink? You had a strike. You had an election. No one was shot.' However, there was a good deal of stress at the time, which played a part in the illness which put William Armstrong out of action at one stage during these events.

There was a desperate but unsuccessful search for a compromise or formula which might get the miners back to work without destroying the incomes policy. At a meeting of the National Economic Development Council, which had acquired a new importance as the only meeting place where members of the government and trade union leaders still talked together, Len Murray, who had become General Secretary of the TUC, appeared to offer an olive branch in the form of a statement to the effect that, if the miners were given special treatment, the TUC would not use that as an argument for special treatment in other cases. This fell short, of course, of saying that the trade unions would not seek special treatment in other cases – as distinct from not citing the miners as a precedent – but if one takes the view that there was a possible opening there which could have been explored, and that events might just conceivably have been different if that had been done, the fact appears to be that the Chancellor of the Exchequer, who was in the chair, did not seek to build on the TUC proposition.

In January 1974 the miners' leaders held a ballot of their members to get their backing for an all-out strike. Having neither beaten the miners nor come to terms with them, the Prime Minister went to the country to get a fresh mandate which might somehow strengthen his hand for dealing with them. The miners' strike was suspended for the election. The result was inconclusive enough for Edward Heath to spend some time seeking an alliance which would enable him to stay in office, but the Liberals under Jeremy Thorpe would not join him and Heath conceded defeat. Harold Wilson became prime minister, and later in the year called another general election which gave him a working majority.

That year was the close of what had been – taking the post-war period as a whole, and in spite of stop–go and sterling crises and relative decline in the world – something of a golden age in terms of high employment and rising standards of personal and public consumption. It was also a period which had seen the rise and fall of the PESC system of public expenditure planning.

5

The Wilson/Callaghan Years

FROM THE SOCIAL CONTRACT TO INCOMES POLICY

The Labour Party manifesto for the election that brought Harold Wilson back to office promised an irreversible shift of wealth and power to working people and their families, though probably very few Labour voters (who in turn were a minority of the electorate) were conscious that that was what they were voting for, as distinct from an end to the three-day week. The implication of this formula was that, not merely would the new government overturn their predecessors' policies, as had happened before, but that this time they would somehow carry out their own measures in such a way that they could not be overturned by a successor government.

'The social contract' was a phrase which was much more on people's lips, without acknowledgment to Rousseau. The thought was that, in place of statutory control of incomes, which was repealed, the cooperation of organised labour would be secured in return for government policies favourable to their cause, in which the trade unions themselves would have a powerful voice; and in fact their involvement in the determination of policy in that phase of government – especially, but not exclusively, as regards labour legislation such as the Employment Protection Act – went far beyond the influence exercised by any pressure group before or since, even the agriculture and aircraft lobbies.

The Treasury team of Ministers consisted initially of Denis Healey as Chancellor and Joel Barnett as Chief Secretary, both of whom stuck it out there throughout the life of the government, with John Gilbert as Financial Secretary and Robert Sheldon as Minister of State. Later on, John Gilbert moved to Transport, Robert Sheldon replaced him as Financial Secretary, and Denzil Davies came in as a promising young Minister of State. In addition, Edmond Dell served as an extra Treasury Minister, second in seniority only to the Chancellor, filling the portfolio of Paymaster General. A precedent for this had been set in the latter days of the Heath government when Maurice Macmillan returned to the Treasury as Paymaster General. However, given that the Chief Secretary retained his specific responsibility for public expenditure, I believe that neither Maurice Macmillan nor Edmund Dell found their roving commission altogether satisfactory, and the arrangement was not continued after Edmund Dell became Secretary of State for Trade in 1976.

Still wedded to the idea of having some counterweight to the Treasury, Harold Wilson made Harold Lever Chancellor of the Duchy of Lancaster as an extra source of financial expertise and advice, with a very small personal staff located in the Cabinet Office. This was to prove a nuisance to the Treasury from time to time, as no doubt it was meant to be, since Harold Lever was no believer in hair shirt policies but a man for ingenious solutions rather than hard choices; and Cabinet, impressed by his reputation for financial wizardry in his private affairs, invariably supported his ingenious, even if expensive, solutions for problems of public finance. However, he was such an engaging person, and one so free from malice, that there was nothing in the atmosphere of the 'creative tension' of the DEA days.

Harold Wilson also brought Bernard Donoughue from the London School of Economics into No. 10 as head of a new Policy Unit, thus providing yet another source of non-Treasury advice – on top of the CPRS, which was kept on. However, the Policy Unit's function was essentially to give advice to the Prime Minister, not normally to Cabinet as a whole, nor did Donoughue report to a separate economic policy Minister, so this arrangement also fell short of re-creation of the DEA.

Early in the life of the new government William Armstrong, having sought and received clearance under the usual procedures, left the Civil Service Department to become chairman of the Midland Bank and to receive the life peerage due to a former head of the civil service as Lord Armstrong of Sanderstead. The move came in for a certain amount of criticism in quarters hostile to private sector appointments for former civil servants, but it saved the government some embarrassment, since William Armstrong was *persona non grata* on the left after his role in incomes policy. Douglas Allen moved from the Treasury to take over the Civil Service Department and was succeeded by Douglas Wass as Permanent Secretary of the Treasury.

To have the country back at work was a great relief and worth paying for through conciliatory measures such as a generous scheme of compensation for pneumoconiosis, but across the board the price paid for the social contract was very high indeed. Food subsidies were introduced, though not on the scale of the war-time and post-war subsidy bill. There was an immediate rent freeze, at the cost of a sharp rise in housing subsidies, together with increased expenditure on other housing measures such as 'municipalization'. On the social security front, in the words of the public expenditure White Paper of January 1975 (Cmnd. 5879), 'One of the first decisions of the new Government in March [1974] was to bring the 1974 general uprating of benefits forward from the autumn to July . . . The increase in the pension represented a real improvement of about 13½ per cent over the rate established in October 1973'. The government also bound itself by legislation to uprate unemployment and other short-term benefits in future in line with prices and to uprate pensions in line with either prices or earnings, whichever proved to be the more favourable.

'The social wage' was another phrase in currency at the time in connection with the various benefits and subsidies which, it was hoped, would be looked on by work-people as a supplement to their ordinary wage packet and which would therefore be taken into account in their wage demands. One such item was the cost of compensation to the Post Office and to the gas and electricity industries to offset their deficits caused by price restraint, a subsidy for which overt provision was now made under an Act passed in 1974, and which came to about £640 million in 1974–75. (The figure is from the February 1976 White Paper, Cmnd. 6393.) However, a decision was secured to start phasing out these particular subsidies in the following year.

Another of the ideas in vogue was that assistance to industry should be 'socially accountable'. The exact meaning of this term was not altogether clear, but it seemed to go with a prejudice against general schemes of incentives to industry, such as had flourished under the previous Labour government, and in favour of selective assistance involving a high degree of intervention. Nevertheless REP, though unselective as between individual manufacturing firms in the Development Areas, was doubled in response to a recommendation from the TUC.

There had been concern that the three-day week might bring about a widespread collapse of companies throughout industry, which would require some general scheme of emergency financial support, probably operated through the banking system. Nothing as bad as that materialised, and unemployment actually went down in the second quarter of 1974 before resuming its inexorable climb, but private sector investment slumped, there was some fall in output generally, and there was a succession of rescue operations for individual companies. Inevitably, the handling of these cases involved rather energetic negotiations between the Treasury and the Department of Industry (from which the Department of Trade had now regained its independence) under the leadership of Tony Benn as Secretary of State.

Not that the Treasury were at all resistant to active industrial policies. On the contrary, Denis Healey made it clear that he did not accept that governments could have no effect on industrial per-formance, and that he saw a place for micro measures as well as macro policies, while Douglas Wass, after visiting Japan to see how they handled relations with industry there, put in hand a plan for a reorganisation of the Treasury designed to enable it to play a more effective role in this field. Even so, the Treasury could not be unconcerned at the possibility that the handling of these operations through prolonged tripartite consultations between government, management and workers might result in indefinite subsidisation without any prospect of a return to viability. Hard-won collective backing was eventually secured for a set of criteria for assistance to industry; a version of this was put to the Public Accounts Committee which, apparently, knew it as the Pliatzky report and found it reasonably satisfactory. However, as we moved from these holding operations to what was meant to be a fully fledged industrial policy, it was clear that the issues would have to be resolved through the Cabinet Office machinery (rather than bilaterally between the Treasury and the Department of Industry) and in the last analysis under the Prime Minister's aegis; and the committee arrangements were adapted accordingly.

There was a clear political commitment to nationalise the ship-building and aircraft industries. There was also a consensus in the government in favour of a National Enterprise Board with large financial resources and a much broader remit than the IRC had been given. There was, too, political support for the concept of planning agreements between the government and individual companies, based to some extent on a misconception of planning agreements which the French were thought to operate. But a principal unresolved issue concerned the question of compulsion. One idea in circulation was that the government should acquire shares in the top twenty-five British companies, or some other number of top companies. But how was this to be done, and in particular was the National Enterprise

Board to have not merely the right to buy share-holdings but also a compulsory power of acquisition? Similarly, were these to be powers to compel companies to enter into planning agreements, since it was clear that few, if any, of them would voluntarily accept the tripartite agreements involving government, management and trade unions which were envisaged at the Department of Industry? In rejecting the compulsory approach, Ministers as a whole moved a good deal of the way towards resolving what had appeared to be a certain ambivalence towards the mixed economy and the role of the private sector.

In the event, the most important acquisition – leaving aside shipbuilding and aerospace – was not of the government's seeking. It came about when a consortium of clearing banks sought a meeting with the Home Finance side of the Treasury, at which I sat in from the public expenditure side, to report that British Leyland, the principal British car manufacturer, at whose birth the IRC had acted as midwife under the previous Labour government, had run up an overdraft of, if I remember correctly, £50 million, which the banks could not continue, let alone provide the further finance which the company wanted for their future investment plans. So the clearing banks handed the problem over to the government – a remarkably passive attitude in comparison with the role played by the big banks in, say, the United States, Japan or Germany, though it can be argued that British Leyland would have been a hopeless case for even the most dynamic banking system to take on.

Since it was unrealistic to imagine that the government would stand aside from the British Leyland situation to the bitter end, it seemed better to go from the outset for the course which Edward Heath had adopted on second thoughts in the case of Upper Clyde Shipbuilders – that is, to give a guarantee as a holding operation and to appoint three wise men to work out a longer-term reconstruction, rather than leave this to emerge from tripartite consultation under the Department of Industry. Whether, in the light of experience, this was the better course, even in terms of damage limitation, it is hard to judge. When agreeing to the proposed course of action, the Prime Minister put forward his own nomination as number one wise man in the person of Sir Don Ryder, who was an unknown quantity to the Treasury but had been singled out for a new post of industrial adviser to the government. Later on, as Lord Ryder, he became the first head of the National Enterprise Board. The Ryder team put forward an ambitious plan for bringing the company back to profitability under public ownership.

The Ryder plan was presented with the utmost confidence in its success and in the accuracy of its projections down to the smallest detail. The trade unions were said to have pledged their cooperation in carrying it out. As everyone knows, what actually took place over the following years was a series of losses, even before the motor car market slumped in 1979, and a continuing history of restrictive practices and industrial disruption, on which no impact could be made except under the threat of total closure, after Michael Edwardes had taken over as chairman of British Leyland in 1977.

While the private sector was in trouble, investment by the nationalised industries, which the Chancellor saw as a stabilising factor in the economy during the recession, went up sharply. The chairmen of the nationalised industries remained unmollified, however, about the repeated chopping and changing of the expenditure totals by which they were governed, about the delays caused by the PESC timetable, and about the detailed intervention by sponsor Departments which, in their eyes, acted as though they knew more about running the industries than the people in charge of them. There was not much that the Treasury could do about the interventionist tendencies of sponsor Departments but, following an initiative in the National Economic Development Council, I headed an exercise designed to streamline a little the timetable and procedures for handling the investment programmes of the nationalised industries; these still came, however, within the public expenditure limits.

As regards the trio of jumbo projects, Britain finally withdrew from the Channel Tunnel project after British Railways' estimates of the cost of the rail link escalated sharply; the plan for a third London airport was cancelled, though not primarily for expenditure reasons; but Concorde still survived. Tony Benn, in whose Bristol constituency Concorde provided a good deal of employment, proposed that all the figures about the project should be published. A good deal of this information had previously been withheld, allegedly on commercial grounds, and it seemed to me that disclosure of the enormous losses involved must surely lead to a decision to terminate the project. For Concorde was a unique phenomenon, defying the notion that, since bygones are bygones in economics, there must be a point of no return after which it is cheaper to go on than to pull out. Even after the vast research and development costs, it would have been cheaper not to go on to the production stage. Even after the losses on production, it would still have saved money not to fly Concorde. Edmund Dell was sceptical, rightly as it turned out, about my prognosis of the results of publishing the figures; in the event it was a great struggle to prevent the production for stock of even more

Concordes beyond the sixteen already in production, several of which still remained unsold. Quite apart from the mystique about the aircraft and the concern for employment, there was anxiety to the last on the diplomatic side about doing anything to upset the French. It was only the palpable lack of further customers which finally enabled the production programme to be limited to sixteen. Of course, Concorde is a marvellously quick way of crossing the Atlantic, and British Airways and its customers are right to use it for this purpose since they do not have to contribute to the losses which have been written off.

The situation in 1974 was like 1964 all over again in the sense that the only sacrificial offerings, as some offset to all the expenditure increases, had to come from 'prestige projects' – with Concorde nevertheless surviving – and from the defence budget. The defence studies already in hand now became the basis for a full-scale defence review under the chairmanship in the first instance of Patrick Nairne, at the time a Deputy Secretary in the Ministry of Defence, with myself as alternate chairman, and with a remit to reduce the share of the national product spent on defence. This did not necessarily entail that the defence budget must be reduced in absolute terms but that, if it increased at all, it must do so more slowly than the rate of economic growth. Naturally, therefore, and in accordance with the principle of believing what it suited them to believe, the supporters of the defence cause argued for an optimistic view about future economic growth.

In the immediate aftermath of the oil crisis and the three-day week the prevailing economic advice in the Treasury was that, though there would be no growth at all for one year, over the medium term the trend growth rate of something like 3 per cent would be achieved, which would mean growth of more than 3 per cent during a catching-up period. The economic projections in the January 1975 White Paper took a 3 per cent growth rate from 1973 to 1979 as the central case, with 2½ per cent and 3½ per cent as, respectively, a more cautious and a more optimistic variant. But by then some at least of the Treasury people had come to a private belief that 2½ per cent would have been a better choice as central case and that lower downward variants had to be allowed for; this possibility was reflected in the text of the White Paper though not in the tables.

In the event the impasse in the defence review over growth projections was to some extent resolved by a new approach based on the principle of overriding priority for our NATO commitment and a minimum credible British capability in the NATO area. Virtually all commitments outside the NATO area were to be given up. In spite of a last minute attempt to reopen the growth rate debate when this plan went forward to the next level in the review – a rearguard action staged not by the Ministry of Defence but by others with the cause of defence research close to their heart – this approach was accepted as the basis of the decisions on defence, and led in due course to a modest reduction in defence expenditure as a percentage of GDP. This can be seen from table 1.1 (p. 15), but the figures for the years after the review reflect not only the review decisions but a whole series of subsequent cuts and restorations of cuts and a quite different pattern of economic growth from that anticipated at the review.

The defence savings were regarded as inadequate not merely in anti-NATO and pro-Soviet circles but also in some quarters where the NATO commitment was supported in principle. The cuts still left us carrying a defence burden which was higher in relation to our resources than in any other NATO country except the United States, though relatively low in absolute terms because of our inferior economic performance as compared with Germany or France. The savings also bore all the marks of having been worked out in the Ministry of Defence on the basis of equality of misery between the three services; this ran counter to the view held by some in the Treasury that we could no longer afford to contribute to NATO both on land and sea and in the air and that, since it was politically impossible to withdraw our Rhine army, the finger pointed at the navy – though from a balance of payments point of view it should have pointed at our forces in Germany, which at that time entailed a bigger foreign exchange loss, as distinct from budgetary cost, than our contribution to the EEC which received so much more attention.

Although Harold Wilson had applied for membership of the Community during his first premiership, in opposition he had become committed to renegotiation of the terms of entry. But at the time of the renegotiation we were still in the transitional period of adjusting to the Community régime, and our net contribution was still quite small. In any event there was never any real possibility of securing different terms in the sense of amendments to either the Treaty of Rome or the Treaty of Accession. The *Report on Renegotiation* presented to Parliament in March 1975 (Cmnd. 6003) had to declare itself satisfied with an agreement which had been reached for refunds of budgetary contributions to any member state which at a future date qualified under a complex formula. Though this was better than nothing, the subsequent experience of Margaret Thatcher's government, when the financial burden of our Community membership had become actual and not merely potential, showed the severe limitations of this safeguard. Moreover, the renegotiation did nothing at all about the common agricultural policy which was such a large part of the problem, beyond securing a fairly worthless arrangement for a stocktaking of the CAP. However, the result was enough to enable the government to recommend and obtain an affirmative vote for staying in the Community in the referendum which followed.

This was also widely regarded as a vote against Tony Benn who campaigned energetically in favour of leaving the EEC. Immediately after the referendum he declared himself willing to abide by its verdict, but this phase did not last very long. Tony Benn had by now gone to the Department of Energy in place of Eric Varley, who in turn replaced Tony Benn at the Department of Industry. Eric Varley, a miner's son, had felt at home at the Department of Energy, and no doubt both of them would have preferred to stay where they were.

All in all, the first year or so of the new administration was a period of frenetic activity. It was also in some ways a period of collective madness. Public expenditure, after rising by 7.9 per cent in real terms in the last year of the Conservative government, rose by no less than 12.7 per cent in Labour's first year, 1974–75, a year in which GDP showed practically no increase. Over the two years together the ratio of public expenditure to GDP rose from 38.5 per cent to 45.0 per cent, the most rapid shift in the whole period covered by this book. To this increase in real terms we have to add the increase in money terms because of accelerating inflation. In the 1974–75 wage round earnings went up by 27 per cent. The social wage had done nothing to moderate demands for the actual wage in the individual pay packet. Table 5.1 brings the stagflation tables up to date. The unemployment figures in these tables, being mid-year figures, do not fully bring out how

Table 5.1: Stagflation gets worse

	Retail price index	Wages and salaries per unit of output	Unemployed including school leavers: UK	
	% increase over previous year	% increase over previous year	'000	% change over previous year
1974	+ 16.1	+ 23.9	542	− 5.7
1975	+ 24.2	+ 27.9	866	+ 59.8

unemployment was rising alongside inflation. From mid-1974 unemployment went up continuously. By the third quarter of 1975 it was well over the million mark and has never come down to a million since then.

As to how the increase in public expenditure, including public sector wages, was being paid for, the January 1975 White Paper went into some details about the implications for personal consumption but did not mention the word taxation. The divorce between the collective decision-making process on public expenditure and the Treasury's budget-making processes remained total. Denis Healey had warned the Labour Party's annual conference before the election that there would have to be tax increases, but he cannot have bargained for, and certainly did not like it when it arrived, the taxation which had to be raised from the man in the street. In the words of the February 1976 White Paper: 'In 1975–76 a married man on average earnings is paying about a quarter of his earnings in income tax, compared with a tenth in 1960–61.' On top of this, the employee's social security contribution had much the same effect as income tax, for practical purposes adding about 5 per cent to the basic rate of tax.

Meanwhile another financial aggregate, the Public Sector Borrowing Requirement (PSBR), was achieving a new notoriety. The PSBR was not a wholly new phenomenon nor, unlike public expenditure, a particularly complicated one or a difficult concept to define. It is quite simply the total borrowings of the public sector – central government, local government and public corporations combined, which come together in the way shown in the chart of financial flows in Appendix III. The argument is not about what the PSBR is but about how much it matters and how big a PSBR the country can stand. For two years after Roy Jenkins' measures the PSBR had been a minus quantity – that is there had been net repayment of public debt. Under his successor it rose to over £4000 million in 1973. In 1975 the PSBR was over £10,000 million. What was disconcerting was the way in which projections of the PSBR turned out to be underestimates by a wide margin and had to be replaced by a succession of higher figures.

From the standpoint of the neo-Keynesian orthodoxy, the large budget deficit was the opposite side of the coin to the slump in the private sector and a necessary corollary of the propensity to save. But in fact the growth of public expenditure far outshot domestic savings and was to a substantial extent financed out of the financial surpluses of the oil-producing countries, a new phenomenon on the world financial scene. The willingness of the OPEC countries to place large sums in the London capital market and to lend money to our nationalised industries, with foreign exchange cover from the Bank of England, was due to three things: the fact that they had to do something with the money, the well-organised character of the London capital market, and the expectation that Britain would be restored to financial solvency when we had our own oil from the North Sea.

The position in this respect was that we had still not had a barrel of oil from the North Sea but that the oil companies had put a great deal of money and effort into exploration and development, and production was in sight. This made it increasingly urgent to resolve the twin issues of government participation in the North Sea fields and the tax régime for North Sea oil. At one stage it was being put about that the uncertainty on these two issues was making the North Sea 'unbankable' – that is, there was a danger of choking off the supply of further funds for development, especially as the costs and technical difficulties were greater than had been anticipated. To a large extent, no doubt, this was part of the propaganda campaign that is always and quite naturally mounted by industries such as oil or agriculture or aircraft production when they are at issue with government, and that government, or at any rate the Treasury, equally naturally takes with a pinch of salt. Nevertheless there was a problem for the companies so long as they were dealing with an unknown quantity – as were we on the government side, since a régime had to be worked out for an industry which was totally new, so far as the UK was concerned.

As regards participation, the starting point was a highly unspecific political commitment to acquire a stake in the North Sea for the people, or words to that effect. Harold Lever led a triumvirate of Ministers charged with giving this a concrete form and negotiating it with the companies. The other Ministers were Eric Varley, until his move from the Department of Energy, supported by Lord Balogh, Minister of State in the Department, and Edmund Dell. There was never any question of expropriation, nor was there any serious proposal for old-fashioned nationalisation, in the form of compulsory acquisition of shares or assets in return for cash or government stock, as the compensation bill would have been extremely difficult to settle and possibly prohibitive in amount. Instead, in a series of urbane presentations to the major oil companies, Harold Lever invited them to let the government have a half share in the oil on terms which would leave them 'no better and no worse off'. On the face of it there was no reason why the oil companies should do any such thing, but it was tacitly understood that they would be dependent on the government's goodwill in such matters as future exploration licences and that they would therefore do well to humour the government now.

There was some mystification as to what the terms might be which would leave them no better and no worse off and what point there would be in negotiating such terms if at the end of the day they changed nothing. I worked out a sophisticated formula for achieving that effect without making it too obvious, but it was too subtle for most people, including the Department of Energy. Eventually the Department of Energy broke through the impasse by negotiating a series of sale and buy-back deals, under which no money would change hands but the companies would sell half their oil production to the state, in the shape of a new British National Oil Corporation, with a right to re-purchase it at the same price. On the face of it the point of these terms also might have seemed a bit unclear, but they satisfied the political commitment and they also gave the government, through BNOC, physical control over the sale and buy-back of oil which could be of special value in another oil crisis but which it might have been difficult to secure in a more direct way – or so, at any rate, it was thought – without falling foul of EEC rules on non-discrimination in oil supplies. In addition, BNOC was to have a seat on each of the consortia developing the various fields, an arrangement which was to help it acquire know-how so that it could take part on its own account in future rounds of exploration and development.

On the taxation front Edmund Dell headed the Treasury and Inland Revenue team. The first problem was to get authentic esti-mates of costs and probable revenues; this was tackled by rather novel forms of consultation with the oil companies. A second problem was to devise a tax régime which was not too generous to the rich fields but not too onerous for the marginal fields. Finally, a rate of tax had to be fixed, in advance of any actual experience of North Sea production, which would maximise the government's take but leave the companies with a reasonable return on their investment and give them an incentive to continue exploration and development. Some years later, in the House of Lords, Lord Balogh criticised the Treasury, 'especially Sir Leo Pliatzky, who painted the blackest picture of the consequences on the activity in the North Sea if there was any increase in taxation,' thus preventing an increase in the rate of Petroleum Revenue Tax to the extent that Lord Balogh thought necessary – a possibly unique case of public criticism of a former official by a former Minister. His remarks also did less than justice to Edmund Dell's leading role in this exercise, since he was a Minister accustomed to making up his own mind at the end of the day on matters for which he was responsible.

The oil companies, for their part, were concerned among other things to get assurances that the tax would be adjusted in the event of a fall in the price of oil, which had stood at $2 to $2.50 a barrel before 1973 and was at this time about $12. Now that the oil price has fluctuated between $30 and $40 during the writing of this book, it may seem hard to credit that oil men were in genuine doubt as to whether the price could stay as high as $12 and tempting to believe that this was part of their propaganda campaign; but in fact there would have been no point in getting those assurances if they could have foreseen the price increases which were to come, and which enabled the Conservative government to adjust the tax upwards rather than downwards – to the accompaniment of the same kind of forebodings from the oil men as were being uttered then.

But to go back to 1975, even though the decisions taken made the outlook for North Sea oil more secure, the gains were still to come. Meanwhile the upward spiral in public expenditure, wages and prices, unemployment, and overseas deficits could not be allowed to go on indefinitely. It was on incomes policy that the first action to turn the situation round was taken. In the summer of 1975, after the referendum on the EEC was out of the way, policy on this front developed rather quickly. After much toing and froing on the question of statutory pay policy versus voluntary pay policy, the decision came down in favour of a voluntary policy with statutory powers in reserve. In the event, the reserve powers dropped out of the picture when trade union agreement was secured for a voluntary policy involving a flat rate increase of £6 a week for everyone earning up to £8500 a year, with no increase at all above that. This had the serious disadvantage of giving high percentage increases to the lower paid while compressing differentials for skilled workers and managers; the advantages were that it was a readily comprehensible scheme and that it had powerful backing in the trade union movement itself in the person of Jack Jones.

It was put about at one time that the Treasury had staged a coup to get a Cabinet decision in favour of a statutory incomes policy to which it was doctrinally addicted. The Treasury at official level were in fact not at all monolithic on this. Whichever type of incomes policy was adopted, the problem was to make it stick. After the trauma of the closing days of the Heath government, we were highly conscious of the problems of enforcing a statutory policy. If a voluntary policy failed, it would be a defeat for incomes policy; if a statutory policy were tried but could not be enforced, that would be a defeat both for incomes policy and for the rule of law. On the other hand there would be no point in a voluntary policy which amounted to no more than another Solomon Binding. I dare say that the Treasury officials directly advising the Chancellor were sceptical about the kind of voluntary policy which was initially on offer from the trade unions, and I doubt whether the unions would have delivered an effective voluntary policy but for their awareness that otherwise the government would have had no choice but to take statutory powers. As for the so-called Treasury coup, this is another instance of talking about the Treasury as though the Department was somehow separate from its Ministers and could operate without them. In fact the Treasury has no access to the Cabinet except in the person of the Chancellor of the Exchequer, or of the Chief Secretary if he is also a member of Cabinet, and cannot circulate papers to it except in the name of the Chancellor or Chief Secretary or under a covering note from one of them.

It was Denis Healey who made the running to get Cabinet decisions on Stage One of incomes policy and who bore the heat of the day in carrying the trade unions with it and with Stage Two and Stage Three which followed. As in the days of Edward Heath's statutory policy, from that point on the administration of incomes policy, and the effort to make it stick through all manner of governmental sticks and carrots short of direct statutory control of wages, was a continuous Whitehall preoccupation until the end of the government's life. But for part of this time it was public expenditure which held the centre of the stage.

THE MISSING BILLIONS

At the end of 1975, on Douglas Henley's departure to become Comptroller and Auditor General, I took over as head of the public expenditure side of the Treasury. Although, as I have commented before, promotion is generally good for morale, I had mixed feelings about this particular promotion, on a number of counts. For one thing, the Treasury's reputation now stood at a low point, reflected in an extended *Times* leader under a banner headline 'Spending is out of Control'. On top of this, the Treasury reorganisation had led to another Second Permanent Secretary appointment, which I would have preferred and had hoped to get, in charge of a new grouping which brought together all aspects of Treasury work which were related to industrial policy, including some expenditure programmes as well as taxation. The Treasury's leading role in industrial strategy and incomes policy, with a strong personality in charge of that side, together with the absence of any established guidelines about relationships between the two sides, was bound to create some ambivalence about the relative priority of the Treasury's objectives in these various fields and to add a fresh complication to the thankless task of trying to bring public expenditure under control. Moreover, though I had by now a great deal of accumulated experience of dealing with particular expenditure programmes and projects – more perhaps than my various predecessors in the job – I was no lover of the PESC system and had never served as one of its high priests presiding over public expenditure as a whole. I had never expected to inherit responsibility for Otto Clarke's creation and found a certain irony in this situation.

The occasion for the *Times* headline was a report in December 1975 on *The Financing of Public Expenditure* from the Expenditure Committee of the House of Commons. This report gave prominence to evidence from Wynne Godley, who until six months previously had been an economic adviser in the Treasury and one of the PESC high priests, to the effect that the actual out-turn of public expenditure in 1974–75 had been more than £5 billion in excess of what it had been planned to be in that year, allowing for price changes, in the public expenditure White Paper of 1971; and the bulk of the excess could not be linked with specifically announced policy changes. The Committee felt 'bound to conclude from this that even allowing for unannounced policy changes the Treasury's present methods of controlling public expenditure are inadequate in the sense that money can be spent on a scale which was not contemplated when the relevant policies were decided upon'.

It should be added that this escalation of expenditure had taken place in spite of repeated cuts exercises. As I commented at the time, controlling public expenditure was like the task of Sisyphus who, in Greek mythology, was condemned to roll a huge stone eternally up a hill but never to reach the top because each time, before reaching the summit, it rolled back down – only our Sisyphean task in reverse was to push public expenditure downhill, only to find it roll back up again to an even higher point.

The Sisyphean cycle was still at work. Programmes for the current financial year, 1975–76, were by then about £1600 million more than had been allowed for in the January 1975 White Paper. As regards the year ahead, despite the fact that in his last Budget speech the Chancellor had announced cuts of £1100 million in the White Paper programmes for 1976–77 in order to reduce the future borrowing requirement, that £1100 million had already been added back to other programmes with another £500 million on top.

Up to a point, but only up to a point, it was not unfair to hold the PESC system, and the Treasury as the Department which had created it and was its custodian, responsible for the missing £5 billion. It was a system which placed emphasis on planning rather than control, on the medium-term future at the expense of the here and now, on so-called resources to the exclusion of money. The convention under which the 'recosting of existing policy' took place during each public expenditure survey facilitated the process through which, in the Expenditure Committee's phraseology, money could eventually be spent on a scale which was not contemplated when the relevant policies were originally decided upon. Although the separation of Cabinet decision-making on public expenditure from the Treasury's Budget decisions was something not altogether in the Treasury's hands, there was force in the Expenditure Committee's criticisms of the failure to establish the necessary connections between public expenditure, taxation, borrowing, the money supply and inflation.

On the other hand it would have been astonishing if expenditure in 1974–75 had turned out as it had been planned three years earlier, with a U-turn and a change of government and the social contract in between. Even with different conventions, the PESC technology would not have been able to contain the political pressures for more spending which were exerted both at the 'PESC' stage – that is, during the annual survey exercise – and 'inter-PESC', as I thought of it – that is, throughout the year between the survey decisions. The Sisyphean increases of the past year had taken place 'inter-PESC'. When it came to the point neither the previous Conservative government nor the present Labour government had paid any attention to their White Paper plans or allowed PESC or PAR to frustrate the will to spend.

If any future plans were not to go the same way, something had to change, but what? As one commentator, Rudolf Klein, observed, it was not a crisis of Treasury control; it was a crisis of political management. The failure to stick to any public expenditure plan had in fact gone a long way towards discrediting the whole process of government. It was unfair that responsibility for this should be laid at the door of the Treasury as a Department. So the changes needed had to be such that, although the technological process could never override the political dimension, the government in its political aspects would be unequivocally responsible at every stage either for sticking to existing plans or changing them by conscious decision.

A number of important developments which had been put in hand in Douglas Henley's time were in fact already in the pipeline. A major and prolonged cuts exercise had been carried out during the 1975 public expenditure survey. This had been what the same *Times* leader described as 'the occasion for the bitter battles over spending with which the Cabinet has been absorbed in recent months'. This did not mean that public expenditure was actually to be reduced even in real terms, let alone in terms of cash. It was in fact to continue growing in the year ahead, 1976–77. But the further increases which would otherwise have taken place in the years after that had been eliminated from the plan. To get decisions on 'cuts' even in this special sense was something of an achievement and went beyond what I would have expected in the feverish political climate of the time – an achievement to which I had made only a limited and intermittent contribution, being absent from the scene for two spells of surgery, one of which turned out rather disastrously. That I had remained a candidate for promotion had been an act of faith on the part of those concerned. However, now that I had returned to the scene, the question was how these decisions were going to be made to stick. What was there to stop the stone from rolling uphill again?

One major innovation which was being planned was the introduction of cash limits. What this meant in principle was that, when volume programmes for the year immediately ahead had been settled at constant prices, and were being translated into cash provision at the prices of the day, a limit would be placed in advance on the price increases to be covered and the amount of cash to be provided. In the case of those programmes which were financed out of Departmental Votes, a limit would be placed in advance on the amount to be provided through Main Estimates and Supplementary Estimates combined. Instead of waiting to see what the rate of inflation turned out to be and providing extra cash to cover it when the time came, the government would, in snooker terms, be calling its shots on inflation and declaring in advance what cost increases it would be prepared to finance.

Denis Healey and Joel Barnett were both keen on cash limits, which they rightly saw as an important back-up for incomes policy in the public sector by gearing the scale of cash provision to the target rate of wage increases. The White Paper on *The Attack on Inflation* (Cmnd. 6151) had envisaged that cash limits would 'contribute to countering inflation by making it clear to both spending authorities and to suppliers that the Government's purchases of goods and services will have to be cut back if prices rise too high'. Moreover, Denis Healey was more sensitive to the monetary dimension of p than some of his advisers, while Joel Barnett, as an accountant by training, seemed to me to be more at home with cash, even after years of having to cope with the PESC system, than with the funny money of constant prices. They had in fact been rather impatient at the rate of progress in preparing the new system.

However, cash limits could not in any event be introduced until the beginning of the next financial year, 1976–77, which was some three months away, and the whole plan could go wrong in that time unless something was done to make it stick. Moreover, cash limits seemed to me to be a second-stage discipline, designed to ensure that the amount of cash spent on volume programmes did not exceed the approved cost. They were not designed in themselves to determine the volume or physical size of programmes. What was needed was a first-stage discipline to prevent Ministers from increasing the volume programmes beyond the figures which had just been agreed with such difficulty. If that were to happen, it would hardly be feasible for Treasury Ministers to concede, say, an additional motorway or a new aircraft project, as hypothetical examples, but to say that there would be no increase in the cash limit – as distinct from refusing to increase cash limits for an existing motorway or aircraft project in order to keep them within their estimated cost.

One proposal which was urged upon me, and which had been put forward in the *Times* leader, was to try to secure a rule that no new expenditure commitment could be approved unless compensating savings were approved at the same time. I did not believe that this would work. Even if we got the rule, it would not be made to stick. It was a formula which could encourage a relaxed rather than a tough attitude towards new commitments. These would be approved and would go ahead on the basis that the savings would be identified later, but in practice the savings would never materialise. There could well be times when the Minister who secured approval for a new commitment would obviously have no scope for making offsetting savings; there would then be a long and fruitless trawl for savings from other spending Ministers, who would resist bitterly. I had seen these things happen before. Part of my problem was to resist no doubt well meant interventions which ran counter to my own experience and judgment.

My own analysis, as I have said, was in terms of 'PESC' on the one hand and 'inter-PESC' on the other. When we came to the next survey the task would be to prevent an across-the-board escalation of programmes. Meanwhile the objective should be to prevent new *ad hoc* commitments altogether or, failing that, to ensure that they came out of the contingency reserve, which must be made an effective limitation of new expenditure. The idea had to be put across that, when we got to the bottom of the contingency reserve, there would be no more money, not even any more funny money. This meant that the contingency reserve must be husbanded and not used up at the beginning, as had happened in the past, sometimes even before the new financial year began.

But how to achieve this? Out of a process of talking to everyone who might have thoughts on the subject the idea evolved of a new Ministerial finance committee with responsibility for monitoring the state of the contingency reserve and vetting all new expenditure proposals in relation to the amount left in the kitty. The precedents were not encouraging. Although Otto Clarke gave a favourable write-up to the group of non-spending Ministers who supported James Callaghan in sorting out competing expenditure bids in 1965, it did not prove a useful arrangement after that initial operation. On one account its fall from grace dated from Dick Crossman's addition to the group. When Roy Jenkins had to clear his expenditure cuts with an inner group of senior Ministers before putting them to full Cabinet, he found this procedure the reverse of helpful. Anthony Barber had at one time held discussions with a group of Ministers who were not big spenders, but with the limited objective of securing some moral support for the Chancellor in Cabinet. However, something had to be done, and the hope was that a formal new Cabinet committee with a specific mandate and something close to executive responsibility would be a more effective brake on excess expenditure than any of the earlier arrangements.

Denis Healey would have been prepared to back this idea, which I discussed with John Hunt, the Secretary of the Cabinet, and others in the Cabinet Office. It was given a sympathetic hearing but two difficulties were pointed out: the lack of non-spending Ministers of sufficient stature and authority to take on this invidious function, and the problem of fitting yet one more committee into the already overcrowded timetable of senior Ministers. The counter-suggestion was put to me that the Prime Minister should be asked to promulgate a new ruling to the effect that Treasury Ministers could not be overruled on financial matters in Cabinet committees. This might on the face of it seem a fairly small change as compared with the old situation in which a Treasury Minister, if defeated on an expenditure issue in Cabinet committee, could reserve the right to take it to full Cabinet. But, in fact, shifting the onus of appeal on to the spending Minister would make a great psychological difference. I was therefore prepared to drop the idea of a finance committee and recommend this alternative suggestion to the Chancellor, provided that it was coupled with an arrangement under which, whenever claims on the contingency reserve went to Cabinet, they were considered on the basis of a progress report on the contingency reserve as a whole. In due course the Prime Minister promulgated the new rule to Cabinet orally at the end of its proceedings. He later referred to it briefly in his book on *The Governance of Britain,* and in conversation he spoke of it as giving the Treasury 51 per cent of the votes. Rules of procedure for Ministers are always promulgated afresh to Ministers when there is a change of administration, but I should expect this particular ruling to have survived the change of administration. In its own sphere it was quite a significant constitutional change.

This took place within my first three weeks in the new post. Meanwhile work was going ahead on the White Paper setting out the results of the recently completed public expenditure survey and giving details of the 'cuts'. I was concerned that the text should signal our intention of 'making and holding to medium term plans'. If we succeeded, the plan would 'stabilise the level of resources taken by expenditure programmes after 1976–77' and 'public expenditure will fall as a proportion of national output from its present exceptionally high level'. But the figure which was to appear for the contingency reserve for 1976–77 was impossibly low, at no more than £300 million, reflecting a view of the contingency reserve as a statistical concept rather than an operational constraint, and this would at the outset have robbed our intention to keep within this limit of all credibility. So it was raised to £700 million, which seemed the very minimum for credibility, but even so the contingency reserve was equivalent to only 1½ per cent of the programme figures, and we were setting ourselves, in the circumstances of the time, a very difficult task.

The White Paper was also to fire the first salvo in a campaign to put over the theme that 'popular expectations for improved public services and welfare programmes have not been matched by the growth in output'. A number of newspapers responded to this theme when the White Paper appeared. The leader in the *Observer* on 22 February 1976 began with a quotation: 'Getting and spending, we lay waste our powers.' 'There has been too much spending and too little getting,' it went on. 'When the economic jargon has been stripped away from the public expenditure White Paper, that is what remains.' The *Daily Telegraph* also used 'Getting and Spending' as the headline for a leader on 27 February.

Nevertheless the White Paper got a bad press on two counts – first, the delayed-action character of the cuts, and secondly a deep scepticism as to whether they would be carried out. 'Semi-credible, semi-adequate' was the headline of a *Financial Times* leader on 20 February. 'Less jam after to-morrow' was its headline a week later. 'Spending cuts – Whitehall farce' proclaimed the *Daily Express* on 19 February, even before the White Paper had appeared.

Within Parliament the White Paper was attacked from both the right and the left. The battle lines had been drawn up in advance, with the Conservative Opposition predicting that the cuts would be too little and too late, and even spurious, while the government's own left-wing supporters had raised the alarm that the government were preparing the betrayal of socialism and of their election manifesto. When the White Paper actually appeared, it confirmed the worst fears of both. 'These cuts', said one left-wing spokesman, 'represent a fundamental shift of wealth and power away from the working people and their families.' When the government tabled the customary resolution seeking endorsement for the White Paper, the left-wingers joined with the Conservatives to defeat the motion. The government responded to this emergency by tabling a vote of confidence, which the left wing were forced to support for fear of bringing the government down and letting the Conservatives in, but only after exchanges of great acrimony between the left and the Chancellor of the Exchequer.

Soon after this, on the morning of 16 March 1976, the word went round the Treasury that the Prime Minister, Harold Wilson, would be issuing a statement later that morning that he intended to resign as soon as the Parliamentary Labour Party had elected a new leader who could succeed him as Prime Minister. News of this kind always causes a little tremor to run round Whitehall. It is a matter not of the personal standing of the particular holder of the office but of the place of the head of government in the country's life and affairs.

Denis Healey was among the entrants for the leadership contest, with Joel Barnett campaigning busily on his behalf. However, it was James Callaghan, at that time Foreign Secretary, who won the succession – predictably, in my view, notwithstanding the view taken by some who were better qualified politically on such questions that his years would count against him. Michael Foot came next in the leadership election and became second in command in Callaghan's Cabinet. Whatever Denis Healey's chance of success, it had suffered from the antagonism created by his robust attack on the left over the public expenditure cuts. In the Ministerial shake-up which followed, Tony Crosland became Foreign Secretary, Roy Jenkins presently left for Brussels to become President of the European Commission, and Denis Healey remained at the Treasury.

The next milestone along the arduous expenditure route was the White Paper on *Cash Limits on Public Expenditure* (Cmnd. 6440) in April 1976, which gave Parliament a description of the new system and the cash limit figures for the various programmes. A crucial passage came in the penultimate paragraph, which dealt with the circumstances in which individual cash limits might have to be reviewed. This part of the White Paper text could not be settled at the Cabinet meeting which approved the rest of the White Paper and had to be negotiated outside the meeting. Spending Ministers naturally wanted as many loopholes as possible, and in any event it would not have been possible, at the start of the experiment, to say that in no circumstances would cash limits be revised. But if it were believed that they could be exceeded with impunity in the expectation of a higher cash limit, we should be no better off and there would be no point in the new system. The eventual formulation was that 'spending Departments will not be able to rely, as they have in the past, on supplementary provision if this would take their total provision for the year beyond the cash limits'.

The only previous experience with this system had been with several public sector building programmes, on which cash limits had been imposed in 1974–75 and 1975–76. This was an *ad hoc* response, agreed between the Treasury and the Departments concerned, to the escalation of tender prices by 88 per cent in the previous two years, following the relaxation of monetary control and the property boom, made worse by the take-off in the price of oil products. It was still impracticable to apply cash limits across the board. Demand-responsive programmes, especially social security, had to be left out of the system; it would not have been feasible to say that, if there were more people sick or unemployed than had been allowed for, there would be no benefit left for those who came last in the queue. In the case of the nationalised industries, cash limits, later renamed external financing limits (EFLs), were applied to the money which they raised by borrowing or from government grants, since it would have been out of the question for the government to put rigid controls on the total outgoings of these businesses on investment, working capital and operating costs. As regards the local authorities, cash limits were put on their capital programmes, at first in the form of limits for their loan sanctions and later as limits on the capital expenditure itself. So far as their current expenditure was concerned, the cash limits applied to the rate support grant which the government provided; these limits governed both the amount initially authorised under the annual Rate Support Grant Order and the supplementary amount authorised later in the year in the annual Cost Increase Order. But there was no way of putting cash limits on the total current expenditure of the local authorities out of grant and rate revenue combined.

Local government, where the manpower employed had risen from 1½ million to 2½ million over a period of fifteen years (an increase of 67 per cent – or on average an addition each year of 65,000, equivalent to the population of a fair sized town), was a sphere in which it was particularly difficult to bring home the reality that the country simply could not stand a continuation of this process, and that programmes for a local authority's various departments must be framed within a budget for the local authority as a whole, rather than letting the budget emerge as the total of the departmental expansion plans. I set out to put this message over in a talk on 1 March 1976 to a conference of local government officials organised by the Institute of Fiscal Studies:

There is a need [I began] for a great campaign of popular education about the realities of the economic situation of this country . . . If, over the ten years up to 1975, our GDP had grown exactly in line with the French GDP, we should have had 20 billion pounds extra of resources to dispose of in 1975. These are the missing billions that are the real source of the problem.

As the year progressed, the idea that cash limits were going to stick gained ground. Cash limits and incomes policy were reciprocally supportive. In an interview with one journalist I quoted the slogan 'Cash Limits Rule, OK?' which Patricia Brown, the Under Secretary in charge of public expenditure statistics, had suggested that I ought to wear on a T-shirt. The slogan appeared the next Sunday as the headline of the journalist's regular column.

Rumblings began to come, in fact, from the staff side that cash limits were going to cause programmes to be underspent and were a form of crypto-cuts, a charge which, in good faith, we repudiated. We did not in reality have any reliable means of monitoring outlays in relation to cash limits on an up-to-date basis. Preparations were being made to introduce a sophisticated new reporting system to keep track of cash outlays on individual programmes, and to compare these with profiles for programme expenditure over the year as a whole, but a great deal of work still remained to be done before these arrangements could be put into effect. However, I was assured that, if there were any substance in the staff side's allegation, we should long ago have had Departmental Finance Officers knocking on our doors to demand a relaxation of cash limits.

While we were still fighting these battles to make the last White Paper stick, we were already engaged in the early stages of the 1976 survey which would eventually lead to the next public expenditure White Paper. The most important change in the guidelines for the survey was that there was to be no automatic re-costing of existing policies. The general rule was that programmes would go into the new survey, revalued at 1976 survey prices, but otherwise no bigger than they had emerged from the previous survey except where an increased allocation from the contingency reserve had been specifically approved. A certain amount of sophistication was needed in applying this approach to demand-responsive programmes, especially social security. But in general anything extra, whether to finance a new policy or a re-estimation of the cost of existing policies, had to be tabled as an additional bid; Cabinet would have to choose between competing bids when decisions on the survey were taken later in the year. No programme increases would be allowed to creep in under the wire if they could not gain admission at the main gate. In addition, the rules focused attention on decisions for the year immediately ahead, rather than some focus year later in the period; all figures beyond the coming year were to be treated as increasingly provisional. In these ways the emphasis was being shifted from medium-term planning to short-term control, though still against the background of a medium-term dimension.

I would dearly have liked to get away from constant prices and have the new survey carried out in current prices, that is, in terms of the prices expected to be current in future years when the time came – in other words, to substitute cash programmes for volume programmes throughout the survey period. This was the way in which the Germans did their forward planning, but they could rely on an inflation rate not exceeding 5 per cent a year. If we were to do our cash projections on the assumption of 5 per cent or 10 per cent inflation, and if prices actually went up by 15 per cent a year, it was not to be expected that the government would cut the physical size of programmes year by year to fit the cash projections. It was one thing to enforce cash limits fixed for a single year; it would be a different matter to fix cash limits for several years ahead and stick to them even if it meant massive cuts in volume programmes. But if the initial current price projections had to be adjusted as we moved along in time, these 'current price' programmes would become a sort of bastard constant price programme – an especially funny kind of funny money – and it was doubtful whether we should be any better off. So the conclusion was that we had to stick to volume programmes for the survey, at any rate for the time being and until inflation was more predictable and under control.

But our overriding preoccupation during those months was to enforce the new drill for claims on the contingency reserve. We had periodical stocktakings with the Chief Secretary who from time to time put progress reports to Cabinet. Although in our view the Treasury had not renounced the right to approve a claim on the contingency reserve without prior reference to Cabinet, the Chief Secretary preferred to require Cabinet collectively to endorse all decisions on proposals affecting the contingency reserve, including those which the Treasury accepted as well as those which were being pressed against Treasury objections. If a claim on the contingency reserve was accepted, that carried with it more or less automatic adjustment of cash limits; the two went together.

It was a period of great stress and tension. As the claims mounted, some of them irresistible, the outlook for containing them all within the contingency reserve of £700 million for 1976–77 seemed increasingly hopeless. If we failed in this, the flow of information which we were now supplying to the Expenditure Committee would have made it difficult to fudge the result even if we had wished to. So we felt ourselves under a spotlight.

The Treasury's split personality, functionally and organisationally, added to the stresses. The Chancellor – unable, in his own words, to resist an appeal to his *amour propre* – had committed himself to the objective of bringing expenditure under control, but this had somehow to be reconciled with his objectives as *de facto* Minister for Incomes Policy, Minister for the Social Contract and Minister for the Industrial Strategy. The tension was further heightened by what appeared to be leaks to the press from Whitehall 'moles' about our problems on the expenditure front. There was a spate of leaks on the Department of the Environment front, some of them about excess expenditure by local authorities.

The compact size and the cohesiveness of the Treasury's public expenditure side were great strengths in responding to these difficulties. It would be difficult to match in any organisation the hours and the effort which went into their unrewarding task – and, I imagine, still do. Heads of all the Divisions that covered between them the whole of public expenditure could be got together round the table in my office either for regular meetings or for special exercises. The regular meetings took on the character of operational reviews rather than chat shows while the crisis lasted. Following one of our stocktakings we advised the Chief Secretary that, if we could hold the line on the contingency reserve for 1976–77 a little longer, we had a fair chance of getting through the financial year without exceeding it. The reason for this was that the time-lags in pubic expenditure were now beginning to work in our favour. As the year moved on, new commitments increasingly tended to involve expenditure in future years, which would come out of the contingency reserve for those years, rather than the current year.

I felt that we had made a great psychological breakthrough when the record of a meeting between the Prime Minister and the head of another government showed that, in connection with a joint financial undertaking proposed by his opposite number, the Prime Minister observed that on our side the money would have to be found out of the contingency reserve. I could not imagine previous Prime Ministers being influenced by such mundane constraints when discussing their grand designs at top level.

Altogether, in spite of the continuing pressures which made it impossible to relax vigilance for an instant, we could feel by the summer that we had turned the corner, and that both cash limits and the public expenditure plan in real terms would hold. It was at this point, when incomes policy had stemmed the orgy of wage claims, when control of public finance was being restored, even if at a high level of taxation and borrowing, and the uncertainties about North Sea oil had been overcome, giving us the prospect of self-sufficiency in oil by 1980, that a loss of confidence which had started in the spring perversely came to a head. The inflow of foreign funds, which had continued while inflation and expenditure were out of control, now turned round, the exchange rate plummeted, and in the summer of 1976 we found ourselves in a new financial crisis, with public expenditure once again at the heart of the storm.

THE IMF CRISIS

During the early months of 1976 the exchange rate for sterling had been fairly stable at around $2.05 to the pound. By July there had been a depreciation of sterling of 12 per cent against the dollar. The immediate cause which inadvertently triggered off the decline was said to have been a move by the Bank of England to 'cream off' dollars at a particular juncture when the pound was thought to be relatively strong, that is, to take advantage of this situation by offering sterling from the Exchange Equalisation Account in order to buy a quantity of dollars to augment the foreign exchange reserves held in the EEA.

The foreign exchange markets interpreted this as a signal that the British authorities were not prepared to support the pound, and holders of sterling began to rush to sell their holdings and move into other currencies. As soon as a move of this kind begins, with a currency such as sterling which is widely used in foreign trade, the process is intensified by 'leads and lags' – that is to say, people who are going to need foreign currency buy it in advance before it gets dearer, while people who are going to need sterling leave the purchase as late as possible in the hope that sterling will by then have become cheaper.

It is true that the pound, at above $2, had been overvalued from the point of view of the competitiveness of British industry and that a prevailing economic view in the Treasury favoured progressive depreciation in order to offset the escalation of our domestic industrial costs. But nobody had wanted or bargained for the slide in the exchange rate which now took place and could not be halted. Although there were rational grounds for concern about Britain's underlying industrial performance and the longer-term outlook for controlling inflation, there was also a certain irrationality, with which it was difficult to cope, about the psychology of the break in confidence and in particular the belief which had got into currency that our North Sea oil had now all been mortgaged. There were no figures to support this idea and, as events were to show, the foreign exchange benefits of North Sea oil would be enough in a few years to enable Britain comfortably to pay off even the huge overseas indebtedness which we were running up meanwhile. However, whatever the rationality or otherwise of the run on sterling, it was a fact and it had somehow to be staunched.

As always happens in these crisis situations, events moved rapidly, argument was heated and opinion went first in one direction and then another. The scene of discussion shifted between the Treasury building and No. 11, frequently involving Harold Lever as well as the Chancellor and the Chief Secretary.

One opinion which was urged upon the Chancellor with characteristic persuasiveness was that the most sensible and also the most painless course was to borrow our way through the situation; we should raise loans enabling us to put funds in the shop window on a scale large enough to demonstrate that there was plenty of backing for the pound and that speculators against it would burn their fingers. However, though in June the Bank of England negotiated central bank lines of credit with their opposite numbers amounting to $5.3 billion, this did not have the desired effect on the foreign exchange markets, and moreover the amounts actually drawn on these credits would have to be repaid in six months' time.

Further measures to restore confidence therefore had to be considered, and public expenditure cuts, going beyond the last White Paper cuts and starting earlier, were the front runner, since it was the size of our expenditure programmes and of the borrowing to finance them which, in the eyes of the financial world, were at the heart of our problem. Argument was now increasingly focused on alternative packages of expenditure cuts in the year ahead, 1977–78. There was no question of making cuts in what remained of the current financial year.

There was a conflict between what was required from the point of view of restoring financial confidence and what was considered feasible and negotiable in Cabinet, and there were fairly strong differences of view on the question of feasibility. A possible package of £1 billion at 1976 survey prices was the starting point for discussion. This was the minimum which might have any hope of making the required impression, but there could be no assurance that it would do the trick. One maverick point of view was that there would be no point in a £1 billion package and that we should either raise it to £2 billion or do nothing at all on the expenditure front and find other ways of financing ourselves out of trouble. But one look at a £2 billion package was enough to rule this out of consideration. Though £1 billion might be the minimum from one point of view, it looked like the maximum from the point of view of acceptability to the Cabinet – especially as the Chancellor proposed at the same time to find room for still further micro measures to help industry and employment. He did not accept that the composition of public expenditure was immutable and aimed to overshoot the £1 billion mark in making the cuts so as to be able to 'add back' the spare amount to those programmes which were dear to his own heart and might make the package a little less unacceptable vis-à-vis the trade union leaders on whose support he counted on the incomes policy front.

At a late stage, and to the chagrin of the industrial strategy side of the house, the Chancellor decided to top up his proposals for a net £1 billion expenditure package with an addition of 2 percentage points to the employers' national insurance contribution, which would yield around a further £1 billion – somewhat less in 1977–78 but rather more in a full year. These measures would enable him to announce a reduction in the prospective PSBR in 1977–78 to £9 billion from the £10½ billion which it was otherwise expected to be.

The increase in selective assistance to industry was to take place at the expense of general schemes of assistance. As part of this shift of emphasis, the weekly rate of regional employment premium was reduced from £3 a man to £2 a man, though at the same time the woman's rate was to be increased from £1.50 to £2, thus producing a single rate and furthering equality of the sexes. In conjunction with the national insurance surcharge, which in 1981 was still with us, this reduction meant a further increase in the cost of labour at a time when unemployment was still rising.

After a hectic round of negotiations in Cabinet and outside it, the Chancellor announced his package in the Commons on 22 July 1976. Looking again at the detailed figures which were issued with the text, which not many readers would want me to go into in detail after this lapse of time, I see that, allowing for all the pluses and minuses and for the revaluation from White Paper prices to 1976 survey prices, we were able to validate our assessment that we were keeping enough in hand in the contingency reserve to get through the year without exceeding it. There was one reference in the Chancellor's statement to the need 'for us to maintain the confidence of those from whom we may have to borrow to finance our external deficit', but the principal justification which he put forward for his measures was that the degree of deficit financing which had been appropriate during the worst of the recession had to be reduced as recovery developed during the coming eighteen months. The measures would 'make certain that this recovery can be sustained until full employment is achieved', and would enable resources to be made available for exports and productive investment. He expected GDP to increase at an annual rate of about 4½ per cent and manufacturing production at a rate of about 8½ per cent. At the same time, the rate of inflation and the growth in the money supply would come down.

The announcement of these measures brought only a short respite. The outflow from the reserves and the fall in the external value of the pound were soon resumed. The Chancellor believed that the crucial reason for the failure of the July package was the omission of any money supply targets from his statement. There were some who argued that the view which had been taken on the feasible size of the package of expenditure cuts had in itself been a reason for the inadequacy of the package, and that bigger cuts should have been put to Cabinet and could have been negotiated. But the fact was that Cabinet had not been prepared to approve in full even the package of reductions which the Chief Secretary had eventually chosen as the basis for collective decisions. The net reductions announced on 22

July, after allowing for the 'add-backs' to help industry and employment, came to £952 million. Moreover, the biggest single item in the
package was a mini-package of cuts amounting to £157 million in the
capital expenditure of the nationalised industries, and this package
within a package had been put together only by excluding BNOC
which, on the advocacy of the Secretary of State for Energy, was
treated as 'a special case'. If the extra capital expenditure required for
BNOC had been brought into the arithmetic, the net total of reductions would have fallen significantly short of £1 billion.

It is difficult to express what an anxious and worrying time that was.
The pound appeared to be in free fall and there was no knowing at
what point it would touch bottom. Intervention by the Bank of
England on the foreign exchange markets, which involved using
foreign exchange reserves to buy sterling which others wanted to sell,
thus supporting the exchange rate, had at best only a temporary effect
and merely depleted further our scanty reserves without restoring
confidence. The Prime Minister and the Chancellor put the Bank on
an increasingly short rein as to the extent to which they could use the
reserves for intervention.

The question now on the agenda was whether to apply to the
International Monetary Fund for support in the form of a drawing or a
standby – that is, an immediate loan or a credit which we could draw
down in due course. Technically, a drawing or borrowing from the
Fund by the UK is a purchase by us of the foreign currencies put into
the Fund by other member countries, which we pay for with sterling;
repayment is effected later by re-purchasing our sterling with foreign
currencies which by then we should be able to spare through an
improved balance of payments. The amount which any member
country can draw is related to its quota in the Fund. The quota in turn
is made up of a number of tranches. The first of these (that is, the gold
tranche – equivalent to the amount which the member country has
itself put into the Fund in gold) can be drawn unconditionally, since in
a sense the country is drawing its own money out. Successive tranches
are subject to increasing conditionality. We had at that time already
drawn, in the previous year, the sum available without conditions,
and in any event the amount now needed would have taken us well
into the conditional credit tranches.

The question of going to the Fund was therefore bound up with the
question of the terms on which, if we did apply, they would insist in
order to improve our balance of payments and put us in a position to
make repayment. The dramatic story of the application and the
negotiations which followed is amply documented elsewhere. Most of

it was public knowledge at the time, either because the events were, by their nature, in the public domain or because the divisions within the government were such that the press were kept even more accurately and more promptly informed of what was going on by various of the parties involved than is normally the case when Ministerial discussions are going on. At the end of the negotiations a number of financial and political journalists, each assuming the persona of one of the leading Ministers involved, were able, for the purpose of a television programme called 'The Cabinet in Conflict', to reconstruct convincingly the Ministerial arguments which had taken place. An account of those events as seen through American eyes, giving an insight into the role of the United States, was provided in March 1977 by a staff report for the Senate Committee on Foreign Relations. A more recent account is to be found in a well-informed book called *Who Runs the Economy?* by William Keegan and Rupert Pennant-Rea (Maurice Temple-Smith, 1979). There was also a detailed piece of investigative journalism by Stephen Fay and Hugo Young called 'The Day the £ Nearly Died', which appeared in the *Sunday Times* in June 1978.

There were some on both sides of the Atlantic who wanted the UK to have to go to the Fund, rather than raise further foreign loans from other sources, so that we would come under the financial discipline of the IMF's terms. Such people were unimpressed by what we had done on public expenditure, even if the cuts were made to stick. Moreover, cuts or no cuts, our borrowing requirement remained very high, and the estimate of the prospective PSBR had moved up again since the time of the July measures. William Simon, the Secretary to the United States Treasury, was said to regard the British nation state as on a par with the insolvent municipality of New York City, which was vainly seeking help from federal funds. But in any event there were no further loans from other sources which would be made available without better evidence of our creditworthiness. We needed not merely the Fund's money but 'the IMF seal of good housekeeping' which would enable us to get credit from other sources as well. Nevertheless, there was no disposition in the government to make concessions on their policies in order to get an IMF loan. Denis Healey told the Labour Party conference in the last week of September that we would go to the Fund 'on existing policies'.

The situation came to a head that week when the pound dropped sharply to $1.64 and Denis Healey turned back at Heathrow airport from the journey which he had planned to Manila for the IMF annual meeting, which takes place outside Washington one year in three.

Douglas Wass, rather than another Treasury Minister, delivered a speech on the Chancellor's behalf at Manila, a slightly surprising arrangement. On 29 September a formal application was made to the IMF for support amounting to $3.9 billion, the largest sum ever requested of them.

The IMF team arrived in London at the beginning of November, led by Alan Whittome, who had formerly been in the Bank of England and was now head of the Fund's European Department. His second in command was David Finch, an Australian. More than a fortnight was spent on preliminaries, ground-clearing or fencing, according to how one cares to put it. Formal negotiations were not opened until 19 November, and I did not meet Whittome or Finch until that day. I had not been anxious to become involved in detailed discussions with them, since it seemed to me that my function was to advise Treasury Ministers rather than the IMF on cutting public expenditure.

Conceding that we had performed a small miracle in bringing public expenditure under control, the IMF proposed that further reductions should be made of £3 billion in 1977–78 and £4 billion in 1978–79 at 1976 survey prices in order to bring down the PSBR forecasts for those years. These survey price figures would of course have to be translated into cash figures when the effects of the reductions on the PSBR were worked out. Any cuts which could be made in the current year, 1976–77, would be a bonus. It was conceded that it was for the British government to choose between different ways of reducing the PSBR, but expenditure reductions would have a better effect than tax increases on financial opinion and on the economy. It was clear that, in Whittome's mind, the negotiation was about terms which would not only give the Fund a reasonable prospect of repayment by the due dates but would also give the British economy a new lease of life. With expenditure and credit under control, our newly competitive exchange rates would launch British industry on a surge of export-led growth.

The figures put forward by the Fund team represented cuts of 6 per cent rising to 8 per cent on public expenditure programmes totalling something like £50 billion. It was never on the cards that Treasury Ministers would put such proposals to Cabinet, let alone succeed in getting approval for them. Anyone who remembered how the terms thought necessary for foreign loans and financial survival in 1931 had led to the break-up of Ramsay MacDonald's Labour government could not doubt that comparable damage would be done if these terms were imposed in order to get the IMF loan, with unforeseeable political and social consequences. This did not mean that, apart from the current year, which we believed to be too far advanced, nothing could be done. In particular, there should be scope for carrying through the effects of the July measures into programmes for 1978–79, since we had not so far extrapolated these cuts beyond 1977–78. But the negotiating gap was immense. Nevertheless the pound had touched a new low point of $1.56, and terms had somehow to be worked out which on the one hand would produce agreement with the IMF and on the other hand would not destroy the government.

The negotiations had turned into something of a war of attrition. The American report to which I have referred describes them as 'a simultaneous two-tiered set of negotiations: one between the British Government and the IMF negotiating team . . .; the other, and perhaps the more difficult, took place within the British Cabinet itself as the Government struggled to agree on a negotiating position'. As the days and weeks went by, a third tier of negotiations developed, in this case between the Prime Minister on the one hand and President Ford and Chancellor Schmidt on the other, by various means of communication. His objectives were not merely to persuade them to exercise a softening influence on the Fund's hard line, but also to pave the way for a 'safety net' of support arrangements for the sterling balances to supplement the IMF loan.

There can be little doubt that these representations resulted in a softening of the initial hard line of the US Treasury and, through the informal mediation of the American and to some extent the West German representatives in the Fund, to a greater flexibility in the Fund's negotiating position. According to the staff report to the Senate Foreign Relations Committee, 'The evolution of the U.S. position from the early relatively "hard" line of demanding tough conditions of the Labour Government . . . may well have reflected the fact that from the beginning of the negotiations, the State Department evaluation of the political feasibility of implementing the program was factored into the evaluation process'. On this evidence there was a better appreciation of what was politically feasible in the State Department than in some quarters on this side of the Atlantic. On the other hand, the United States and West Germany would not seek to influence the Fund beyond a certain point or support our application unless we could negotiate terms with the IMF team which they could bring themselves to accept and put to the IMF Board of Directors; this would still have to include something substantial on the expenditure side. But all the indications were that Cabinet were still in no mood to agree to any expenditure cuts or at any rate to more than a token package of cuts.

The situation in the Treasury was in many ways like July all over again – the same scene, and the same actors, but with an increasingly weary and frustrated Whittome now in the wings, and the same internal debates, but more intense and going on longer, late into the night and over the weekends. There was also the same issue as to what package of expenditure cuts was feasible on top of what had already been done in July.

One severe limitation on the room for manoeuvre was the virtual untouchability of social security, by far the largest single programme. So far from being reduced, the main benefits would go on rising in line with prices or, in the case of pensions, in line with earnings, unless new legislation could be passed; but the political judgment was that, not only would Cabinet turn this course down, but even if they went along with it the government's supporters in the House would not stand for it.

There was initially a greater disposition to suspend the inflation-proofing of civil service pensions, until it was appreciated that this too would require legislation, and that the indexation scheme applied not merely to top civil servants but to large numbers of civil servants and local government and health service workers on pretty low pensions, along with the armed forces, the police, judges and Members of Parliament. A statement in a *Financial Times* article that the mandarins fought to preserve their index-linked pensions was the reverse of the truth.

The current expenditure of the local authorities was another large area which we had to leave untouched, as we had done in July, for the practical reason that there was no way of ensuring that cuts in this expenditure would take place. In previous exercises we had too often seen spending Ministers offer up reductions in programmes such as education on the basis that these would be effected through paper cuts in the current expenditure of local authorities on these programmes rather than through reductions in expenditure within the control of Ministers themselves. But the more items that were ruled out for political or practical reasons, the more we faced the possibility that a crude across-the-board moratorium on capital projects would have to feature prominently in any package – if, in the end, Cabinet were prepared to cut public expenditure at all.

I still somehow have in my possession a scrap of paper on which, at one meeting of Ministers and officials in the Treasury, in despair of our ever getting agreement on anything, I had the following scribbled exchange of comments with whoever was sitting next to me:

'I think that this Government must be finished.'
'Nearly, but not quite yet? Thursday?'
'Yes, I meant in principle, leaving it to the forecasters to put numbers on it.'

The forecasters were in fact involved in a number of these meetings, when they presented successive updatings of the short-term forecasts and variants which simulated the effects on the economy of possible fiscal and monetary measures. The Chancellor showed a consuming interest in the line-by-line details of their computer print-outs.

When eventually he put proposals to Cabinet on which it was believed that a settlement could now be reached with the Fund, it was common knowledge that resistance came not only from Tony Benn and other supporters of the 'alternative strategy' of import controls but from others also, especially Tony Crosland, who held that there was no economic case for cutting expenditure while unemployment was high. So Ministers turned at the next stage to consideration of the alternative strategy on the basis of a neutral paper by the CPRS setting out the pros and cons, but it did not offer them an alternative any less painful than the IMF terms. Even so it is doubtful whether there was a general realisation of the overwhelming problem of financing the balance of payments, with liabilities greatly in excess of the reserves and a continuing current account deficit on top. It might seem unthinkable that we should be reduced to the condition of a chronically bankrupt country like Turkey, financing its overseas trade on a hand-to-mouth basis, but what was there to prevent that if we failed to get some fresh foreign exchange financing?

Throughout all this the Prime Minister, by all accounts, held his hand in Cabinet until, at the end of a running debate spread over several meetings, he came out in support of the Chancellor. It may well be that he had intended to do so all along from the time that the Chancellor had put his proposals forward, but the fact remained that until then Denis Healey had had to bear the heat of the battle. Cabinet as a whole now either accepted the Prime Minister's judgment or at least swallowed their objections. Crosland was reported – for instance in the television reconstruction of that meeting – to have said that, while still unconvinced of the case for cuts on that scale, he would not go against the Prime Minister on the grounds that, if the Prime Minister were to be overruled by Cabinet and this were to become known, the effects on confidence would be disastrous. One left-wing Minister was believed to have considered resigning but to have been talked out of it by friends.

The public expenditure element in the proposed terms involved reductions of £1 billion in 1977–78 plus the sale of £500 million of government-owned shares in the British Petroleum Company. (It was legitimate to treat this special item as reducing the public expenditure figures since we had counted it as a public expenditure cost when the

Bank of England had acquired for the government the BP shares
which the Burmah Oil Company had to sell when they needed funds.)
For 1978–79 the reductions were to be £1½ billion, with a provisional
undertaking to make a further but unspecified fiscal adjustment in
1978–79 of £½–1 billion at 1976 survey prices if the situation at the
time so required. On the monetary side there were to be targets for
domestic credit expansion (DCE).

A hectic round of further discussions took place to settle the
composition of the £1 billion to be cut in 1977–78 and the £1½ billion
from programmes for 1978–79. The base-line for the cuts was provided by the programme figures which had emerged from the 1976
public expenditure survey, which it had been essential to complete
notwithstanding some resistance on the grounds that the then
imminent IMF negotiations would make the survey exercise futile.
Putting the package together was again complicated by the Chancellor's determination to make room for add-backs to help industry and
employment. The defence budget, which had already been reduced
by the July measures below the level agreed after the defence review,
was now further reduced. Food subsidies were to be brought to an
end. The overseas aid programme, which had survived the July
measures intact, now made a modest contribution. The regional
employment premium was to be terminated on 2 February 1977
except in Northern Ireland. Thus James Callaghan, who in his time as
Chancellor had announced the birth of REP, on which so many hopes
had been placed, now presided over its funeral rites. Opinion about
the effectiveness of REP had shifted during the life of the scheme.
There was now a tendency to argue that failure to increase the rate of
premium in line with inflation had eroded its effectiveness. But the
fact was that, since the days when Nicki Kaldor had been at the zenith
of his influence, there had been a philosophical shift in the Labour
government in favour of selective rather than general schemes of
assistance to industry and employment.

But there was still no way of making up the final package without a
moratorium on construction projects, that is, a postponement for six
months of all new starts in a wide range of programmes such as roads,
health and water and sewerage – a measure which led the Expenditure
Committee to observe that 'The Government is thus itself acting like
those industrialists it criticises for failing to invest. Indeed, even
worse, it appears to be cutting capital expenditure and selling off
productive capital assets (e.g. BP shares) in order to sustain current
expenditure, the classic action of an ailing industrial company'. However, as the Chief Secretary told the House, we had to consider the
practicalities.

On this basis the IMF approved the $3.9 billion, to be made available in instalments. The public expenditure cuts were announced in a statement by the Chancellor on 15 December 1976. The following month the safety net for sterling was negotiated in the form of medium-term 'swap' facilities, enabling the Bank of England to exchange sterling for foreign currencies from other central banks if there were another run on the pound, on the basis that the swap would be reversed after the agreed period.

After an interruption for Christmas and a brief but traumatic further encounter with the surgeons, which however did not end as disastrously as it might have done, the next event was the White Paper on the *Government's Expenditure Plans* (Cmnd. 6721) which appeared towards the end of January 1977. This White Paper had a new look in a number of respects. Part I and Part II, respectively the general part and the part giving details of individual programmes, appeared in separate volumes. The slim first volume gave figures for only two years ahead instead of the customary four years. The reason for this was not merely to emphasise that the more distant projections which emerged from the annual survey must in any event be more shadowy in their nature, but also because on this particular occasion they had not been 'further reviewed' in the light of the results of the IMF negotiations. The programme figures for the full survey period were therefore relegated to the second volume. For 1977–78 and 1978–79, programmes in total were to be brought down, following the July and December measures, to a reduced level as compared with the precedng two years, instead of being levelled off as had been intended under the previous White Paper plan. The ratio of public expenditure to GDP would now fall, a significant reversal of the previous trend.

The new-look White Paper also dispensed with the paraphernalia of a medium-term assessment. There were no projections showing different patterns of growth on a variety of assumptions. There was, however, a short section on Public Expenditure and the Economy in which we said that the objectives announced for the PSBR 'were determined on the basis of a forecast that GDP would increase by above 2 per cent in 1977–78 and by 2½–3 per cent in the following year'. The figures in Appendix I show that the growth of GDP in market prices in these two years was in the event 2 per cent and 2.4 per cent. This section of the White Paper put the expenditure plans in the context of a stabilisation programme, extending over two years or more, to restore confidence, bring the economy back into balance and reduce the strains that the financing of the public sector was imposing in financial markets.

We were ourselves astonished by the speed with which, following the relatively limited though politically difficult adjustments agreed with the IMF, confidence was resurrected, the adverse financial trends were reversed, and we sailed suddenly from the eye of the storm into unusually calm water, financially speaking, though it remained choppy enough in other respects. The pound began an upward climb which continued throughout 1977 and took it back above $2 in 1978. There was an equally dramatic movement in the opposite direction in interest rates, which had been pushed up during the crisis to levels unprecedented since the war and now came down again in 1977 with beneficial effects on such things as housing subsidies and the cost of homes.

We did not know it then but, as was established later, the reductions in public expenditure were a great deal less limited than we had believed. This came about because of shortfall, or underspending, which is difficult to allow for in advance and which was also, under the information systems available at the time, difficult to measure with any accuracy while it was taking place. Unknown to us at the time, unplanned shortfall was much bigger than the planned reductions which had brought the government of the country to crisis point. Throughout 1976 the view was consistently taken that nothing could be done to reduce expenditure during the current year. At the time of the January 1977 White Paper it was still too soon to make a firm assessment of the out-turn for 1976–77, but the estimates at that stage suggested that there had been some moderate underspending. Putting together the information later contained in the 1978 and 1979 White Papers, we find that in the event total expenditure in 1976–77 in volume terms (constant prices) but excluding debt interest was about 3½ per cent less than in the previous year (2½ per cent less when debt interest is brought into account) and a similar percentage, involving an underspending of £2¼ billion at 1977 survey prices, below the level which had been planned for 1976–77.

It is difficult to assess how much of the credit or the blame for this should go to cash limits. Certainly cash limits proved more effective as a general financial discipline – and not merely as a deterrent to unbudgeted cost increases – than I for one had anticipated. In January 1978 it was estimated that those central government programmes covered by cash limits had been underspent in 1976–77 by about 2 per cent or £600 million. A year later the underspending in 1976–77 on those programmes, and on local authority capital expenditure which was also cash limited, was put at 3 per cent. It is reasonable to believe that the cash limit on rate support grant was influential in avoiding an excess on local authority current expenditure which had at one time been feared. Over £600 million of the total shortfall occurred in government lending to the nationalised industries in 1976–77, which was accompanied by a switch to overseas borrowing by these industries for balance of payments reasons, but there was also a downturn in their underlying capital expenditure. Finally, there was underspending in a variety of programmes which were not cash limited, such as new schemes of assistance to employment which built up slowly.

In 1977–78 there was an even larger fall in public expenditure in real terms as compared with the previous year and an even larger shortfall. The January 1979 White Paper (Cmnd. 7439) reported that 'Actual expenditure in 1977–78 is now estimated to have been about 7 per cent (over £4 billion) below the plans in Cmnd. 6721'. It is tempting to make the sensational statement that this shortfall was four times as big as the cuts of £1 billion in 1977–78, excluding the sale of BP shares, which had been negotiated with the IMF, but that would not be comparing like with like. The £4 billion included 'another large shortfall in nationalised industry borrowing', an item which featured in the public expenditure figures only from the time of the 1977 White Paper. There was also 'a saving of about £700 million in refinancing of export and shipbuilding credit, partly due to changes in the agreement between the Government and the banks'. But even excluding these items there had been a shortfall of over £2 billion, or twice the amount of the planned cut.

As regards 1978–79, the March 1980 White Paper (Cmnd. 7841) reported that the volume of expenditure was estimated to have been about 3½ per cent (around £2½ billion) below the level planned in the January 1978 White Paper. This figure again exceeded the £1½ billion of cuts agreed with the IMF for that year.

The occurrence of shortfall was not unforeseen. It had tended to happen even in those years when expenditure plans were continually being revised upwards; that is to say, out-turn had tended to fall short of the revised programme figures. An allowance for shortfall is usually made in the White Paper figures, and the Treasury forecasters usually make a larger but unpublished allowance for it in the PSBR projections. There was no adjustment for shortfall in the future plans set out in the 1977 and 1978 White Papers because we were committed for the first time to deliver those plans and not to exceed the published figures. We did not want to be held to have failed if we scaled the figures down in anticipation of shortfall and it did not materialise. In my experience, the year when a programme is scaled down on

grounds of 'realism' is likely to be the year when the original programme is after all fully spent and misplaced realism leaves you short
of financial provision. On this occasion, the year when we cut out
provision for shortfall was the year when it occurred on a scale far
beyond the customary provision. It was the scale of the shortfall
which took us by surprise.

There can be no knowing what difference it would have made, and
how the IMF negotiations would have gone, if we could have anticipated this outcome. Nor can there be any knowing whether and by
how much this actual underspending reinforced the psychological
effects of the settlement with the IMF in bringing about the dramatic
turn-round on the financial front between 1976 and 1977.

WHAT IS PUBLIC EXPENDITURE?

It will be clear from the story so far that different definitions of public
expenditure have been used over the years and that the choice of
definition is anything but an academic question. It determines what
comes within the government's expenditure limits, and we have seen
how time after time spending Ministers and Departments have fought
to get round the limits by arguing that particular items should not
count as public expenditure – sometimes successfully, as in the
treatment of BNOC as a special case for the purpose of the July 1976
cuts. At a more general or psychological level, the definitions affect
the size of the total figures, which in turn can affect the public
perception of whether the government is spending too much. After
the Conservative victory in 1979, when the money supply became the
great talking point, gatherings in City boardrooms would switch on a
broadcast of the monthly money supply figures with the same expec-
tancy as an aficionado tuning in for the latest test match score. But in
the financial crisis of 1976 it was public expenditure which was at the
heart of the economic debate.

A great deal of prominence was given at that time to a passage in
the 1976 White Paper which stated that public expenditure had risen
to 60 per cent of GDP. Milton Friedman cited this as further evidence
that Britain was going down the road to ruin, and that things were no
better here than in Marxist Chile. Yet, after a visit to Canada, when I
reported back in the Treasury that the Canadians were as worried
about the size of their public expenditure as people over here,
although in their case it accounted for no more than 42 per cent of
GDP, I was told that, on Canadian definitions, the UK percentage

would probably not be much more than the Canadian figure, which excluded, for instance, the Canadian Crown agencies.

There were then no internationally agreed comparisons. Later on, in 1978, the OECD filled this gap with a study on *Public Expenditure Trends* which published comparative figures of 'general government expenditure'.

[These were] intended to be consistent with the definitions given in the internationally agreed system of national accounts, where general government refers to the various departments of central, state or provincial and local governments which do not produce goods and services for sale in the market . . . The main exclusion from public expenditure, defined in this way, is the expenditure of those government-owned enterprises or public corporations which primarily sell the goods and services they produce in the market. (p. 11)

Following the mini-package of cuts in nationalised industry investment which formed part of the total July package, and which was the cause of some dissension quite apart from the BNOC business, the Chancellor's announcement of the cuts included a statement that 'We believe the time has now come to review the treatment of the nationalised industry programmes generally in our public expenditure figures so as to bring our practice more closely into line with that of other countries. The Expenditure Committee will of course be consulted on this review.'

Even without the benefit of the OECD study, it was clear that we were out of line with other governments in counting as public expenditure the whole of the capital investment of the nationalised industries, including that part of it which is financed from internal resources, that is, depreciation funds and trading surpluses; these of course come from revenue and therefore from the consumer, not from the taxpayer. There was no doubt that the capital investment figures as such should cease to be included in the White Paper totals of public expenditure. This made it possible to treat the annual investment reviews as a separate exercise from the annual PESC operation, though they would run in parallel with it and the results would appear in a separate part of the public expenditure White Paper.

The next question was how to treat government funds provided to the nationalised industries. The Treasury proposal was that funds provided from Votes – that is, grants and also public dividend capital (PDC), which is a form of pseudo-equity – should count towards the White Paper totals, since these are an actual or potential charge on the taxpayer like other Voted money, but that loans raised from the market and on-lent through the National Loans Fund, with a statutory obligation on the nationalised industries to pay full interest and repay the principal, should not so count. This was later to be the distinction adopted in the OECD figures. However, the sponsor Departments which provided PDC to their nationalised industries took a stand against treating it differently from loans, on the grounds that to do so would imply that PDC, unlike hard loans, was soft money; their posture was that PDC was investment capital which must in due course show a good return. In fact it was clear even then that PDC was more pseudo than equity, and most of it has since, predictably, been written off. The Treasury could clearly not agree to leave this type of financing outside the public expenditure constraints. Since it had to be all or nothing, the conclusion was that the main public expenditure totals should include NLF loans as well as all Voted money provided to the nationalised industries; their market and overseas borrowings were to be shown separately as a below-the-line item. This compromise involved storing up a certain amount of trouble for the future, because of the variation from year to year in the proportions in which the nationalised industries raise their loans from the NLF on the one hand and from market and overseas borrowings on the other.

The primary concern of this review had been operational, not presentational. The object was to get away from a system which exacted a contribution from investment in, say, the energy industries and the transport industries whenever the hat was being passed round to make up a target figure of expenditure cuts, and which caused the annual investment reviews to get bogged down in the overall PESC exercises. At the time the nationalised industries welcomed the new arrangements, which seemed to hold out the prospect of more flexibility. For instance, if their government financing had to be cut, they might have the option of increased self-financing, through higher prices or economies in current expenditure, rather than cutting investment. As we shall see, it was a case of 'Now they ring the bells, but soon they will wring their hands'.

However, the new treatment also had the presentational effect of reducing the White Paper totals by some billions of pounds, the exact amount in any year depending on how much the industries borrowed from the National Loans Fund and how much from other sources. This was accompanied by another and even more dramatic change in the arithmetic, which came about in the following way. At the time when interest rates were shooting up, and we were wrestling with the problem of the increased housing subsidies which would be needed to meet the higher interest charges on the capital cost of council houses, this prompted the question whether we were going to have the same problem with other programmes also. Debt interest – that is, the cost of servicing the national debt and local authority debt – was obviously another problem area. At that point, in the same way that the theory of gravity came into Isaac Newton's head when the legendary apple dropped on it, it came into my head to ask whether we were double counting.

The answer was that double counting on a large scale was in fact involved in treating as part of the public expenditure total both the debt interest on loans raised to build council houses and the housing subsidies which went towards paying this interest. The subsidies from the Department of the Environment and from the rates were paid into the housing revenue accounts of local authorities, along with revenue from council house rents, and the two together – subsidies and rent receipts – financed the whole of the interest charges in this field. Therefore, if we were interested in the net amount of debt interest which had to be met out of taxation, the interest costs of public housing had to be excluded altogether, since either they had already been charged up to the taxpayer once in the subsidy figures or else they were a charge on the tenant and not on the taxpayer at all. Thus we moved from a gross treatment of debt interest to a net treatment.

When the net treatment is applied to money borrowed by the National Loans Fund for on-lending to the nationalised industries, we find that the whole of the interest borne by the NLF on these loans is automatically offset by interest paid to the NLF by the nationalised industries. This in turn comes out of their commercial revenues and thus from the consumer of gas, electricity, etcetera, not from the taxpayer, and is no more a public expenditure cost than any other current outgoings of the nationalised industries which are paid for out of trading revenues – the cost of wages and materials, for instance.

When we have netted off that part of gross debt interest which is balanced by interest receipts or other automatic offsets, we are left with the net figure of debt interest on the deadweight national debt, which has to be financed out of taxation or out of new borrowing, which adds still further to the deadweight national debt. The effect of switching from a gross basis to a net basis in the 1977 White Paper was dramatic. On the old basis the debt interest figure for 1975–76 would have been £5.5 billion; on the new basis it was £1.1 billion. The change was of course purely presentational. It did not save any money, since in reality the government was already bearing only the net cost of debt interest, but the change brought the presentation into line with the reality.

Although the Expenditure Committee chaired by Michael English gave their blessing to these changes, some of the Conservative members of the Committee may have gone away with some suspicions about them. If so, it was a pity, because, though no government is above presenting figures in the light most favourable to its policies, statisticians in the Treasury and the Central Statistical Office are capable of almost perverse tendencies in the opposite direction in the cause of statistical purity as they see it.

The net treatment of debt interest is, I believe, not only essential in order to avoid double counting, but also more illuminating. If we look at the Budget figures for 1981–82, we see (from Table 21 of the Red Book) that the gross service of the national debt had roughly doubled since 1975–76 to about £11 billion. But the net figure – the cost of the deadweight national debt – had gone up more than five-fold in that time to over £6 billion. It is this latter figure which gives a true indication of the budgetary problem created for the Chancellor of the day by the accumulated effects of a series of high Budget deficits in previous years combined with high interest rates on the outstanding debt.

We were fortunate in the intelligent response to these presentational changes from informed financial journalists such as Peter Jay, at that time editor of the *Times* Business News, and Samuel Brittan of the *Financial Times*. Peter Jay's article in *The Times* on 28 October 1976 was headed 'De-cooking the books'. In the *Sun* on the same date there was a less technical article by Roger Carroll with an equally intriguing heading 'Zip goes four billion'. An article by Anthony Harris in the *Financial Times* on 11 November was headed 'Public spending: smaller figures make better sense'. They would have made even better sense but for the pious but misguided stand of the industrial Departments on the treatment of public dividend capital, which prevented us from excluding the loans which are made by the NLF purely as an intermediary and which have no taxation implications. Even so, a certain logic could be claimed for the new public expenditure totals as representing general government expenditure (but going beyond the OECD definition through including government loans to trading bodies) which has to be financed out of taxation or government borrowing.

When it came to expressing the expenditure total as a percentage of GDP, a further change was made and has now become accepted practice, in that from the 1977 White Paper onwards the figures for both expenditure and GDP have been calculated on the same basis, i.e. at market prices. The previous figures had shown GDP at factor cost, thus comparing like with unlike. This purely statistical adjustment reduced the expenditure/GDP percentage by about one-tenth. Thus, the alarming 60 per cent figure was brought down by the new treatment of the nationalised industries and debt interest to an expenditure/GDP ratio for 1975–76 of 51½ per cent of GDP at factor cost; by putting GDP on the basis of market prices, the ratio for that year was further brought down to just under 46 per cent.

On either basis the share of GDP taken up by public expenditure had risen by 10 percentage points over the previous ten years. Changing the way in which this ratio was expressed did not change the actuality of what had taken place or the increase in taxation and borrowing which it had entailed, but it enabled a true comparison to be made with the position in other countries. The OECD study which appeared in 1978 showed that the growth in public expenditure had not been something special to the UK but had been common to the OECD as a whole. Over the twenty years covered by the study, the OECD average percentages for three specimen periods were as shown in table 5.2. In the last of these three-year periods the United Kingdom's figure of 44.5 per cent (a little lower on the OECD

Table 5.2: Public expenditure as a percentage of GDP, 1955–1976 (current prices)

Three-year period	OECD average	United Kingdom
1955 57	28 5	32 3
1967–69	34.5	38.5
1974–76	41.4	44.5

Source: OECD, *Public Expenditure Trends*, 1978.

definitions than on our revised definitions), though somewhat above the OECD average, was roughly on a par with Germany's 44 per cent and Italy's 43.1 per cent, and below the figures for the Scandinavian countries and the Netherlands, which topped the league with 53.9 per cent. Japan, top of every league for industrial performance, came last in these figures with 25.1 per cent. The United States came rather low in the overall rankings with 35.1 per cent, but spent 5.8 per cent of

GDP on defence, a higher figure than that of any other country except, remarkably, Greece.

The similarity between our experience and, say, Germany's in this respect has to be taken in conjunction with the dissimilarity in economic performance. The proportion of national resources allocated to public expenditure cannot be independent of the level of productive capacity. If a primitive country living at subsistence level were to allocate the same proportion of its resources to public expenditure as a very productive country, its people would fall even below subsistence level, and that is of course what happens in poor countries with large armies and self-indulgent rulers. Though the difference between Germany and Britain was not as extreme as, say, the difference between Britain and some of the primitive economies of Africa or Asia, Germany's much higher growth made possible a rapid improvement in both public services and private living standards and still left room for a balance of payments surplus, without the strains experienced in Britain when the growth in public expenditure outstripped the growth in the economy as a whole.

Moreover, even in the high-growth OECD countries the 1974–76 triennium marked the end of the optimistic era of expansion. By 1980 the changing mood was reflected in a framework paper for an OECD seminar on controlling public expenditure, which read: 'There is now a general and widespread concern in Member governments over the level and growth rate of public expenditure . . . Between 1970 and 1977, due in large part to the recession and to the oil crisis which induced external imbalances, the internal balance between public expenditure and receipts has become seriously threatened.'

The new definitions were introduced in the 1977 public expenditure White Paper (Cmnd. 6721). Thanks to help from friends and old colleagues, a statistical appendix appears at the end of this book (Appendix I) which includes a specially prepared table setting out the development of public expenditure in the United Kingdom since 1959 on the basis of those definitions. This table is calculated so as to take account of both volume changes and what is known as the relative price effect (RPE). This series of figures thus shows the growth of 'public expenditure in cost terms'; this is the best measure of the real cost of public expenditure after taking account of inflation generally and of the extent to which the prices which enter into public expenditure (such as civil service wages or the prices of defence equipment) have risen either faster or more slowly than the general inflation rate. If they go up more than other prices, there is a 'positive RPE'; if more slowly, the RPE is negative.

Governments cannot bind their successors; nor can Permanent Secretaries. After I had left the Treasury, in circumstances to be explained in the next section, the new presentation held good only until the 1979 White Paper (Cmnd. 7439). Since then the White Paper tables have been rearranged; moreover, there are differences in coverage from one table to another. I deal with the different White Paper presentations in the statistical appendix, but it need not be regarded as required reading for any but the most dedicated public expenditure scholars.

THE WINTER OF DISCONTENT

The latter part of the government's term of office was marked on the one hand by an unprecedented freedom from worries about sterling and on the other hand by a preoccupation with getting legislation on devolution for Scotland and Wales through a House of Commons in which the government no longer had a working majority. They kept office only through the Lib–Lab pact, under which the leaders of the Liberal Party in the Commons had to be consulted about which measures they would support. In one sense this was helpful in containing the dissidents within the government who, if not open to persuasion on other grounds, accepted the brute fact that Liberal support could not be obtained for further left-wing measures.

At the same time there was an increasing rebelliousness in the Commons against the authority of the executive and a growing frustration among backbenchers at not being involved in policy-making. It was a backbench initiative which led to a provision in the Scotland Act 1978 and the Wales Act 1978 that there must be an affirmative vote from the majority of the Scottish and Welsh electorates in the referendum on devolution before the devolution arrangements could come into effect. The result was that all that political manoeuvring came to nothing when devolution failed to secure the required majority even in Scotland, where the devolutionists may still have retained some long-term hope of hypothecating the revenue from North Sea oil for the exclusive benefit of Scotland, though they had not succeeded in getting any such provisions into the 1978 Act.

The Treasury had their own special problems. In the early months of 1977 the question of splitting the Treasury, by transferring its public expenditure functions to the Civil Service Department, became a live issue. The Expenditure Committee, in which Michael

English took a broad view of the sphere of interest of his General Sub-Committee, received evidence in support of the proposal from two former Prime Ministers, Edward Heath and Harold Wilson, and ambivalent evidence from John Hunt, the Secretary of the Cabinet, which was taken as a pointer that the Prime Minister of the day whom he served must be thinking quite hard about the idea.

The Treasury seemed to have more defenders in the press than within Whitehall. A *Times* leader on 2 March 1977 was headed 'The centre must hold'. Under a heading 'How not to split the Treasury' Anthony Harris in the *Financial Times* on 4 March described the proposed split as decidedly odd.

Remembering the economic record [he went on] of its two best-known exponents, Mr Edward Heath and Sir Harold Wilson, only makes it odder . . . The main reason given for the notion – that it is nonsense to have civil service pay and manning settled in isolation from the main spending decisions – has the sort of superficial appeal which always arouses those who think that the secret of government is to keep the civil service on the run by disorganising it every few years; but it is strictly superficial.

The outcome remained in suspense for some time. A month later, on 4 April, the *Financial Times* printed a feature article on 'The Treasury under fire' in which Peter Riddell wrote:

The Treasury has recently faced criticism of an intensity unusual even for such a traditionally friendless department . . . The decision within less than a month by two of the Treasury's top five civil servants to leave for the private sector – with another only working part time – has inevitably fuelled the flames of this controversy . . . Ironically, this is occurring just at the time when the Treasury's efforts to tighten control over public spending has been clearly shown to be a considerable success and when the financial environment has changed out of all recognition compared with last year.

The part-timer in question was Bryan Hopkin, the Chief Economic Adviser, who had left the Treasury some years previously to take up a chair in economics at Cardiff, and who had been brought back to succeed Ken Berrill as Chief Economic Adviser when Berrill moved to the Cabinet Office to take over from Victor Rothschild as Head of the Central Policy Review Staff – an arrangement which occasioned Berrill's valedictory remark: 'I go to make way for an older man.' Bryan Hopkin was now past the civil service retiring age and had agreed to stay on only until the summer on a part-time basis while arrangements were being made to replace him, after which he would return to Cardiff. So in fact three of the top five men were to go. The other two were Alan Lord and Derek Mitchell, who went, respectively, into industry and the City. 'To lose one Second Permanent Secretary may be regarded as a misfortune,' wrote the *Guardian*, adapting Oscar Wilde, in a leader on 1 April, 'To lose two, and in the space of a month at that, looks like carelessness.'

Knowing that Derek Mitchell had been the front-runner for the Permanent Secretary post at the Department of Trade, when I learned of his plans to leave the service I made it known that I should like to be considered for the Department of Trade job. Coming on top of the other departures, this would mean a clean sweep of all four Treasury posts at Second Permanent Secretary level, and was bound to cause a certain amount of further embarrassment. Moreover, by the time I went to the Department of Trade I would have only a couple of years left before reaching retirement age, and that was regarded as rather a short period for an appointment of that kind. The reaction to my request was therefore unenthusiastic. Nevertheless, Douglas Allen, as Head of the Civil Service, did not stand in the way of my name going forward along with the others in the field, and in the summer of 1977 I moved to the Department of Trade and renewed my involvement with the international scene which I had so much enjoyed in my time on Overseas Finance. Frances Cairncross, writing in the *Guardian* on 29 June about 'one of the most extraordinary bouts of musical chairs that Whitehall has ever seen', concluded that 'the most astonishing thing about the change is how small are the ripples it has left behind.' I was succeeded at the Treasury by Anthony Rawlinson. The Treasury was not split and the fuss died down.

At my new Department I also resumed my working relationship with Edmund Dell who, as I have mentioned earlier, had left the Treasury to become Secretary of State for Trade. However, the following year he was to leave the government, having decided to accept the offer of the chairmanship of a large private sector company. He was replaced by John Smith, a Scottish member who, as Minister of State at the Privy Council Office, had played a large part in the devolution legislation.

From this point on I ceased to be involved in public expenditure from the inside, but I was still involved as Head of a spending Department. The Department of Trade was a sort of conglomerate and, apart from international trade, it had responsibilities for shipping, civil aviation, a miscellany of other industries such as tourism and films, the Patent Office, company law and finally, our biggest growth area, the insolvency service. Although the Department was not in the same league as big spenders like the Department of Health and Social Security or the Ministry of Defence, it had a sufficient stake in the annual public expenditure exercises to enable me to keep my hand in.

When the 1977 expenditure exercise was being planned, before my move to Trade, the programme totals for both the current year and the following years, 1977–78 and 1978–79, were regarded as predetermined by the figures agreed with the IMF. At some stage after that it seemed reasonable to expect that public expenditure could be allowed to grow again at a rate of, say, 2 per cent per year and that this would be within the rate of growth in the economy. It was perhaps optimistic, and yet not necessarily altogether foolish, to think in terms of a decade liberated by North Sea oil from balance of payments crises and therefore from stop–go in economic policy, and to believe that, with these two constraints removed, British industry could start on the long haul of raising its performance. Nevertheless, rather than fall once again into the trap of planning for growth in expenditure in anticipation of future economic growth, it seemed sensible to allow for a transitional year in 1979–80 in which total expenditure would be roughly stabilised before expansion was resumed.

In the event, when the next White Paper appeared in January 1978 (Cmnd. 7049), it showed that, so far from making the further downward adjustment in 1978–79 which had been agreed with the IMF as a possible contingency measure, the Chancellor had made a number of upward adjustments which added over £1½ billion to the planned expenditure for that year. This was designed to produce a growth, in round numbers, of 2 per cent over the previous year's expenditure, and this growth rate was to be sustained over the following years. This could still be regarded as relatively prudent compared with the U-turn and social contract periods. Moreover, shortfall in 1978–79 produced a result which, in real terms, was still somewhat below rather than above the figures agreed with the IMF. However, because of the even greater shortfall in the 1977–78 figures, there was a quite unforeseen year-on-year variation. After falling by 6.9 per cent in real terms in 1977–78, government expenditure rose by 6.0 per cent in 1978–79 After a period of years in which the government expenditure/GDP ratio had been brought down from its peak, it now started to move up again, as the figures in table 5.3 illustrate.

By most measurements, 1978 was a year in which the efforts of the previous years, especially the comparative restraint in incomes and public expenditure, were bringing their rewards. The stagflation indices were more favourable at last, in that the rate of inflation was down to single figures for the first time since 1973, and the annual unemployment figures, although still much higher than the level to

Table 5.3: Government expenditure as a percentage of GDP, 1973–74 to 1978–79 (real terms)

1973–74	39.9
1974–75	45.0
1975–76	45.4
1976–77	43.0
1977–78	39.3
1978–79	40.4

which Denis Healey had aspired, were also a little down on the previous year, for the first time since 1974. There was a bigger increase in real personal disposable income than at any time since the boom of 1972. And yet, paradoxically, the closing months of 1978 were the point at which the trade unions overthrew the government's incomes policy, or failed to prevent the shop stewards and picket organisers from overthrowing it, and we were back into the inflationary spiral. Table 5.4 illustrates how victory was won and lost.

As 1978 ran its course, and the government came nearer to the end of their permitted term of office, there were growing expectations of an October election. But the Prime Minister, after teasing the public with that prospect, decided to stay on through the winter and to defer the election until the spring. This meant that the government had to embark on one more round of incomes policy. The Prime Minister – in emulation, according to some accounts, of West Germany's success in keeping wages and price inflation to 5 per cent – announced a 5 per cent norm for the coming wage round. On one view it was this turn of the screw, added to the lack of authority of a government with only a few months of office left, which sealed the fate of the voluntary incomes policy. On another view, that policy had contained the seeds of its own eventual disintegration, through the compression of differentials and through the sense of deprivation of trade union leaders who had to a large extent lost their traditional role as wage negotiators. On this view the demand for a return to so-called free collective bargaining would in any case have been irresistible.

Attempts by employers to comply with the 5 per cent norm were met not merely by direct industrial action against the employers themselves but by hostile secondary picketing of anyone attempting

Table 5.4: Stagflation versus incomes policy

	Retail price index	Wages and salaries per unit of output	Unemployed including school leavers: UK	
	% increase over previous year	% increase over previous year	'000s	% change over previous year
1976	+ 16.5	+ 9.8	1332	+ 53.8
1977	+ 15.8	+ 6.5	1450	+ 8.9
1978	+ 8.3	+ 10.6	1446	− 0.3
1979	+ 13.4	+ 15.3	1344	− 7.1

to deal with them. Industrial action by the road haulage workers caused widespread disruption. The country's seaborne trade, apart from the roll-on roll-off ferries, was brought to a halt through almost total closure of the ports – though there was as yet no dispute in the ports themselves – as a result of secondary picketing by the lorry drivers. There was nothing that the Department of Trade, or the Department of Transport who were responsible for the ports, could do about this. The leaders of the transport workers, with whom as a Department we did not have direct dealings, were reported to be unwilling or unable to intervene in response to the representations made to them by Ministers.

The collection of sticks and carrots on which the government had relied to secure compliance with incomes policy by private sector employers – in the field of government contracts, for instance, or financial assistance or export credit guarantees or by the potential use of reserve powers on prices – were ineffective in the face of this action by the employed, against whom there were no sanctions. In the public sector the government had been prepared, with mixed success, to accept confrontation in particular disputes, and in some cases to use the armed forces to carry out essential services. The present industrial action appeared to be on too great a scale for the use of the armed forces to provide alternative services, even if Ministers had been prepared for such a course. But over and above their lack of instruments to enforce their policy, a government which had come to office on the basis of a social contract with the unions now appeared to lack the will or authority to deal with the situation without even the moral support of the trade union leadership, for what it was worth when they could no longer deliver compliance by their members.

There was selective industrial action in the civil service in support of a claim to catch up with pay increases outside the service. The withdrawal, for instance, of a limited number of staff in the Companies Registration Office was enough to bring to a halt the whole of the service to the public provided by the CRO. There was nothing here to match the terrors of the flying pickets or the frightfulness of the refusal of workers in the Merseyside area to allow the burial of the dead. Nevertheless, what took place was out of keeping with the traditional behaviour of the civil service. Even some of those in the middle grades appeared to be undergoing some mental conflict about whether or not to support the industrial action.

A settlement of the protracted dispute was eventually negotiated on the basis of a staged pay increase which, even when phased over more than a single year, could not be accommodated within provision for a 5 per cent norm. Nevertheless, cash limits for the next financial year, 1979–80, were meanwhile being fixed on the basis of an increase of 5 per cent in staff costs and an inflation rate of 8½ per cent for goods and services. That is to say, the new White Paper programmes for 1979–80, which were planned to rise by 2 per cent in real terms, would be translated into cash provision on the basis of these increasingly unrealistic projections of inflation. Ministers were beginning to make rather Delphic statements that, if the increase in civil service pay worked out at more than 5 per cent, they would withhold at least part of the adjustment required to bring cash limits into line with the actual rate of inflation. In that case there would have to be a volume squeeze on programmes, whether through staff cuts or other economies, and the real rate of increase would be less than the planned 2 per cent.

There can hardly have been any intention on the part of the Labour government to stick ruthlessly to the announced cash limits. The sort of idea in the air was that, if the actual increase in staff costs exceeded the allowance made for it by, say, 5 per cent, cash limits would be increased, but only by 2 per cent less, ie by 3 per cent. I must have been about the only person in Whitehall outside the Treasury to support this idea. While still at the Treasury, when asked in a session with the Expenditure Committee what we would do about cash limits if there were no incomes policy, I had answered to the effect that in that case perhaps cash limits would be our incomes policy. What I had in mind, for instance, was that, if ever there was a danger of a return to the 1974–75 situation, the government should refuse to provide the money to finance wage inflation at a rate of 25 per cent or more. But that was not the situation in the spring of 1979, since the government did still have an incomes policy, though it was no longer an agreed policy. They could not sensibly have professed to stick to the 5 per cent norm while increasing cash limits to allow for pay increases of twice as much.

We can only speculate how far the Treasury Ministers of that time, if returned to office, would have been able to stick to their intention to hold back part of the excess, or what new incomes policy, if any, the Labour government could have rebuilt on the ruins of the old. They were not put to the test because the Conservatives under Margaret Thatcher came to power in May 1979. If one accepts the judgment, which was implied by James Callaghan's decision against an election the previous autumn, that Labour would not have won then – a judgment not universally shared – the events of the winter could not have made a decisive difference to the outcome. Yet it is difficult to doubt that they had an important effect on the voting and that, just as many in 1974 had voted against the three-day week, a good many of the votes in 1979 were cast against the winter of discontent.

6

The Margaret Thatcher Years – A First Term Report

THE MONETARIST REVOLUTION

The Conservative victory in May 1979 was more than just another change of government; in terms of political and economic philosophy, it was a revolution. The first victim of this coup was the commitment to full employment. It can be argued that this commitment had become a dead letter since the first oil crisis of 1973 and that no government could undertake to restore full employment as we knew it before then – though there are those who do not accept this – or that at the least it is necessary to specify a substantially higher unemployment figure as the level at which we can be said to have full employment. However, as recently as 1976 Denis Healey had hoped to get unemployment back to 600,000 and, as we have seen, in his statement of July 1977 he held out the prospect of returning to full employment without inflation.

The new administration was the first government since the 1944 White Paper on *Employment Policy* not to make full employment one of its objectives. In November 1979 it published a short White Paper on *The Government's Expenditure Plans 1980–81* (Cmnd. 7746) showing the results of its first scrutiny of spending plans after six months in office. Opening with the statement that 'Public expenditure is at the heart of Britain's present economic difficulties', the White Paper set out the government's 'three central objectives'. The first was to bring down the rate of inflation by reducing the growth of the money supply and by controlling government borrowing. The second was to restore incentives by holding down and if possible reducing taxes, particularly on income. The third was to plan for spending which would be compatible with the objectives on borrowing and taxation, and with a realistic assessment of the prospects for economic growth.

Thus there had ceased to be any trade-off in government policies between the counter-inflation objective and the employment objective. The counter-inflation objective was overriding. Not only was there no mention of full employment as an objective; the word 'employment' did not appear at all in the short White Paper except in the section-heading 'Industry, energy, trade and employment', and in one of the paragraphs in that section which stated that 'No provision is made for the extension of the Small Firms Employment Subsidy'. The first full-length statement of *The Government's Expenditure Plans 1980–81 to 1983–84* issued in March 1980 (Cmnd. 7841) restated the three central objectives and again, in Part 3 which deals with the expenditure plans as a whole, the word employment was mentioned only in the context of 'a substantial reduction in Government assistance to industry, and in the provision for employment and training . . .'.

This omission was not inadvertent, but reflected the explicitly anti-Keynesian monetarist doctrine which was associated on the other side of the Atlantic with the name of Milton Friedman and the Chicago school of economists, and which had been preached in Britain in a tireless stream of publications from the Institute of Economic Affairs and by the monetarist minority in the academic world. Advisers from this school of thought had secured the ear of the Conservative economic policy makers during their recent period of soul-searching in the political wilderness and, from being cranks who were irrelevant to the real world of practical affairs, they had emerged as opinion-makers who had access to the decision-makers and who had great influence on their thinking. No doubt full employment remained an aspiration, as one of the economic Ministers put it in conversation, but it was no longer a commitment. Once inflation had been squeezed out of the economy, it was argued, achievement of the government's objectives on the money supply and taxation would bring about a new entrepreneurial atmosphere which in turn would produce – in a favourite phrase of another Conservative Minister – real jobs, not cosmetic jobs such as had been provided under the Labour government's job creation schemes. Thus full employment, however defined, had ceased to be an objective in its own right. It was not to be pursued by 'throwing money at problems', another term of criticism much heard about this time.

There were a number of remarkable things about this situation.

One was the fact that, in what was traditionally a party of practical men rather than theorists, which not many years earlier had in Sir Alec Douglas-Home a Prime Minister reputed to do his economic arithmetic by the use of match sticks, policy was now dictated by an abstruse doctrine on the money supply, which even on the basic question of definitions was capable of still more variants than public expenditure. Another remarkable thing was the fact that monetarist theory gained such an ascendancy when from the first only a minority of the Cabinet positively subscribed to it, and even among the minority there were different degrees of philosophical commitment. The attitudes of the rest ranged from acquiescence, through support for the Treasury team's policies in principle coupled with dislike of their practical manifestations (especially high interest rates), to an outright preference for the political middle ground or traditional Tory paternalism or Heath-type interventionism. The new administration was unique among modern Conservative governments in displaying internal differences so openly and so early in its life.

The monetarist minority nevertheless prevailed in economic and industrial policy because they had strategic control of the key Departments and Cabinet committees; as in previous administrations, only the Prime Minister and Treasury Ministers were effectively involved in taxation policy and, in conjunction with the Bank of England, in interest rates and exchange rate policy. The doubters and dissenters were either given no opportunity to mount a challenge in full Cabinet or were unable to do so effectively.

But as one moved on to other areas of policy, and specifically public expenditure, the monetarist writ ceased to run. The Friedmanite propagandists had in fact never received from the Conservative policy makers the same commitment to their prescriptions on public expenditure as to their recipe for dealing with inflation. For their objective went far beyond cutting public expenditure. It was to re-draw the boundaries not merely of the public sector of industry, by denationalisation or privatisation, but of the public services. There is no necessary connection between a belief in the cardinal role of the money supply and the collection of other beliefs which tend to cluster round it, but in general it does tend to go with a vision of a market economy free from restrictive practices imposed by government, trade unions or cartels and a competitive low-tax society motivated by profit and loss, consumer's preference and the spread of private ownership of property. Monetarist doctrine, therefore, rejected not only the Keynesian commitment to full employment through demand management but also the Butskellite consensus on the welfare state; it called into question the whole case for state provision of services beyond defence and internal security. Wherever possible other services should in some way be put back into the market, if not left to charity and private patronage.

On many aspects of policy this philosophy was reflected in the 1979 Conservative manifesto – on control of the money supply, trade union reform, cutting income tax, a property-owning democracy, de-nationalisation and fair trade – but the elimination of public services never became Conservative policy, except to the extent of favouring the contracting out of services such as refuse collection and opposing local direct labour schemes, which is far from being an exclusively monetarist viewpoint. There was a commitment to better value for money, and the promise of an enhanced role for private medicine and independent schools, but in coexistence with the National Health Service – which was not to be cut – and the state education system.

Nevertheless it is likely that monetarist doctrine had some impact on Conservative thinking about the public services and provided part of the rationale for cutting public expenditure. 'Most aspects of public spending are worth while, if the nation can afford them', said the Chancellor in his Budget speech on 27 March 1980. 'Our choices have been guided by the belief that government should provide efficiently and realistically those services which it alone is able, and best fitted to provide.' But in practice, outside the field of support for industry, services were to be cut rather than cut out. There was, therefore, the prospect of a compromise between the Butskellite consensus on the welfare state and the monetarist rejection of it, as a result of which the whole range of public services would be kept in being, but grudgingly. This was an outcome which the monetarist purists did not welcome.

The Government's monetary policy requiring the Budget deficit to be reduced will be condemned, and the Government will expose itself to vilification by plausible critics, if it appears to be responsible for harsh cuts in welfare and other desired services.

The quotation is from an open memorandum to the Prime Minister and the leader of the Opposition, which appeared in *The Times* on 9 January 1980 above a score of signatures which made up a monetarist roll call of the great and the good. Their proposed remedy distinguished between those government services which, like defence, law and order and street lighting, are 'public goods' and those, from education and medicine to refuse collection and libraries, which are not. The latter, being 'personal, private, family services', should be paid for by charges on the user.

The poor could be financially enfranchised by selective cash subsidies by the use of a reverse income tax, and perhaps where there are children by the issue of education and health insurance vouchers. All could then confront the costs of choice and decide the cuts – or increases – for themselves and their families.

This policy of 'putting personal services supplied by the government into the market', along with curbs on trade union power and exposing the nationalised industries to more competition, was one of the essentials 'for easing the path of monetary policy and increasing the efficiency of the supply side of the economy'.

There is of course no reason why the state should not provide and charge for market-orientated services, as is of course done with public utilities such as gas, electricity, public transport and the postal service, but a scheme for converting a whole range of public services, including education and medicine, to commercial public utilities, without putting them out of reach of the poor, would have been hopelessly impractical. The monetarist memorandum was singularly devoid of costings, but earlier work in Whitehall on more conventional tax credit schemes had indicated that the cost would be high. One would expect a scheme sufficiently generous to enable those on lower incomes to enjoy reasonable parity of services to be prohibitively expensive. Such detailed study as has been given to a scheme of education vouchers suggests that this too would be an expensive way of providing freedom of choice of school.

Thus, in terms of hard line monetarist philosophy, what had taken place was after all only half a revolution. The objective of reducing the public sector borrowing requirement would have to coexist with what would still be, in spite of all the cuts and disposals of publicly owned assets, a very large public sector.

Let us now see how this problem of coexistence has worked out, but I should first make it clear that by this point in the story I had ceased to have any personal involvement in these matters. The circumstances were as follows. Unlike previous Prime Ministers, Margaret Thatcher did not start off by treating Whitehall as a set of building blocks, dismantling Whitehall Departments and reassembling the pieces so as to create new ones. Though, the wheel having come full circle, it was the turn of the Civil Service Department to be threatened with absorption by the Treasury, it survived until 1981. But the one head to fall was that of the Department of Prices and Consumer Protection.

This was a tiny Department which shared common services and 'common citizenship' for the staff with the Department of Trade and the Department of Industry, the three Permanent Secretaries sitting as a triumvirate to deal with staff matters. It had been set up by Harold Wilson in 1974 to provide a suitable Ministerial role for Shirley Williams, but it had never been a satisfactory creation as a Department in its own right. Its winding up was long overdue, but moves to bring this about under the Labour government had foundered on questions of personalities.

Under the new government the DPCP was integrated into the Department of Trade. As a result of the reallocation of posts which followed I was summarily informed by the Civil Service Department that, since I was within a few months of retirement, I was to be treated as a supernumerary Permanent Secretary for that period, which I therefore spent on special assignments in the Department, receiving expressions of condolence – which was not how I had expected to wind up – from the many people who went out of their way to say how badly I had been treated by my colleagues. I was then invited to stay on for six months after my normal retirement date in order to carry out a review of so-called quangos, that is to say, the thousands of public bodies, large and small, executive or advisory or judicial in character, which had come into existence outside the normal Departmental structure. For this assignment, which attracted a disproportionate amount of public interest, I was attached to the Civil Service Department, in which I found a certain irony, but worked direct to the Prime Minister, thanks to whom I ended my time in Whitehall on something of an upbeat after all. However, throughout this period I had no part in what went on in Whitehall outside these special assignments, and in January 1980 my delayed retirement from the service took place, since when I have followed the events discussed in this final chapter with a mixture of regret and relief at being no longer involved.

THE GREAT DEPRESSION

Inheriting cash limits for 1979–80 which allowed for pay increases of 5 per cent, the new government did something rather similar to what the outgoing government had threatened to do. In revised cash limits, the total civil service pay element in the inherited base-line figures was reduced by 3 per cent. The result was an indirect cut in programmes in volume terms, with the exception of the defence budget, which had its cash limit increased. As a complementary measure, there was a temporary ban on recruitment into the civil service. Given the breakdown of incomes policy, this approach was the only way open to the new government to limit the size of the pay bill. But this merely lowered the base-line to which the cost of new pay settlements would have to be added, for the Conservative government also inherited studies which their predecessors had put in hand for the civil service, the armed forces and certain other groups, and these led to awards designed to enable these public services to catch up with other groups in the national workforce that had done better in pay. The new government did not repudiate these awards but paid up, though by stages, and, having scaled cash limits down, were obliged to scale them up again.

In addition to the indirect volume cut, there were to be direct volume cuts in planned programmes in order to achieve a temporary standstill. The short White Paper of November 1979 described this as a strategy 'to stabilise public spending for the time being'. There was a good case for a holding operation of this sort by the new government. It was the first year after the period covered by the IMF cuts, and the breakdown of incomes policy had created a fresh situation, but a standstill was going to be much harder to achieve than was generally appreciated. The White Paper arithmetic was helped by taking credit, legitimately, for special sales of assets and, less legitimately, by including the nationalised industries' market and overseas borrowings; large net repayments were to reduce these borrowings (known as NIMOBS for short to the public expenditure statisticians) to a minus figure. But on the other side of the account there were a number of major programmes which the Conservative government were committed to increase, in particular defence and law and order, or not to cut, as in the case of the National Health Service. Social security, the largest single programme, would also keep rising in spite of the government's intention to de-index unemployment benefit. Finally, our contributions to the European Community were rising steeply now that the transitional period for our entry into the Community was over; unless a new deal could be negotiated, the cost would rise from £750 million net of receipts (£1300 million gross) in 1978–79 to about £1000 million (£1800 million gross) in 1980–81, and, if the Community was given its head, could go on rising to over £1500 million net by 1983–84.

But a standstill did not satisfy the government's supporters. When interest rates were raised steeply to enable the government to sell the amount of gilt-edged securities required to finance the PSBR, and at the same time to discourage the financing of inflationary cost increases in the private sector, the Treasury team came under increasing pressure to cut the PSBR and in turn exerted pressure for further spending cuts. The results were announced in the full-length White Paper which appeared in March 1980, the first to be synchronised with the Budget so that the government's detailed proposals on expenditure and on financing were for the first time presented together. 'The Government intend to reduce public expenditure progressively in volume terms over the next four years', was the key statement in the White Paper. As a start, the plans for 1980–81 had been reduced since the earlier short White Paper. At the same time the *Financial Statement and Budget Report* set out a medium-term financial plan under which the rate of growth in the money supply would also be progressively reduced over the next four years.

The main reductions were to come from housing, which was to be nearly halved over the four years; from government lending to the nationalised industries; from the industry, energy, trade and employment block; and from education. After allowing for an extra £3 billion for the growth programmes, and a contingency reserve of £2 billion for other possible increases, an absolute net reduction of the order of £3 billion in real terms – either more or less than this figure according to what items were counted in – was planned by 1983–84 as compared with the estimate for 1979–80.

There was a familiar look to this spending profile, in that only a marginal reduction was planned for the first year ahead, and it was not until the later years that there was to be significantly less jam. On top of the direct volume cuts, an indirect cash limit squeeze on volume programmes was planned for the second year running; volume programmes for 1980–81 were translated into cash limits which provided for a rate of inflation of 13–14 per cent, substantially below the actual inflation rate. The difference between this figure and a new civil service pay rise of over 18 per cent was made up partly by delaying payment of the increase for a month and partly by a staff cut of about 2.5 per cent. But provision was also made for the full financial year effect of the previous year's staged pay settlement, so that altogether civil servants' pay rose year on year by about 25 per cent, which was regarded as no more than justice within the civil service but scandalised some outside it. At the same time the government were now moving, in spite of their overt rejection of anything which could be called an incomes policy, to an explicit position on the target rate for new pay increases and not merely a position implicit in the fixing of cash limits.

Meanwhile the standstill for 1979–80 had failed to materialise. In real terms, expenditure (on the Getting and Spending definitions) rose by well over 2 per cent in the Conservative government's first year.

Let us now jump a year and move on to the White Paper on *The Government's Expenditure Plan 1981–82 to 1983–84* (Cmnd. 8175) which was issued at the time of the March 1981 Budget. It showed that, within a year of the failure of the planned standstill, the plan to cut total public expenditure had also failed.

The totals of expenditure, both the outturn now estimated for 1980–81 and the planning totals for future years, are higher than in Cmnd. 7841 and higher than the Government would wish in the light of their financial and economic objectives. (p. 3)

In fact, on the Getting and Spending definitions, total government expenditure rose by 2.1 per cent in 1980–81.

So once again the question has to be asked – what went wrong? Experience shows, of course, that there is a natural tendency for plans to go wrong, and that the multiplicity of government objectives makes it extremely difficult to achieve all of them. Some of the difficulties were predictable from the outset: the commitment to increases in particular programmes which meant that the government would have to run hard just to stand still; the improbability of a turn round in the financing of the nationalised industries on the scale proposed; the uncertainty of those savings which required the cooperation of the local authorities; and the tendency of spending Ministers to want to spend once the pressure of events became more potent than the Brownie points awarded for cutting their pro- grammes. But on top of these factors it was the slump, gathering momentum rapidly as the year progressed, which had not been antici pated in the 1980 Budget – whether or not it was foreshadowed in unpublished Treasury forecasts – and which wrecked the expenditure plan. In the calendar year 1980, while the exchange rate went from strength to strength, total output fell by more than 10 per cent, manufacturing output by 15 per cent and employment in Great Britain by over 1 million or nearly 5 per cent.

The recession upset the expenditure plan in a number of ways. The social security programme in the 1980 White Paper assumed that the unemployed (excluding school leavers, etc.) would average 1.8 million in 1981–82 and subsequent years, with another 200,000 school leavers, adult students and temporarily stopped. By the time of the 1981 White Paper, the unemployment assumption had risen to 2.5

million for 1981–82, and 2.7 millon for each of the next two years, with a further 200,000 school leavers, etc. Each increase of 100,000 in the unemployed was estimated to increase the cash cost of unemployment benefit by about £140 million in 1981–82. Thus the extra 700,000 unemployed would involve about an extra £1 billion in a full year.

An important factor in the results for both 1979–80 and 1980–81 was the non-occurrence of shortfall on the same scale as before. This could be partly explained by the cuts themselves – the more that programmes were cut, the less room there was left for shortfall. But the increasing slack in the economy also played a part, since it improved delivery dates and caused the defence budget in particular to be overspent rather than underspent as in the past.

The recession also played a large part in the disappearance of two major programme cuts on which the government had relied for a large part of their total savings. One was government lending to the nationalised industries which, as a group, were to be transferred from net borrowers to a source of net repayments to the government; as part of this programme, the British Steel Corporation, which had required injections of external finance approaching £2 billion in all over the three previous years, was set a target of operating at a profit in 1980–81. The other was support for industry and employment, which was to be nearly halved. As part of these cuts, the boundaries of the assisted areas were to be changed so as to cover, by 1982, 25 per cent of the employed population of Great Britain, instead of 44 per cent. Regional development grants were to be maintained in the Special Development Areas, reduced in the Development Areas, and abolished in the Intermediate Areas. The functions and budget of the National Enterprise Board were reduced. No provision was made for major rescues by the Department of Industry. Programmes operated by the Department of Employment and the Manpower Services Commission were to be scaled down. The MSC's staff was to be progressively reduced.

In the short space of time between the 1980 White Paper and the 1981 White Paper these cuts had gone into reverse. About £1 billion had been added back to the projected borrowings of the nationalised industries in 1981–82, and about £1¼ billion to support for industry and employment. The cost of employment and training measures rose sharply, partly because of increased take-up of demand-responsive schemes and partly because of new MSC programmes, especially to help the young. After a series of cliffhangers, British Leyland, now redesignated simply BL, had its funds replenished. The ambitious financial target for British Steel was replaced by a write-off of old capital and a major injection of new money. It is difficult to credit that the injunction to BSC to turn itself round from mammoth loss-making to profitability in a single year was ever seriously intended.

The *ad hoc* concessions on industrial policy created speculation about the possibility of a volte-face on demand management in the 1981 Budget. There were hopes, for instance, of relief for industrial costs by removal or reduction of the national insurance surcharge, which had continued in force since its introduction by Denis Healey as an expedient in 1977 – another case of *rien ne dure comme le provisoire.* It therefore came as something of a shock when Geoffrey Howe presented a disinflationary Budget, designed to reduce the public sector borrowing requirement from around £13½ billion in 1980–81 to £10½ billion in 1981–82. Direct taxes were to be increased in real terms by withholding any increase in personal allowances to take account of inflation. Indirect taxes were to be increased in the form of higher petrol duty. Cabinet were informed of these measures, in the customary manner, only at the last minute before they were announced to Parliament. This led, it was reported, to a demand that Cabinet should in future be involved in policy-making on the Budget in the same way as on other policies for which they accepted collective responsibility, a move which on the face of it would have carried to its logical conclusion the concept of bringing together the planning of public expenditure and of its financing. However, the demand appears to have been firmly rejected.

The failure of the public expenditure strategy, still not fully acknowledged, had come about not through a deliberate U-turn, still less as a result of advice from the civil service, which had never had so little influence, but through force of circumstance. The cuts were still being pressed home wherever possible, for instance in education, even to the point of confrontation with the local authorities. Money was not easy to get out of the Treasury, as it had been at the time of the Heath–Barber contracyclical measures or in the heyday of the social contract. Administrative economies were being pressed with unprecedented energy in the civil service, with the help of Derek Rayner, borrowed from Marks & Spencer to mobilise scrutiny teams in each Department. The cash limits fixed for 1981–82 allowed for pay increases of only 6 per cent, and the government were surprisingly successful in getting settlements in the civil service and local government not much above this figure. They had now moved even closer to an incomes policy, imposed not agreed, but not so formalised as to prevent bigger increases for groups with a special case or special industrial muscle – the police, the firemen, and the water workers.

But all these efforts were more than offset by the additional expenditure which the government had to meet either from choice or through *force majeure.* The Budget was the response to this situation dictated by the monetarist half-revolution. If expenditure could not be cut, it must be financed without inflating the money supply. But in principle the government still regarded 'their commitment to constrain public expenditure in total as the overriding consideration' and the past year's development in this total 'as one which requires the most serious attention during the 1981 annual survey, when the plans for 1982–83 onwards will be reviewed'.

So the 1981 public expenditure exercise was put in hand with those behind crying 'forward' and those before crying 'back'. There was mounting pressure on the government, and from those within the government who were now at least as much concerned about unemployment as about inflation, for a greater or lesser degree of reflationary expenditure. But the Treasury team, still committed to the objectives of reducing the PSBR and the growth in the money supply, and all the more so their supporters who thought them not monetarist enough in their handling of the public sector and the trade unions, argued for fresh public expenditure cuts.

As the summer recess approached, it became clear that the Treasury team were fighting a rearguard action. Two-thirds of central government expenditure was accounted for by three major programmes (social security, the National Health Service, and defence) which, unless the government were prepared to reverse existing political commitments, would go on increasing. The social security figure would have been £1.5 million higher but for legislation passed to end earnings-related unemployment benefit and to end the obligation to increase basic unemployment benefit in line with prices. The obligation to increase state pensions in line with prices or earnings, whichever was the more favourable, had been replaced by a commitment to upratings solely in line with prices – which would still leave pensioners in a better position than those at work if real wages fell. In spite of these changes the social security bill was still going up with the rise in the number of pensioners and of the unemployed. As regards the NHS there was a frequently reiterated 'pledge to keep total spending on the Health Service in line with the plans of our predecessors and so maintain a modest level of annual growth'. Even after higher charges, this would entail some increase in the net cost. At the Ministry of

Defence the appointment of John Nott in place of Francis Pym, who had spoken heretically about the sanctity of cash limits, led to the use of more respectful language on that subject and, after some months, to the announcement of a severe curtailment in conventional navy strength and support facilities. But there was no going back on the undertaking given to NATO that we would increase the defence budget by 3 per cent a year in real terms. An undertaking on these lines had in fact been given by the Labour government in their final phase, after the forces had come back into favour through keeping essential services going during industrial disputes, and when the employment created by the defence budget had taken on increased importance. At 1981 prices this commitment meant that an extra £1 billion a year would be added to the defence budget every three years. The naval economies would merely help to meet the rising cost of defence equipment, and especially the new Trident nuclear deterrent.

As regards the remaining third of central government expenditure, the White Paper plan already took credit for large unspecified reductions in support to industry and employment and in loans to the nationalised industries in 1982–83 and 1983–84, which would very probably fail to materialise, as had happened so far. One saving which had been achieved, as a result of the Prime Minister's persistence in the face of an initially hostile reaction from the other Community Heads of Government, was a negotiated refund of part of our contributions to the EEC budget up to 1981, with a less specific prospect of continuing remedial measures after that date. But the 1981 White Paper already took account of this result; it would not count towards any further reduction.

If we turn now to local authority expenditure, by the summer of 1981 a critical point had been reached in the relationship between central and local government. There was now a system of cash limits on the aggregate capital expenditure of local authorities within which, apart from a few exceptions, they could determine their own priorities. As regards current expenditure, cash limits were still applied to the rate support grant, not to the current expenditure which the grant helped to finance – the balance of the finance coming from the rates. But a drastic new curb had been introduced in the form of powers under which Whitehall set target figures for the current expenditure of each local authority and could reduce the amount of grant to an individual authority as a penalty if the target was exceeded; this was now being done in an increasing number of cases. This could, however, produce the reverse of the wished-for effect on rate charges, since a local authority which could not or would not achieve the required reduction in current expenditure could make up for the loss of grant by increasing the rates, thus further worsening the financial plight of British industry. The government countered with a statement of intent to impose still further cutbacks on the freedom of action of local authorities.

The idea of abolishing the rates altogether, which the Conservatives had favoured when in opposition, and replacing them by a block grant, was also being revived in some quarters, but it was not easy to see when any Chancellor of the Exchequer would feel able to switch the financing of over £10 billion from local rates to central government financing. Moreover, the logical conclusion of this thinking would be in effect a national service, or set of services, centrally financed but locally administered, rather like the National Health Service but involving twice as much money and with the same kind of problems of control and accountability. The intractable question of alternatives to the rates as a local tax was reopened, but with no better results than in the past. In this situation, the government were having to exert themselves to secure the savings already projected in local authority expenditure, let alone making further cuts.

The great expenditure debate went on through the summer of 1981. Industrialists who, out of the need to survive in a harsh economic situation, had achieved economies in manpower in individual companies and a realism in wage bargaining not previously negotiable, argued that massive savings could be achieved without drastic policy changes by a further squeeze on numbers and the pay bill in the public services. The Treasury team's supporters asked whether all the sacrifices which had been made were to be wasted and the gains were to be lost through premature relaxation.

But the gains were not evident in the performance of the economy as a whole. Output continued to decline in the first half of 1981, though more slowly and with the possibility that bottom might soon be reached. The rate of inflation had been brought down in 1981 below the 1980 peak, but was still in double figures, while unemployment continued to reach new peaks unknown since the 1930s. Stagflation had turned into slumpflation.

Sentiment against expenditure cuts crystallised further among the non-monetarists as the summer brought with it outbreaks of rioting by young people in one inner city area after another. There was a fairly general belief that unemployment among the young, and especially coloured young people, and the urban squalor in which they lived were among the causes of the riots and that there was a need to spend more money, not less, on dealing with them. Against this background, immediately before Parliament adjourned for the Royal wedding and the summer recess, the Prime Minister announced a major expansion in the Youth Opportunities Programme and other job-creation measures. The budget of the Manpower Services Commission, a quango which earlier in the government's life had been under a cloud and had suffered cuts in staff and programmes, was now being re-expanded as an essential instrument in these measures.

1981 was the low point in the slump and in the political fortunes of the government and the Prime Minister. Their position would have been even more difficult but for the Labour Party's suicidal choice, in November the previous year, of Michael Foot rather than Denis Healey as leader of the party in succession to James Callaghan. Those moderate Labour Members of Parliament who voted for Michael Foot – a man well liked as a person within the Parliamentary party, but ineffectual in office and as a party leader – did so in the belief that he would be the better choice to unite the party; but in the event he presided over a shift to the left which led to the defection of a number of the moderates in 1981 to the newly formed Social Democratic Party. On the other hand, the alliance of the SDP with the Liberal Party, which initially did well in the opinion polls and some by-elections, while weakening the Labour Opposition, presented a potential new threat to the Conservatives.

In September 1981, the Prime Minister's hand was strengthened by a purge which she carried out of the Cabinet dissidents, and by the winding up of the Civil Service Department and a reallocation of its functions between the Treasury and a new Management and Personnel Office under the Secretary of the Cabinet. This move – which was the very opposite of the splitting of the Treasury that some had argued for in 1976, and which restored to the Treasury some of the functions which it had lost on the creation of the Civil Service Department – gave the Prime Minister and Treasury Ministers more effective control over civil service pay and manpower.

In the autumn Ministers came back to their desks to take up where they had left off – except those who were moved to different desks or none at all in the Cabinet reshuffle – and to resume the negotiations on public expenditure cuts. But the brute facts of the situation had not changed. The outcome was that, in a statement on 2 December 1981, the Chancellor had to report further additions to planned expenditure and, in anticipation of his 1982 Budget, measures to raise extra revenue by higher charges and contributions, so as to contain the borrowing requirement with which he would be faced in his 1982 Budget. However, in the Budget paper he announced a number of measures to help industry (especially small businesses), including a long-awaited cut in the national insurance surcharge from 3½ per cent to 2½ per cent.

Much the same pattern was repeated in the following twelve months, which, as it turned out, proved to be the run-up to the general election. In September 1982, the Chancellor put to Cabinet gloomy Treasury projections of the longer-term outlook for expenditure and taxation, together with a CPRS paper on possible radical options for cutting services, and sought a remit for a substantive study of options for reducing expenditure; but Cabinet blocked this move, which was well leaked to the press, no doubt by its opponents. In the shorter term, the Chancellor faced a fifth consecutive increase in public expenditure (on the Getting and Spending definitions) in 1983–84. In the autumn of 1982, while announcing – in advance of the Budget – a further cut in the national insurance surcharge to 1½ per cent, the Chancellor also had to announce increases in normal national insurance contributions. Subsequently, in the Budget proper, he announced a third cut in the national insurance surcharge to 1 per cent, some important reliefs for North Sea oil exploration and development, and some concessions on personal taxation. Unemployment benefit, which on an earlier occasion had been increased by less than the rise in the cost of living, now had that abatement restored; but the base-date for uprating pensions, which had been changed (from the 'historical method' to the 'forecast method') as part of one of the Labour government's rounds of expenditure cuts, was changed back, now that the original method suited the Exchequer better.

If we take personal taxation and national insurance contributions together, the total burden had increased during the government's term of office. But the Chancellor preferred this outcome, unpalatable though it was, to reducing taxes by higher borrowing. (The option of reducing taxation by reducing expenditure, as we have seen, had been denied him.) By forgoing lower taxes, he was once again able to plan for lower borrowing. From over £13 billion in 1980–81, which was a peak figure in money terms – though as a percentage of GDP (5.7 per cent) it had been exceeded in the 1970s – public sector borrowings had been brought down to £8.8 billion and £9.2 billion (something over 3 per cent of GDP in each case) in the two following years. Now, in the March 1983 Budget, he was able to announce a planned public sector borrowing requirement of £8 billion for 1983–84; as an estimated percentage of GDP (2¾ per cent), this would be the lowest figure since 1971–72.

THE FALKLANDS FACTOR

The events of 1979–81 provided one more illustration of the way in which plans and projections come to grief and expectations are disappointed. The events of 1982, in contrast, are a dramatic example of developments which no one planned or forecast. (We have to go back, perhaps, to the Yom Kippur war and the oil crisis of 1973 for an equally dramatic example.) In April 1982, Argentina invaded the Falkland Islands, a British possession in the South Pacific with a tiny population, of British stock though not enjoying full British citizenship. The Argentinians had laid claim to the territory for many years, but it had not been foreseen that they would actually occupy it with a large garrison, as they now did. Equally, the Argentinians did not anticipate that, faced with a *fait accompli*, the British would seek to re-take the islands, 8000 miles away. However, spurred on by sentiment in Parliament, the government promptly despatched a task force to do just that. If it had failed, as it might well have done, we can only speculate how long Margaret Thatcher could have survived as Prime Minister. In the event, in spite of the traumatic sinking of part of the British fleet by the enemy air force, the British navy – after sinking the cruiser Belgrano – deterred the Argentinian ships from leaving port, and the professional British army routed the demoralised enemy soldiers and secured their surrender.

This was a vindication of resolute government and a cause for national pride. The Prime Minister's personal authority and reputation were enormously enhanced, and the government's loss of standing in the country was sharply reversed. Whether the 'Falklands factor' would persist was a popular talking point; it turned out to have a more lasting effect than many expected.

The re-occupation of the Falklands left Britain with an expensive new commitment. After what had taken place it was out of the question to resume the negotiations with Argentina about the status of the Falklands which had been going on before the war. On the other hand, the defence of these small islands for an indefinite period and at such a distance was a costly business and entailed at least a partial reversal of the planned economies in the surface fleet. The costs of the Falklands war and the subsequent protection of the islands were treated as additions to the defence budget, on top of the NATO commitment to an annual increase in defence expenditure of 3 per cent a year in real terms up to 1985–86. Defence expenditure, which had been under 5 per cent of GDP since 1969, now started to rise above that mark (see Table 1.1 on page 15). However, at that stage this was accepted as a price worth paying for a rare national success.

The government was now also having increasing success on at least one aspect of economic policy – getting inflation down. By the middle of 1982 the rate of price inflation, though still higher than the government had inherited, was below double figures; it continued to fall rapidly to a low point of under 4 per cent by the middle of 1983. This took place in spite of the earlier failure of the money supply to conform to the growth targets set for it, and thus falsified the predictions of that school of monetarists which believes that the growth of the money supply at any time inexorably determines the rate of inflation two years later.

Most of the elements of the medium term financial strategy had in fact gone wrong. Apart from the deviant behaviour of the money supply, neither the objective of cutting public expenditure nor the objective of cutting taxation had been achieved. However, by forgoing the tax objective, the government had adhered through thick and thin to the objective of reducing the borrowing requirement as a percentage of GDP. In war, too, it can happen that plans go wrong but objectives may nevertheless be reached by pressing on, though at the cost of casualties. The casualties of the slump and the conquest of inflation were the unemployed, of whom by mid-1983 there were more than 3 million. Moreover the numbers of unemployed were still growing, though the rate of increase was slowing.

The conquest of inflation and the disaster on the unemployment front are illustrated by table 6.1, which carries the story forward from the stagflation tables in earlier chapters. However, in order to overcome a problem of statistical continuity in the unemployment figures, this particular table goes back to 1976, before the time of the Conservative government with which we are concerned in this chapter. In these years we move from stagflation to outright slumpflation and then to a new phase, in which inflation comes down rapidly but unemployment keeps going up. Thus, though the stagflation tables suggest a link between rising wage costs and rising unemployment, these latest figures show that the opposite had not yet occurred. That is to say, there was nothing yet to suggest that squeezing out inflation would by itself restore employment; the monetarist camp might argue that the squeeze could not be expected to have this effect until it had run its full course.

Just as, in an earlier chapter, we had to ask: what is public expenditure?, so at this point we have to ask: who are the unemployed? In

Table 6.1: Slumpflation and after

	Retail price index	Wages and salaries per unit of output		Unemployed including school leavers: UK	
	% increase over previous year	% increase over previous year		% increase over previous year[d]	
		manufac-turing	whole economy	'000s	
1976	16.5	10.6	9.8	1302	+38.4
1977 ave.	15.8	8.6	6.5	1403	+7.8
1978	8.3	13.4	10.6	1383	−1.4
1979	13.4	14.0	15.3	1296	−6.3
1980	21.5	24.6	23.3	1445	+14.5[e]
1981 Q2	11.7	10.1	11.3	2392	+65.5
1982	9.4	6.1	5.8	2796	+16.9
1983	3.7	3.3[a]	4.6[b]	3068[c]	+11.4[e]

[a]3 months ending May 1983.
[b]1983 first quarter.
[c]Affected by 1983 Budget provisions: estimated value on pre-Budget basis 3156.
[d]New basis (claimants) with adjustments for the change to fortnightly payment of benefit and for the 1983 Budget provisions.
[e]Estimated underlying change.

other words, as I have already indicated, there is a problem in producing a long-run series of unemployment figures for the UK including school leavers. A new basis for the figures was introduced in November 1982. Before then the figures were based on records of people registering for work at job centres and career offices, but in October 1982 registration ceased to be a compulsory requirement for claiming benefit and therefore ceased to be a usable basis for the unemployment figures. After the change, the figures were derived from records of claimants to benefit (meaning unemployed people claiming unemployment benefit, supplementary benefits and national insurance credits) at Unemployment Benefit Offices. As a result of further changes announced in the 1983 Budget, men aged 60 and over no longer had to sign on at an unemployment benefit office in order to qualify for the higher long-term rate of supplementary benefit or to secure national insurance credits. A further complication during this period arose from the switch to fortnightly instead of weekly payment of benefits.

Critics of the government argued, naturally, that the changes in the figures were designed to obscure the true magnitude of the unemployment problem. However, whether or not that was a convenient side-effect of the new statistics, it was not the reason for them. The 1983 Budget changes, for instance, spared the over-sixties the pointless ritual of regular signing on.

The Department of Employment had revised their unemployment series back to 1971 to take account of some of these changes, but some discontinuities remained in their series at the time of this appraisal. The unemployment figures in table 6.1 from 1976 onwards represent an informed estimate which takes account of all the changes; these figures are thus different in coverage from any unemployment figures quoted earlier in this book.

BACK FROM THE ABYSS?

Why did unemployment, which in the heyday of the post-war full employment period thirty years earlier had been no more than 300,000, rise to ten times that figure or more? If we dig into the causes, we find a number of layers.

In part at least the slump in Britain reflected a recession in the whole of the industrialised world. The oil crisis of 1973 was a watershed in the economic history of the OECD countries, and the successive OPEC price increases since then have both stimulated inflation and depressed growth in the non-oil-producing countries, in much the same way as if the OPEC countries had imposed a vast indirect tax on the rest of the world. The oil-importing countries have had either to pay the tax through transferring resources in return to the OPEC countries or to cut down their use of oil. There has been a general tendency for them to take a tougher line on monetary and fiscal policy in order to keep inflation in check and protect their balance of payments.

Nevertheless, it is not the case that the growth process was switched off at a stroke in 1973. After a pause, the growth of industrial output in the OECD countries and the growth of world trade were resumed, though at a less phenomenal rate (see table 6.2). But then the OPEC countries turned the screw again. In 1977, the OPEC 'marker' price for light Arabian oil was $12 a barrel. By 1979 it had crept up to over $13. In the course of 1979 it jumped to $24, and by 1981 it had gone up

Table 6.2: Economic growth before and after the
oil crisis (percentage growth per annum)

	GDP OECD countries %	Exports of manufactures (volume terms) from main industrial countries %
1964–73	4.9	10.4
1973–79	2.7	5.3
1979–82	0.7	1.2

further to $34 a barrel. Though in one sense this fell short of the quadrupling of oil prices in 1973, in fact it involved a bigger price increase and a bigger extra payment by the oil-importing countries since OPEC was now multiplying an already much multiplied price.

This had a depressing impact on industry – more severe on some sectors than on others – through its effects on costs, prices and demand and through the more stringent economic policies adopted by governments in response to the situation. Excess capacity led to intensified trade competition, and this in turn to growing protectionist pressures throughout the world. In particular sectors of trade the newly industrialised countries presented special problems. Even so, the severe fall in output and trade in the industrialised countries after this second escalation in oil prices did not, overall, go as far as Britain's negative growth; and, though unemployment rose throughout the OECD countries, the increase in Britain at the beginning of the 1980s was exceptional. Moreover, self-sufficiency in oil has exempted the United Kingdom from the resource cost effects (though not from the price-inflationary effects) of OPEC policies; that is to say, when the oil price goes up, the 'tax' stays in the UK. It seems unlikely, therefore, that the precipitate take-off of unemployment in Britain in 1980 is to be explained solely by reference to the oil crisis and its aftermath or to the state of the rest of the world.

Let us therefore consider other explanations. There has been a vogue recently for theories about the displacement of human employment by new technology. Historically, new techniques and products have not led to fewer jobs but have employed a growing working population. But the changes involved have required great adjustments in society; if the pace of technological change is speeding up, the required rate of adjustment may be harder. Moreover, the new jobs do not always employ the same people or in the same places as the old ones. Industrial change in the UK has, over the generations, involved great shifts between regions, some growing and some declining. Such shifts must now be occurring, to a greater or lesser extent, not merely between regions but between different parts of the world. But developments of this kind do not take place overnight and could not by themselves account for the sudden fall in economic activity in 1980 and the upsurge in unemployment which followed it. It is much more plausible that, like earlier recessions, this was precipitated by straightforward economic and monetary phenomena operating to depress demand.

Some relatively small proportion of registered unemployment has no doubt resulted from a preference for untaxed social security benefits (possibly topped up in some cases by untaxed earnings from 'moonlighting') rather than taxed pay; and it would be sensible to aim to remove any such disincentive to work when decisions are taken about social security benefits on the one hand, and tax rates at the bottom of the scale on the other. But the rise in unemployment since 1979 cannot conceivably be explained by a sudden rush to join the ranks of the voluntary unemployed.

This rapid rise was superimposed on the development of stagflation over a dozen years or so. The upward trend of wage costs, price inflation and unemployment does not in itself establish that 'workers have priced themselves out of jobs', but if we also go by common observation and the testimony of people in industry it is reasonable to believe that this has been a factor in the situation. We should not use phrases like 'pricing themselves out of jobs' too literally, because the young people who have been coming on to the labour market for the first time are not the people who have produced this situation. Nevertheless, if there has been a shift in the relative cost of labour, this will make it all the more difficult, even with a relatively high level of aggregate demand, to get unemployment back to anything like the levels of the fifties and early sixties. Future pay restraint will not in itself reverse this development, though it could prevent it from getting worse. But we have still to explain why, after inflation had been held in check for the time being, and unemployment had turned down in 1978 and 1979, stagflation gave way to slumpflation in 1980.

If we look for factors special to that point in time, the finger surely points to the soaring exchange rate, linked with the high interest rates which were regarded as a means of discouraging borrowing from the banks, thus damping down the growth in the money supply and inflation. Following the wage explosion of the winter of discontent, it would have required the very opposite – a fall in the exchange rate for the pound – to maintain the price competitiveness of British industry. But instead the rate went up – at times as high as $2.40 in 1980 and early 1981. Roughly 30 per cent of our GDP is accounted for by foreign trade in goods and services. Some companies are affected differently than others by foreign exchange movements, and some coped better than others with the appreciation of sterling, but for much of our industry, and not merely manufacturing industry, it brought a loss of price competitiveness in home and overseas markets which they could not offset by measures within their own power.

This view of the situation was not universally shared at the time. The paradox of a strong pound and a weak economy was bound up with the fact that North Sea oil had been coming rapidly on stream and strengthening the current account of the balance of payments. In one view it was inevitable that other industries should decline to make room for North Sea oil. It was also held that North Sea oil was bound to push the exchange rate up, not so much by its direct effect on the current account as by attracting foreign funds into the UK on the strength of the North Sea revenues which would guarantee the soundness of these holdings; the effect of high interest rates on the standing of the pound was discounted. On either view there was nothing to be done about the exchange rate. However, though the role of North Sea oil – compounded by the volatile psychology of the financial world – was no doubt crucial, all experience suggests that exchange rates *are* influenced by interest rates. Past experience in this country also shows that the balance of payments does better when demand is depressed by a low level of economic activity, as was the case at that time, and this too must have played some part in the current account surplus and the strong exchange rate.

In 1981, the exchange rate and interest rates came down from their peaks and in the second half of the year industrial output began to creep up slowly from its low point. Market forces began to take their revenge on the OPEC cartel. Impelled by the high price of oil, producers everywhere drilled for new supplies; users everywhere economised on oil and bought less. A glut of oil developed and in 1982 the price broke. Early in 1983, the OPEC marker price was reduced to $29 a barrel, and even this could be held only by a drastic cutback in supplies from Saudi Arabia, the dominant producer. Financial markets reacted with their customary volatility to this reduction in

Britain's oil revenues, while relative interest rates were no longer working in favour of sterling. Markets were affected also by speculation about the date of the next general election. The pound, so recently at $2.40, plummeted below the 1976 crisis level – though the effect this time was less critical – and at times fell below $1.50.

By the summer of 1983 industrial output (apart from construction) was a couple of points better than a year earlier, and several points above the mid-1981 trough of the slump, though still far below pre-slump output – all the more so if we take output other than oil and gas. The construction industry remained very depressed. Spending by the consumer public was buoyant, but much of this was going on higher imports. Industry was arguing for a further reduction in interest rates, which had not come down as sharply as price inflation and which were therefore felt to be high in real terms.

The modest revival in output was reflected in higher productivity, especially in manufacturing, rather than higher employment. National statistics did not indicate productivity gains as widespread in industry generally or as impressive as individual experiences might suggest. However, there had been important examples of dramatic reductions in workforces through more efficient use of manpower rather than through cutting output. These were survival measures forced on companies by the slump rather than one of the causes of the slump in the first instance; but, if the shake-out of labour proved more durable than had been the case after earlier and milder recessions, that too would make it the more difficult ever to get unemployment back to where it had been before.

What part did public expenditure policy play in the loss of employment in 1980 and after? If, as I have argued, there was a diversity of factors in the situation, it is unlikely either that the government's expenditure measures – ineffectual, as it turned out – were dominant among them, or that a high public expenditure strategy would have been the right response to all these factors. In practice, though the government broke with the past in rejecting deliberate contracyclical expenditure measures to counter the slump, they found themselves willy nilly financing higher expenditure, not merely on those programmes to which they meant to give priority, but also on unemployment benefit and other unintended programmes resulting from the slump.

Apart from the growth of social security payments, the increase in the defence budget maintained the flow of orders for companies involved in weapons systems, electronics and such like, while the health service continued to expand – though there was a question mark over how long this would be allowed to go on. Thus the three largest programmes all grew. Education, the next largest, was among the programmes which were cut. The severest reductions were in the housing programme; cuts in construction programmes generally, which had already suffered from Labour's cuts in capital programmes, directly affected employment in the private sector. Cuts in civil service and local government manpower – like manpower savings in the private sector – though not among the causes of the slump in the first place, reduced the job opportunities open to the new generation coming on to the labour market. So, within the total of public expenditure, different programmes fared differently, but the total, viewed as a crude aggregate, was not cut, in spite of the government's intended strategy, but increased, whether measured in money terms or real terms or as a percentage of GDP. It was the government's decision not to finance the extra expenditure by extra borrowing, but on the contrary, after that peak borrowing figure in 1980 81, to reduce public borrowing in the depths of the slump, which represented the effective break with neo-Keynesian policy and which was at the heart of the financial strategy – and therefore at the heart of the controversy surrounding it.

The government believed that persistence in this strategy and the conquest of inflation would create the conditions for spontaneous and sustained growth without any financial stimulus from itself. At various earlier stages, during the darker hours of the slump, some Ministers had claimed that we were already emerging into the sunshine, but each time it had proved to be a false dawn.

It is interesting to compare the course of policy in Britain and in the United States. There President Reagan had come to office with policies based on 'supply side economics', not unlike the Conservative government's, relying on cuts in welfare programmes and in taxation to stimulate the economy. But he also embarked on a large increase in defence spending, without securing economies in other programmes on the scale which would have been needed to offset both the tax cuts and the extra defence spending. Unlike the British government, he went ahead with the tax cuts just the same, producing a budget deficit and government borrowings which were enormous by American standards. At first, to counter the inflationary effects of excessive total borrowing, the Federal Reserve Bank raised interest rates to levels which intensified recession in the private sector and slowed down recovery in other countries because of the effects on interest rates there. Such high world interest rates swelled the debt service burden of countries such as Mexico, Brazil and Argentina to unmanageable dimensions, and the prospect of default on their debts raised the spectre of the potential insolvency of major United States banks which had lent enormous amounts to those countries. It was this threat to large parts of the banking system which finally induced the Fed to abate interest rates, and this, together with lower oil prices and the budget deficit, led to a strong upturn in the United States economy by mid-1983 without, as yet, a revival of price inflation. Growth appeared to be making something of a come-back in other major economies also, though mostly at a rate which was probably nearer to our own recent improvement than to the pace of the American upturn.

The question mark in the United States was how long this relaxation of monetary policy could last; cynics held that it would last until after the next Presidential election. In Britain the question in the summer of 1983 was whether the rather Delphic economic indicators[1] signified that the upturn which had taken place would develop into sustained recovery. Whatever the answer, the outlook for the unemployed remained discouraging, though the rate of increase in their number was slowing down considerably and there was a prospect that unemployment might soon reach a plateau.

ALL YOU EVER WANTED TO KNOW ABOUT THE PSBR

What is the public sector borrowing requirement – the PSBR for short? It is a creation of the Treasury's – the concept is not used at all in France or the United States, for instance, where attention is focused on the central government budget deficit, and was not in use in this country until the late 1960s – and it is what the Treasury say it is, i.e. borrowing by public sector bodies. It is who does the borrowing that counts, not where the borrowings come from. Thus the PSBR is the sum of the three bottom lines in the flow-chart in Appendix III: it consists of the central government borrowing requirement (the CGBR), plus the market and overseas borrowings of the nationalised industries and certain other public corporations, plus the market and overseas borrowings of the local authorities.

Although the government has shareholdings in undertakings such as

---

[1] Statistics for the first half of 1983, which became available later, showed an unusually large discrepancy between the output measure of GDP (which is generally considered the best indicator of short-term trends) and the expenditure measure. The average measure of GDP was 3 per cent higher in the first half of 1983 than a year earlier, but still 3 per cent below its peak level reached in 1979.

BL which operate as companies, the nationalised industries such as the National Coal Board and other public corporations such as the New Towns Corporations (in the flow-chart I use the term nationalised industries as shorthand to cover both types of public corporation) are not companies governed by the Companies Acts but are governed by the statutes under which they were set up. All of them fall fairly and squarely within the public sector and the PSBR. Denationalisation or 'privatisation' can be effected by selling off the assets of a public corporation, or by transferring the assets to a government-owned company set up for the purpose and then selling shares in the company. So long as the government keep the shares and keep control of the company, it is still a public sector body and its borrowings should still form part of the PSBR. The criteria used by the Treasury relate to control as well as to ownership. Thus the British Petroleum Company has always been excluded from the public sector figures, even when the government owned a majority of the shares, because of the self-denying ordinance under which the government had declared that they would not intervene in the management of the company. Margaret Thatcher's Conservative government declared themselves ready to follow this precedent if the privatisation of publicly owned industries still left them with a majority shareholding after a minority of the shares had been sold off.

Why did the government attach so much importance to the PSBR? The official answer[2] can be summarised as follows. A reduction in the PSBR over a period of years was to play a crucial part in the medium-term financial strategy, and would make it possible to achieve a progressive reduction in the rate of monetary growth while at the same time reducing interest rates. This would in turn reduce inflation. But it is not immediately obvious why a lower PSBR has this effect on the money supply, or why a higher PSBR, if financed in a non-inflationary way by genuine savings, must have the opposite effect. Let us therefore try to put a little flesh on the bare bones of the argument.

A lower PSBR means that the government can finance its borrowings without either 'printing' money (i.e. without creating too much additional money through the banking system, the inflationary effects of which were discussed in chapter 3, in the section on 'The Limits of Public Expenditure') or pushing up interest rates to attract savings. The government is then left to cope only with private sector demand for money, and it is less likely that interest rates will have to be pushed up to very high levels to damp this down.

Conversely, a borrowing requirement that remains high, and even more so one that keeps going up, will either drive the government into printing money or require continuously rising interest rates to persuade investors to add to their already large stock of government securities. This will tend to undermine confidence in the currency and feed inflationary expectations, because it will not seem plausible that the process can go on indefinitely; even if the government is still funding its large borrowing requirement by sales of securities to savers, there is likely to be a belief that sooner or later it will have to resort to printing money.

As to the further connection, as seen in the official literature,[2] between monetary policy and inflation and employment: '. . . over a period, any reduction in the money stock will eventually lead mainly to a reduction in prices rather than output. But in the shorter run, there may be some loss of output and jobs.' Written in mid-1980, three years later that last sentence seemed in retrospect something of an understatement.

However, monetarist observers believed that, in spite of the discarding of the original money supply targets, the progressive reduction of the PSBR as a percentage of GDP in three successive Budgets could be given credit for the slowing down of inflation, and that this had been achieved broadly through the mechanism described above. A belief that public finances were under control (in spite of the creeping growth of public expenditure, which was less worrying because of reduced government borrowing, and which was to some extent disguised by the lower borrowing requirement) had created increased confidence in the currency and people were more prepared to hold money.

On an alternative view, the mechanism through which reduced government borrowings affected private sector wages and prices was by worsening the deficiency in effective demand, thus adding to the fear of closures and redundancies and weakening wage pressures. A high exchange rate, by making foreign goods and materials cheaper, helped to reduce inflation in two ways – through increasing the fear of unemployment and reducing the cost of living. The break in the oil price also helped. In the public sector, government policy operated more directly to de-escalate pay increases by refusing to provide cash for settlements beyond a defined point, and by a preparedness to see industrial disputes through to the end. Legislation to reduce trade

[2] Cf. an extensive article on 'Monetary policy and the economy' in the July 1980 issue of the Treasury's Economic Progress Report and the Treasury press notice which accompanied it.

union immunities was a further element in the changing industrial climate which reduced inflationary pressures and strengthened the hand of management. Some of these were measures which monetarists had urged in order to reinforce monetary policy but which any hard-headed person might well have favoured.

The next question is why this restrictive policy on government borrowing should extend to the PSBR as a whole and thus embrace the borrowings of the nationalised industries. It is true that the nationalised industries are partly responsible for the size of the central government's borrowings, to the extent that they obtain money through the National Loans Fund which the government has raised on their behalf, but in principle this arrangement could be ended and they could go to the market for all their loan funds. However, they would then be competing for the same gilt-edged funds as the government itself. This would manifestly be the case if – as has been the normal arrangement in the case of their past market borrowings – they enjoyed a Treasury guarantee, though even with a guarantee the nationalised industries have in the past had to pay a fractionally higher rate of interest than the government itself. But even if they went to the market without a guarantee and ostensibly on their own credit, in practice they would still be regarded as having the government behind them. Thus the same total requirements for government and government-backed stock would have to be met. It is worth noting that in the United States – where, as I have said, there is no all-inclusive aggregate of public borrowing – it is the treatment of spending by various public bodies as 'off budget', and the exclusion of federal borrowing to finance them from the general run of budget deficit figures, that attracts some criticism.

Whatever the rationale, the new emphasis on the PSBR gave a new twist to the perennial problem of reconciling the government's objectives on the management of the economy with the objectives of the public corporations in managing their businesses. Throughout the thirty years or more that we had had a large public sector of industry there had been a problem over devising a satisfactory régime for these industries. This was of course aggravated by changes of government and policy, which, for instance, brought us full circle from the Heath government's policy of forcing the nationalised industries into deficit, in order to hold down prices, to the policy adopted in the early days of Margaret Thatcher's government of forcing those industries which were capable of it into large price increases, in the name of economic pricing but also in order to make a financial surplus and reduce public spending and borrowing. Privatisation could be regarded, not only as a method of raising money from the disposal of assets or shares and a means of getting the bodies thus privatised out of the PSBR, but also as a final solution to the problem of relationships.

As the recession deepened, there was increasing frustration, not only among the nationalised industries but also in the construction and project industries which looked to the public sector for orders, at the fact that capital investment that was claimed to be financially profitable, or of importance to the nation, was subject to the constraints of the PSBR and of external financial limits (EFLs) – the equivalent in this field of cash limits – on the amount of money that the nationalised industries were allowed to obtain from the government or the market. The Confederation of British Industries – like many others who favour economy in general but expenditure in particular – while pressing for reductions in total public expenditure, especially in the salary bill for the civil service and other public services, campaigned for more public money to be spent on contracts of interest to their member companies and industries. Frustration was increased when the Treasury were reported to be changing the rules and insisting that any government guarantees for private sector involvement in joint projects must count against the PSBR. This turned out to be a piece of misreporting, but in general the Treasury remained unconvinced about the economic case for most of the disputed projects or the financial case for various unconventional methods proposed for financing them.

The system of EFLs nevertheless has great advantages over the régime which preceded it, when for practical purposes there was at times no control over the financing of nationalised industry deficits from the National Loans Fund. EFLs for public sector industries are as useful an instrument for financial management and pay restraint as cash limits are in Whitehall Departments. But the EFL system sets problems for the nationalised industries which do not arise in fixing cash limits for spending Departments, since the nationalised industries are not just spenders but also revenue earners. Their external financial requirements, like the PSBR itself, are the difference between expenditure and revenue, which can be highly volatile. They are therefore difficult to forecast with accuracy even for the financial year ahead – all the more so when the forecasts are called for well in advance of the financial year – and it would be rather unreasonable if nationalised industries were forced to project their requirements for several years ahead and then held rigorously to these figures.

Most of the schemes which were floated for somehow circumventing the constraints of the PSBR and EFLs in order to secure more funds for public sector investment were likely to prove ephemeral and are therefore not discussed here, but one which was more likely to stay on the agenda was the proposal, at one time taken up by the new Social Democratic Party, for a North Sea Fund as a channel for part of the revenue from North Sea oil. Some versions of the scheme are more explicit than others about hypothecating North Sea revenue, i.e. earmarking it so that it can go only into the Fund and not into the general pool of revenue. The most specific example of hypothecation in the past was the old scheme of Road Fund Licences under which duty paid by each car owner (now paid to the Department of Transport as Vehicle Excise Duty) went into a Road Fund and helped to pay for road building. The nearest modern example is the earmarking of import duties as part of the European Community's *ressources propres*, but these are paid to the Community via the Consolidated Fund and not direct from Customs and Excise.

It is understandable that people are frustrated at the fact that more primitive countries which produce oil have used the revenue from it to finance industrial and social development, while in Britain both have been cut back since North Sea oil came on stream. Nevertheless a North Sea Fund would in itself do nothing, except perhaps presentationally, to remove their frustration. If the required amount of North Sea revenue or any other revenue could be spared, it could quite simply be channelled to increase the amount available for roads, railways, the Scottish and Welsh Development Agencies, and so on, in the conventional way through Departmental Votes and the National Loans Fund. On the other hand, if there is nothing to spare, diverting some of the oil revenue for a North Sea Fund would leave the government short of that amount for their other outgoings and would create a need for extra taxation or borrowing.

A government embarking on a recovery programme might well decide to allocate an extra amount for investment. They might conceivably find some symbolic value in attaching some kind of North Sea label to the allocation. There is nothing to prevent this from being done through the existing public expenditure machinery. Resort to hypothecation would not be helpful from the point of view of control and accountability – the example of the Community's management of its *ressources propres* is not encouraging – and could revive the aspirations of Scottish nationalists to achieve the hypothecation of North Sea revenue for the exclusive benefit of an autonomous Scotland. However, these institutional questions would not make any difference to the judgment required on the size of public expenditure, taxation and the borrowing requirement.

WILL FUNNY MONEY HAVE THE LAST LAUGH?

In the 1981 public expenditure exercise a radical new step was taken which attracted little notice at the time but which could lead into a whole new minefield. During their first two years the Conservative government had operated the PESC system which they inherited practically unchanged, apart from reducing the survey period by a year. This meant that the constant price basis, the much derided funny money, was still used for medium-term planning, in contrast to 'the principle that cash determines volume during the year' which was applied a year at a time through the cash limits system.

But in the 1981 review it was decided to drop constant prices and carry out the survey in cash terms. After a number of possible compromises had been debated within the Treasury, opinion suddenly crystallised in favour of going the whole hog. Programmes for Year 1, the year in which the survey was carried out, were to be expressed in current cash prices. Programmes for year 2, the financial year immediately ahead, were to be calculated on the assumption that the rate of inflation over the previous year would be 7 per cent. The rates of inflation assumed for the following two years were 6 per cent and 5 per cent, giving the sequence shown in figure 6.1.

Survey year	Price basis
Year 1 (1981–82) programmes	1981–82 prices
Year 2 (1982–83) programmes	Year 1 prices plus 7%
Year 3 (1983–84) programmes	Year 2 prices plus 6%
Year 4 (1984–85) programmes	Year 3 prices plus 5%

Figure 6.1

Monetarist philosophy apart, there were good practical reasons for wanting to break away from the old survey prices, which were based on the price levels prevailing some months before the start of the survey, in order to get a firm historical point of departure. By the end of the annual exercise, inflation rendered these price levels all the more out of date. In the 1981 White Paper, for instance, total public expenditure for 1981–82, including net debt interest, was projected at around £84 billion in 1980 survey prices. The projected cash equivalent was over £110 billion, more than 30 per cent higher. There is a certain unreality in taking collective Ministerial decisions in terms of prices so far removed from what is currently happening in the economy. On the receipts side, the natural basis for projecting revenue is in cash terms, on given assumptions about inflation, and there would be obvious advantages in projecting revenue and expenditure in conjunction and on a common cash basis. Moreover, a significant proportion of government expenditure consists of transfer payments, such as social security and debt interest, and under the old system a certain tortuousness was involved in seeking to express these cash programmes in volume terms; to project cash programmes in cash terms is a more natural course.

Conditions were now more favourable for the change than when I had toyed with the idea in 1976 but given it up. To start with there was the changed philosophical climate; I doubt whether the primacy of cash over volume programmes, not merely for one year ahead but for the medium term, would have been negotiable under the previous government. Secondly, cash limits, which paved the way for this further change, were a new thing in 1976, whereas their primacy on a year-by-year basis had now been established. Finally, at the start of the 1976 survey, inflation was still running at over 20 per cent, and at 16 per cent at the start of the 1977 survey. At the start of the 1981 exercise the rate of inflation was about 13 per cent and falling, so that it was a somewhat less heroic undertaking to plan on the assumption of single figure inflation in the years ahead.

Nevertheless, what were the chances that inflation in the subsequent three years would be 7 per cent, 6 per cent and 5 per cent? What was to happen if the inflation rate turned out to be, say, twice as high as that? Would volume programmes be cut to fit this new bed of Procrustes? In that case the real value of programmes would be cut by 15 per cent over the three years. Or would programmes be re-worked on the basis of prices nearer to the actual rate of inflation? In that event the outcome would be one which I had anticipated when looking at this problem in 1976, and the cash prices used for the survey would themselves become constant prices of a sort.

It is of course common practice in industry to prepare forward estimates in cash terms on fairly arbitrary assumptions about future price changes, and to revise the figures from time to time according to how things go, but the problems involved for industry in making projections of this kind are rather different from those involved for governments. If the government appear to be predicting a particular rate of inflation, that has a political significance which does not attach to a company's inflation assumptions. A government fighting inflation is more or less obliged, if it publishes forward plans on a cash basis, to project inflation coming down at a rate which is very likely to be unrealistic.

So my assessment at the time was that the move away from planning in terms of historical constant prices was to be welcomed, and the experiment in cash projections should be given a fair wind, but that, unless and until we could assume low inflation rates with confidence that they would actually happen, there would probably have to be some compromise between cash planning and programming in real terms over the medium term – meaning any period longer than a single year ahead.

In practice, the new cash planning system was implemented more successfully in the first two years than I had expected. Although total planned expenditure was exceeded, that was because of other developments. The original 7 per cent inflation assumption for 1982–83 was replaced, before the start of the year, by a 4 per cent figure for pay, together with a 9 per cent assumption for non-pay items, which corresponded more closely to the way in which inflation was now coming down. These two figures were designed to produce about the same result on average as the original 7 per cent. The intention was that, if actual pay increases proved to be above the 4 per cent figure – which had now ceased to be merely an assumption but was described as a 'pay planning factor' – then the excess had to be found by economies in the provision for staff costs. (Something similar had happened in 1981–82 when pay increases of 7½ per cent were squeezed, after prolonged industrial action, out of cash limits designed to accommodate increases of only 6 per cent.) After the event, the average rate of inflation in 1982–83 (as measured by the GDP deflator, which can produce different results from the retail price index) was judged to be 7 per cent. Thus the Treasury got through the first year under the new system without any general adjustment to the allowances made for pay and price increases.

In the next (1982) public expenditure survey the cash programmes from the survey before, plus or minus any agreed changes in between, provided the base-line figures for the new exercise. With each survey a new final year comes into the survey exercise; in the 1982 exercise this was dealt with by a small percentage increase over the year before which, in effect if not overtly, amounted to provision for inflation in the final year at a reducing rate. Volume programmes no longer appeared at all, but Departments were free to argue for some improvement on the base-line figures if they were inadequate, while the Treasury was free to argue for reductions. So far as 1983–84 was concerned, the original inflation assumption of 6 per cent which had been built into the base-line figures more than covered the actual rate of inflation which emerged during the year. Thus the system appeared to be working well in its second year also.

Nevertheless, by mid-1983 it seemed to me that cash planning, operated in this way, had reached a cross-over point, and that it was likely to run into increasing trouble. The reason for this was that, while the public expenditure exercises rolled programmes forward from one year to another on the assumption of a continuous decline in inflation, in other contexts the government were projecting some upturn in the rate of inflation. Once the cash allowed for inflation dipped below actual inflation, it would be possible to stick to the figures only by squeezing programmes in volume terms.

In the first flush of the Treasury's conversion to cash planning, the down-grading of the concept of volumes was carried to such an extent that, in the 1982 public expenditure White Paper, programmes were expressed in money terms only, even for past periods, so that one had no idea what had actually been happening to programmes in real terms. My own feeling was that, though volumes had been officially outlawed, they had gone underground rather than fled the country. When Departments responsible for goods and services programmes (as distinct from transfer payments programmes) argue with the Treasury about the adequacy of the figures, the concept of adequacy must surely be related to some concept of volume. In the special case of defence, our NATO commitment was to increase the defence budget in real terms, so here quite clearly the dialogue could not be conducted purely in cash terms.

This obscurantism about the real trend in public expenditure was modified in the 1983 White Paper to the extent that, for past years and the year about to start (1983–84), the main cash programmes were supplemented by a table expressing them in cost terms, i.e. adjusted for the general rate of inflation. But programmes for 1984–85 onwards were shown in cash terms only. The Treasury would have claimed that they were not in fact in a position to translate these figures into cost terms in advance of the assumptions about the GDP deflator which were to be disclosed somewhat later, at the time of the Budget. (The brief experiment in publishing the public expenditure White Paper at the same time as the Budget, which had at the time been put down to virtue rather than to mere slippage in the timing of the White Paper, had evidently been discontinued.) When the Budget material did appear, it indicated an expected inflation rate (measured by the GDP deflator) of 5½ per cent in 1984–85 and 5 per cent in 1985–86, as compared with the uplift of 5 per cent and 4 per cent respectively which had been built into the base-line figures for those years. This implied a modest but increasing degree of under-indexation and a consequent modest but increasing squeeze on the real value of programmes, as a result, not of any explicit policy decision to cut real programmes, but of the operation of the cash planning system.[3]

This was in effect confirmed by a table which was produced in response to a Parliamentary Question[4] and which translated future programmes from cash to 'cost terms' on the basis of the expected inflation rates used in connection with the Budget. Expressed in these terms, practically all programmes, including health and personal social services, would have their real value cut after 1983–84, and even defence would increase by less than the 3 per cent in real terms which was regarded as a NATO commitment. It is astonishing that these figures passed practically unnoticed and that the problem inherent in them seems to have been hardly recognised at the time in Whitehall, let alone outside it. Forward estimates of the GDP deflator would no doubt remain subject to revision downwards as well as upwards. But if, when the time came, we had a Chancellor who set out to hold his colleagues to the cash plans for future years, irrespective of the actual trend in inflation and its effects on the real value of the figures, the situation contained a built-in clash with spending Ministers; something quite like this was in fact to take place after the election – but that would take us outside the period which we are covering.

In this situation, though it was too soon to pass final judgment on the new system, it was difficult to see how the assumption of continuously reducing inflation could be maintained indefinitely. This went beyond the German system, as I understood it in my time on this front, of forward cash budgeting on the basis of a low but stable inflation rate, which corresponded to the actual behaviour of the German economy at that time. Without wanting to turn the clock back to the old régime of artificial survey prices, I was reinforced in my doubts as to whether it would be possible altogether to jettison the concept of volume in the forward planning of physical programmes.

---

[3]Admittedly, with the passage of time, the effect on cash programmes of inflation assumptions made in the past becomes harder to disentangle from the many other developments affecting the figures. The 1983 White Paper stated that cash plans for future years 'do not depend on specific assumptions about future price changes . . .' However, apart from the ambiguity of the term 'depend', the same passage concedes that these plans 'are generally consistent with the Government's intention that the rate of inflation should continue to fall' (Cmnd. 8789–1, p. 10).
[4]Hansard, 17 March 1983: Written Answers, Cols 240–242.

My preferred option would have been to continue the new practice of planning programmes for the year immediately ahead in cash terms, but on a reasonably realistic inflation assumption and retaining flexibility to adjust the price assumptions in the closing stages of the survey; any required volume squeeze would be a matter for explicit policy decision. For the later years of the survey period, I should be inclined to assume zero inflation – which would amount to making no assumption about inflation in those years; that is to say, programmes for the later years would be on the same price basis as the first year ahead, but in the following survey a fresh, reasonably realistic assumption would be made for one year ahead, and this in turn would provide the price basis for all future years, until the next survey came round. Let cash limits rule, but for a year at a time, on the basis of figures fixed shortly before the year to which they apply.

It would be unfortunate if the principle of cash limits were to be undermined, either because the idea of cash budgeting as a medium-term rather than a short-term instrument is taken too far, or because too much weight is put on cash limits as an instrument of policy, without a sufficient degree of acceptance for the policies themselves. But dissidents should direct their criticisms at the policies, not at the instrument. For cash limits, which in essence simply put a figure on the rate of inflation that the government will finance in the coming year, have at the same time proved a uniquely effective instrument of good housekeeping.

ON THE EVE OF THE LANDSLIDE

The election was announced on 9 May 1983, when the government had nearly a year left of its term of office, and took place on 9 June. Before we go on let us bring together a few miscellaneous developments of relevance to our public expenditure theme, starting with the fate of the Central Policy Review Staff. Under Margaret Thatcher, it had ceased to have any special role in the annual public expenditure exercise. After Berrill left the CPRS to become head of a firm of stockbrokers, he was succeeded by Robin Ibbs, an industrialist from ICI who, as head of the CPRS, concentrated on industrial issues, on which he was believed to carry a good deal of weight with Ministers, though he kept a low public profile. In due course he rejoined his company, though he was to return to Whitehall after the election, succeeding Derek Rayner as head of what had by then become the Efficiency Unit, reporting direct to the Prime Minister. John Sparrow, a merchant banker, became the third – and, as it turned out, the last – holder of the top CPRS post under this Conservative government. He re-expanded somewhat the scope of the thinktank's work, and it was involved, among other things, in the abortive attempt to persuade Cabinet to look at radical expenditure options in the autumn of 1982. Some regarded the adverse publicity attracted by this incident as the main reason for the Prime Minister's decision to wind up the CPRS immediately after the election; others did not believe that that *affaire* had played such an important part in this decision, but that more generally the Prime Minister did not find the CPRS of any great value in her scheme of things.

Her tendency, rather, was to build up a little the limited resources available to her in No. 10 and to get a more direct hold on some of the levers of policy. In addition to the Policy Unit, she had recruited Professor Alan Walters as economic adviser in No. 10 and, after the Falklands, she acquired for No. 10 a senior diplomat from the Foreign and Commonwealth Office to help in monitoring developments on that front. There was a good deal of public discussion of the question whether we were moving towards a Prime Minister's Department (such as exists in Australia, for instance), but neither before nor immediately after the election did such appointments amount to more than a limited reinforcement of the Prime Minister's office – falling far short of the massive recruitment of problem-solvers from industry to the heart of government which was advocated by John Hoskyns, at one time head of the Policy Unit, who had quit in disenchantment.

In the House of Commons, as part of the replacement of 'subject committees' by Select Committees monitoring particular Departments, the Select Committee on Expenditure was replaced by the Select Committee on the Treasury and Civil Service, which had a wider remit than its predecessor over the whole field of economic and financial policy. Its rather ambitious recommendations on reform of the Budget process[5] led to a much more limited but still quite significant innovation in the form of an Autumn Statement by the Chancellor. This amounted to a preview in November of expenditure programmes for the coming financial year and, in a less detailed way, of the fiscal outlook for that year. As yet, however, the Commons had hardly taken advantage of the Autumn Statement as an occasion for seeking to influence the specific Budget decisions which were still to be made. Little or no progress had been made in developing other

[5] These recommendations were based on a report prepared by the Institute of Fiscal Studies, with William Armstrong (who died not very long after) in the lead.

ideas for giving the Commons an enhanced role – such as a right of approval of the borrowing requirement – in controlling the nation's finances.

On the EEC front, the predictable crisis over the Community budget was now close at hand. Following an escalation in the cost of the common agricultural policy, there was a prospect that the financial resources available to the Community would before long quite simply fall short of the amounts required to finance its programmes. The EEC Commission proposed an increase in the 1 per cent VAT contribution of member countries. (Appendix II should be consulted for a slightly fuller description of the EEC's finances.) There was little appetite among European governments for radical reform of the CAP in the face of entrenched farm interests now joined even in Britain by those farmers, such as growers of cereals, who gained from high CAP support prices. The situation was further complicated by the accession of Greece and the prospective accession of Spain and Portugal, all with special agricultural interests.

Britain started by opposing any increase in the Community's resources. She later came round to the idea of some compromise on this, while still seeking to limit the cost of the CAP, and also stipulating a 'safety net' through which a country's net contribution to the EEC budget would be related to its GDP. As it was, the only two net contributors in most years were West Germany, one of the richer member countries, and (even after refunds) the UK, now reduced to having one of the lowest GDPs per head in the Community. As regards refunds, following the reliefs which had been secured for 1980 and 1981, a similar arrangement was agreed for 1982, but was in part held up by the European Parliament. A meeting of EEC Heads of Government to discuss budgetary problems, which was to have taken place in June 1983, was postponed because of the general election in Britain; when it did take place after the election, a figure was agreed for a refund of Britain's contribution in 1983, but its payment depended not only on approval by the European Parliament but also on a settlement of the wider problems of the Community budget.

On the general public expenditure front, the total had gone up by 2 per cent or more in real terms in each of the four years up to 1982–83, the last full financial year before the election. (These figures are on the Getting and Spending definitions; a series of figures on this basis going back to 1959 is to be found at table A.1 in Appendix I.) A further increase was in prospect during the election year itself. The Treasury tended to quote a rather differently based 'planning total', which gives a lower rate of increase (see table A.2 in Appendix I.) On either basis, the increase was not high compared to the spending explosions in some earlier years, but it had to be contrasted with the government's intention to cut expenditure, not increase it. The government's supporters found some consolation for this setback in the better than expected success of the programme of privatisation of publicly owned industries and companies[6] and disposals of publicly owned assets; this form of cutting the public sector became to some extent a kind of psychological substitute for cutting public expenditure. The receipts from these sales also brought some material help to the government's accounts.

Because the increase in expenditure took place while the national output of wealth was either falling or not increasing very fast, public expenditure grew as a percentage of GDP – from 40½ per cent in 1978–79 to about 44 per cent in 1981–82, and it was still above 43 per cent in the following year (see tables A.1 and A.3 in Appendix I).

As we have seen, during the years of high economic growth there had been an upward trend in the ratio of public expenditure to GDP in the OECD countries generally. There has also been a long-term shift, which will no doubt go on, from employment in production industries to employment in the service industries, as technology enables production to be carried out with less manpower; this has made it possible for more people to be employed in the public services outside the market sector of the economy as well as in service industries in the market sector. But there is an important difference between the two, in that people pay for services provided commercially out of their take-home pay as a matter of choice, while they pay for public services through taxation which reduces their take-home pay. A working woman who may choose to pay the astonishing amount of £5 or £10 for a monthly or even a weekly hair-do, because that is her personal priority, would part much less readily with an extra £5 or £10 a month or a week by way of income tax or national insurance contributions. She might be more reconciled to the loss if she believed that her money helped to pay for services which were not only needed but also economically managed, and that it was not the

---

[6] The privatised enterprises included British Aerospace, Cable and Wireless, Britoil (which took with it the exploration and development interests of BNOC, leaving that body only with its trading responsibilities), the National Freight Corporation (now renamed the National Freight Consortium), the British Transport Docks Board (renamed Allied British Ports), and a company called Amersham International, which achieved fame when the sale of its shares on privatisation was enormously oversubscribed.

METROLAND

Note: Metroland is a closed economy employing 10 million car workers in the market sector and 10 million social workers in the non-market sector.

Key Statistics	£ billion at 1981 prices
Market sector	
Income from cars sold:	
to car workers	50
to social workers	50
Total gross income	100
Tax deducted	45
National savings	5
Non-Market sector	
Value of services provided:	
to car workers	50
to social workers	50
Gross public service pay bill	100
Tax deducted	45
National savings	5
Financial Statement and Budget Report	
Output of goods	100
Output of services	100
GDP	200
Public expenditure	100
Financed by:	
taxes on the market sector	45
taxes on the non-market sector	45
Total taxation	90
Public sector borrowing requirement (= national savings)	10
Ratio of public expenditure to GDP	50%

Figure 6.2

primary purpose of the tax increase to provide more jobs and increased union membership in central and local government.

By way of shorthand let us use the term 'car workers' for everyone in the market sector of the economy and 'cars' as shorthand for all the goods and services they produce. Let us use the term 'social workers' as shorthand for everyone in the non-market sector paid from the public purse. The social workers will of course want roughly the same standards of transport as the car workers, who must produce and sell enough cars for everyone. The car workers must also pay enough tax, or buy enough national savings, to enable the government (who are themselves in the social worker category) to pay the take-home salaries of the social workers. So part of the car worker's output and pay goes on cars for himself: the rest goes on cars for the social workers. In return for forgoing part of his output and pre-tax pay the car worker gets whatever services he needs from the social workers. (See figure 6.2.) If we are to have more social workers, or to supply those we have with more cars, the car workers must produce more cars and divide the extra output and the extra sales income between themselves, through higher take-home pay, and the social workers, through higher tax deductions and national savings.

The parable of the car workers and the social workers is simply another way of making the point that the total of public expenditure which can be sustained, including the public service payroll, depends on the size of the national output and income which can be generated and the proportion of it which can be siphoned off by taxation and government borrowing. This is of course an over-simplified model. Public expenditure does not consist entirely of 'goods and services' programmes, which involve the direct employment of public servants or the indirect employment of people making goods for the public services; the total also includes 'transfer payments', such as social security benefits. In a more sophisticated model (which I may attempt in another work) we would have another category in the non-market sector, whom we will call pensioners, standing for everyone receiving transfer payments. But our parable still applies, because the car workers have not only to produce cars for themselves but must also produce enough cars for the social workers and pensioners and these have to be paid for out of taxation (including national insurance contributions) and government borrowing.

There is no particular figure which is sacrosanct for all time as the ratio of public expenditure to GDP, but experience suggests that the shift of six percentage points between 1964–65 and 1967–68 was too rapid and that the resulting 40 per cent (approximately) of GDP was too high in the circumstances of the time. The same can be said of the shift of nearly eight percentage points from 1971–72 to 1975–76, which produced a ratio of 45–46 per cent. Though this was later brought down to 40 per cent, the taxation required to finance it was still high; at any rate, both major parties felt it necessary to promise to reduce taxation in their 1979 manifestos.

In a slump, other things being equal, it is almost inevitable that public expenditure will rise in relation to GDP. But the money still has to be found to pay for it. Whether the government should be prepared to borrow more in order to finance a stimulus to the economy, instead of reducing its borrowings in pursuit of its anti-inflationary strategy, was a central issue in the election campaign of 1983. The manifesto of the Liberal–SDP Alliance set out a programme of selective additional expenditure and tax reliefs (but also some withdrawals of personal tax reliefs) designed to reduce unemploy ment by 1 million over two years; public borrowing would be in-creased from £8 billion to £11 billion a year. (The extra £3 billion was, incidentally, no more than the margin of error in the Budget forecasts of the borrowing requirement in some previous years, but of course the proposed £11 billion would itself be subject to a margin of error.) The Alliance manifesto also sought a specific mandate for an incomes policy.

The Labour Party's manifesto proposed a massive emergency pro-gramme for expansion at a cost of £11 billion, which was said to entail an additional borrowing requirement of £6 billion. This would lead into a five-year programme designed to provide 2½ million jobs. 'And where will the money come from?' asked the preface to the manifesto. 'Some of it will come from those oil revenues now pouring down the drain. Some of it will come from the billions we waste on the dole queues. Some of it will come from the billions now being allowed to be exported in investment abroad. Yes, and some of it will be borrowed'.

The Conservative manifesto was brief and unspecific about public expenditure. In the next Parliament a Conservative government would maintain firm control of public spending and borrowing; it would continue with a financial strategy which would gradually re-duce the growth of money in circulation – and so go on bringing inflation down. In the course of the election campaign, Conservative Ministers rejected charges (based on the leaked options exercise of the previous September) that they had a 'secret manifesto' involving the dismantling of the welfare state, and the Prime Minister declared that the National Health Service was safe with them. In an earlier statement (in a television interview after her return from a visit to the Falklands) she had indicated that the government's strategy now was to stabilise public expenditure and thus reduce it as a percentage of GDP as the economy grew; this strategy was to be explicitly confirmed by the new Chancellor, Nigel Lawson, after the election. But what were the practical implications of this strategy? The outgoing Chancellor, Sir Geoffrey Howe, had said during the election campaign that the government's expenditure plans were laid out in the public expenditure White Paper for all to see. To see, yes, but not to understand. The last public expenditure White Paper (Cmnd 8789) had shown a continuing increase in cash terms, but it was impossible to tell from the White Paper what this implied in real terms. When adjusted (though not in the White Paper itself) for the expected rate of inflation, the Planning Total did appear to be stable for the rest of the White Paper period. However, within this total, as we have seen in the discussion of the cash planning system, many individual programmes, including health and personal social services, would be cut in real terms, if these were treated as binding figures and if inflation conformed to the latest pre-election forecasts. It was therefore inherent in this situation that there would be a renewed tug-of-war between the Treasury and spending Departments after the election. It was not out of the question that the inflation forecasts would become more favourable after the election, but the fact remained that, under the cash planning system and the chosen method of operating it, the real size of programmes was at hazard and depended on how far actual inflation in a particular year corresponded to the allowance made for it three years earlier.

As everyone knows, the Conservatives won the election with a minority of the popular vote but, because of the divided opposition, an overwhelming majority of seats, creating electoral records galore. On the one hand 'no government this century has achieved an increase in its majority on anything like this scale' (David Blake in *The Times*); on the other hand 'in fact it was the lowest winning percentage of the vote any Conservative leader has had since Bonar Law' (Adam Raphael in the *Observer*). With the prospect of a second term of office in which to do it, the new Chancellor took on not merely the immediate problem of trying to make the White Paper figures stick, but the underlying and longer-term problem of trying to make the financial strategy stick – assuming, as he did, that this remained the right strategy.

WHERE DO WE GO FROM HERE?

The post-war period covered by this book has been, to sum up, one of decline in Britain's relative place in the world and of adjustment from the role of imperial power to membership of the European Community. It was also, up to 1979, a period of relatively slow economic growth compared to the growth rates achieved over much of this time in Europe and Japan and, more recently, in the newly industrialised countries such as Korea or Singapore. Because of the time taken to run down our post-war military commitments and financial liabilities, together with basic weaknesses in industrial performance, development was punctuated by stop–go phases and, until the last few years, recurring balance of payments crises.

History, class structure and the absence of proportional representation resulted in what was in effect, prior to the 1983 election, a two-party system, each of the two major parties taking turns in office. An initial degree of consensus on social and economic policy has progressively given way to an increasing polarisation of policies, with each incoming government attempting to reverse their predecessors' efforts. This discontinuity of policy has not occurred in other major OECD countries, including the United States, Canada, Japan, the Federal German Republic or France since de Gaulle, until the advent of Mitterand. Nevertheless, the force of events drove successive British governments to modify or reverse their manifesto policies and to adopt measures more like those of their predecessors than they would have wished. The creation of the Social Democrat–Liberal alliance as a potential third force in British politics was in part a reaction against this pattern of events.

Against this background, public expenditure developed in a seesaw fashion. Phases in which it shot up ahead of economic growth, were followed by bouts of expenditure cutting. Until the advent of North Sea oil, the cutbacks were generally precipitated by a balance of payments crisis and the need for foreign exchange support from the IMF and foreign central banks, though it is rather hard on the foreign bankers if they are blamed for the fact that we needed their money. In spite of all this, technological change and economic growth (which for much of the time averaged something like 3 per cent) were enough to change consumption levels and the way people live in Britain out of all recognition, and to enable a rising share of the national wealth to be spent on public services side by side with the rise in personal standards of living. The percentage of GDP going to public expenditure has risen from around 33 per cent in 1959 to a figure oscillating between 40 per cent and 45 per cent since 1973, a development in line with the experience of other OECD countries, though the pace and degree of this development in Britain produced problems. It was therefore possible, until quite recently, to argue that these material gains, in conjunction with the quality of life which had been retained (Northern Ireland apart), were not a bad trade-off. But there was always doubt whether it would be a stable trade-off if we could not improve our industrial and economic performance, and the depression in fact brought a deterioration both materially and in the quality of life in the cities.

After over thirty years of more or less full use of productive capacity, in spite of the stop–go cycle, the early 1980s were years of large-scale under-utilisation of resources. Before then the missing billions had been the difference between an actual growth rate averaging something like 3 per cent and the growth rate of 4 per cent or more to which we aspired. In the depths of the slump the missing billions were the difference between a positive growth rate, however modest, and negative growth; after the beginning of the upturn, there still remained the gap between the pre-slump and post-slump levels of wealth creation. It was this loss of national wealth which bedevilled the financing of what was now a moderate rate of increase in total public expenditure.

On the credit side, there had been the great gain in getting the rate of inflation down; although it was expected to turn up again from the low point reached in the first half of 1983, the de-escalation of wage increases had not depended on a pact with the unions or on statutory controls and would not therefore go into reverse purely through a breakdown of such restraints, as had happened in the past. A question often asked was how far the new realism (relatively speaking) in wage claims depended on a continued fear of closures and redundancies.

The productivity gains in industry were a further credit item. But to argue, as some tended to do, that our last state was, on this account, better than our first, in spite of the loss in total output, implied a value judgment that it was better that the total national wealth should be greatly reduced provided that part of it was produced more efficiently. Our last state would be unequivocally better than our first only when we could raise the level of national wealth creation while retaining higher productivity and lower inflation. The question to be put to the test in Margaret Thatcher's second term was whether such a state of affairs would come about spontaneously and at a sufficient rate solely through persistence with the first term strategy.

Appendix I: Statistical Tables

Table A.1: Public expenditure and ratios to GDP in 1981–82 prices

Year	Public expenditure[a] Cost terms[b] £ billion	Year-on-year % change	GDP at 1981–82 market prices[c] £ billion	Year-on-year % change	Ratio of public expenditure to GDP
1959	51.6		155.8		33.1
1960	53.7	+4.1	163.0	+4.6	32.9
1961	56.5	+5.3	168.4	+3.3	33.6
1962	57.7	+2.1	170.0	+1.0	34.0
1963	59.9	+3.8	177.2	+4.2	33.8
1964	63.3	+5.6	186.5	+5.2	33.9
1963–64	61.2	–	180.3	–	34.0
1964–65	63.6	+3.8	187.8	+4.1	33.9
1965–66	67.3	+5.9	192.0	+2.2	35.1
1966–67	71.2	+5.7	195.9	+2.1	36.3
1967–68	80.5	+13.1	201.6	+2.9	39.9
1968–69	79.6	−1.1	208.2	+3.3	38.2
1969–70	79.5	−0.1	211.9	+1.8	37.5
1970–71	81.6	+2.7	216.5	+2.2	37.7
1971–72	83.8	+2.7	222.9	+3.0	37.6
1972–73	89.4	+6.6	232.2	+4.1	38.5
1973–74	96.4	+7.9	241.4	+4.0	39.9
1974–75	108.8	+12.7	241.8	+0.2	45.0
1975–76	109.3	+0.5	240.9	−0.4	45.4
1976–77	106.7	−2.4	248.1	+3.0	43.0
1977–78	99.3	−6.9	253.0	+2.0	39.3
1978–79	105.2	+6.0	260.5	+3.0	40.4
1979–80	108.0	+2.6	266.2	+2.2	40.6
1980–81	110.3	+2.1	257.1	−3.4	42.9
1981–82	112.8	+2.4	256.0	−0.6	44.0
1982–83	115.8	+2.7	264.7	3.4	43.8

[a]Defined as the 'Planning Total' used in Cmnd. 8789 of February 1983 *less* nationalised industries market and overseas borrowing *plus* net debt interest and *plus* an imputed charge for the consumption of non-trading capital. This is close to the definition of public expenditure used in Cmnd. 7439 of January 1979 *plus* the imputed charge for non-trading capital consumption.
[b]In 1981–82 prices, including the relative price effect. This cost terms series is derived by applying a general measure of changes in prices (the GDP deflator) to the public expenditure figures in current prices. The resulting series combines both changes in quantity (volume changes) and any relative changes between prices appropriate to public expenditure and prices in general (the relative price effect). Thus, it differs in character from volume series for public expenditure as used in public expenditure White Papers up to 1981. Such volume series reprice public expenditure in all years at the public expenditure prices obtaining in a single year.
[c]Gross domestic product (GDP) at market prices is the value of the goods and services produced by UK residents, including taxes on expenditure on both home produced and imported goods and services, and the effect of subsidies. It differs from GDP at factor cost which excludes the net value of these taxes and subsidies.

Table A.2: Public expenditure Planning Total

	Cash £ billion	Percentage change on year earlier	Cost terms[a] £ billion	Percentage change on year earlier
Definition in Cmnd. 9143 but excluding market and overseas borrowing of public corporations:				
1963–64	9.9	–	57.1	–
1964–65	10.8	9.2	59.6	4.5
1965–66	12.0	11.4	63.4	6.4
1966–67	13.3	10.7	67.3	6.1
1967–68	15.5	16.6	76.3	13.5
1968–69	16.1	3.9	75.6	−1.0
1969–70	17.0	5.5	75.8	0.3
1970–71	19.1	11.9	78.4	3.5
1971–72	21.4	12.5	80.7	2.9
1972–73	24.8	15.6	86.4	7.1
1973–74	28.6	15.2	92.7	7.3
1974–75	38.6	35.1	105.1	13.3
Definitions used in Cmnd. 9143:				
1974–75	39.3	–	107.0	–
1975–76	48.9	24.6	106.0	−0.9
1976–77	54.4	11.1	104.1	−1.8
1977–78	56.8	4.4	95.6	−8.2
1978–79	65.8	15.8	100.2	4.9
1979–80	76.9	17.0	100.4	0.1
1980–81	92.8	20.6	101.9	1.6
1981–82	104.7	13.0	104.7	2.8
1982–83	113.4	8.3	106.3	1.6
1983–84 (provisional)	120.3	6.1	107.5	−1.1

[a]Cash figure in column 1 deflated by GDP deflator; financial year 1981–82 = 100

Table A.3: Ratios of public expenditure to GDP at market prices from 1973–74 (per cent)

	Planning Total plus debt interest[a]	General government expenditure on goods and services[a]
1973–74	41	23½
1974–75	46	26
1975–76	45½	27
1976–77	44	25½
1977–78	39½	23½
1978–79	40½	23
1979–80	40½	23
1980–81	42½	24
1981–82	44	24
1982–83	43½	24
1983–84	43	23½
1984–85 (estimated)	42	22½

[a]The expenditure totals include non-trading government capital consumption to make them comparable with gross domestic product (expenditure estimate) at market prices.

NOTE ON THE STATISTICAL TABLES

Table A.1 covers general government expenditure, including government loans to the nationalised industries, and thus conforms to the definitions which were adopted in 1976 and used from the 1977 public expenditure White Paper (Cmnd. 6721) to the 1979 White Paper (Cmnd. 7439). The figures are all in 1981–82 prices and enable the real cost of expenditure in each year to be compared after allowing for inflation generally.

The main presentation in the White Papers since 1979 has featured a Planning Total, which differs from these public expenditure totals in two respects. A Treasury series of figures on the Planning Total basis, going back to 1963–64, appears in table A.2. The differences in coverage are as follows. First, the Planning Total adds in the market and overseas borrowings of the nationalised industries. This overcomes the difficulty of comparing one year with another which was felt to arise when the nationalised industries switched their borrowing between one year and the next from the National Loans Fund to other sources or vice versa, but it has the disadvantage of bringing in a financial flow which is not government expenditure and is not an expenditure item at all, except in the books of the institutions and OPEC governments which lend the money. These funds are a financing item, like other funds from which public expenditure is financed, and belong in the PSBR, not in the public expenditure total.

Secondly, debt interest is omitted from the Planning Total, on the grounds that this is the total of the items which can be planned by collective Minsterial decision, and that debt interest is not such an item. However, while it may be reasonable to leave debt interest out of *ex ante* figures presented to Ministers collectively as a basis for spending decisions, debt interest is an outgoing which has to be brought into the Budget arithmetic and into any *ex post* statistics of government expenditure.

The term 'nationalised industries' is used here as shorthand to denote not only the nationalised industries generally thought of as such (coal, steel, the railways, etc.) but also a growing list of further public corporations which are treated in the same way in the public expenditure figures – though there is still a rump of 'other public corporations' which do not get the same treatment and whose total capital expenditure, however financed, is included in the public expenditure totals. The latest and most substantial addition to the list of bodies getting nationalised industry treatment are the regional water authorities; though this change took place in 1983, it has been carried back in the figures to 1973–74 (table A.1) or 1974–75 (table A.2). The difference made by including the market and overseas borrowings of the nationalised industries in the latter table is that, when they are positive, this increases the expenditure total; when there are net repayments of these borrowings, as in recent years, this reduces the total. In neither case do the borrowings or repayments have tax implications, unlike net debt interest which has large tax implications – hence the case for excluding the former from the public expenditure figures and including the latter. However, it is sensible to treat the nationalised industries and the water authorities alike. Under the new treatment, these authorities should not, in principle, be subject to the constraints of the public expenditure limits in renewing the infrastructure needed for the water and sewerage services, provided that they can raise the required finance.

Table A.3 shows public expenditure as a percentage of GDP from 1973–74 to 1982–83 in the same format as in recent public expenditure White Papers. The expenditure figures used for this purpose correspond to the Planning Total plus net debt interest and, for consistency with the GDP figures, an imputed amount for the consumption of non-trading capital. They therefore differ in coverage from table A.1 only to the extent that they bring in the market and overseas borrowings of the nationalised industries, and they are to be preferred to the Planning Total figures as a measure of public expenditure. Although it would be better still to exclude the market and overseas borrowings of the nationalised industries, their inclusion does not seriously vitiate the ratios of public expenditure to GDP in this particular table. Since the 1950s, when the nationalised industries ceased as a general rule to have direct access to capital markets, they have borrowed on a large scale from sources other than the government only during a few years after the oil crisis of 1973, when it suited the government that these industries should take advantage of the funds available from the financial surpluses of the OPEC countries. As the repayment of these loans is completed, and unless there is a further change in the pattern of nationalised industry borrowing, this should cease to be a significant item in the statistics. In any event, the difference in coverage between tables A.1 and A.3 has made a difference of only ½–1 per cent to the ratio of public expenditure to GDP since 1973–74.

A useful feature of table A.3 is that it shows not only total public expenditure, but also that part of government expenditure which goes on goods and services, as a percentage of GDP. Thus, in 1981–82 24 per cent of GDP was spent by central and local government on goods and services embracing manpower, procurement and investment, and a further 20 per cent was spent on transfer payments such as social security subsidies and debt interest.

All the figures in this appendix have been revised to take account of changes in the official statistics up to 1 November 1983, including revised estimates of GDP in past years. The figures from 1981–82 onwards have been further revised to take account of subsequent minor changes up to February 1984, but these latest changes have in general been ignored in respect of the earlier years where they make a difference of only £0.1 billion or 0.1 per cent to particular figures. The GDP figures used for the most recent years are on an expenditure basis and are therefore likely to be somewhat higher than estimates of GDP on an output basis or on an average of the expenditure and output figures. The expenditure figures in Table A.1 and A.3, but not those in Table A.2, include VAT paid by local authorities (which is refunded to them) for the sake of consistency with the GDP figures.

Appendix II: Northern Ireland, Devolution and the EEC Budget

There are special financial arrangements for Northern Ireland, based on the principle of parity of taxation and parity of services with the rest of the United Kingdom of which it forms part. Since Northern Ireland has a lower GDP per head than the UK as a whole, the same rates of taxation produce below-average tax yields in Northern Ireland, and parity of services can be maintained only by supplementing its tax revenue by payments from the rest of the UK. In other words, Northern Ireland has been receiving increasing subventions from Westminster to enable it to pay its way.

These financial arrangements go back to the settlement of Irish affairs which was made after the first world war and the constitution embodied in the Government of Ireland Act 1920. This was drafted so as to apply to the South of Ireland as well as Northern Ireland in the hope that the two, though separate initially, would come together later, but in practice it has from the outset applied only to Northern Ireland. From 1921 to 1972 Northern Ireland had a separate Parliament sitting at Stormont, Belfast, and a separate government, with a good deal of autonomy in internal administration; but 'imperial services', including defence and overseas representation, and all aspects of external affairs remained a Westminster responsibility. Westminster retained responsibility for 'reserved taxes', including income tax and Customs and Excise Duties; Stormont had power to fix and collect 'transferred taxes', including estate duty (now replaced by Capital Transfer Tax) and Vehicle Excise Duty.

The Northern Ireland Ministry of Finance operated (and its successor, the Department of Finance and Personnel, still operates) its own Consolidated Fund, from which money is channelled to the various Northern Ireland services through Departmental votes, on the same

223

lines as on the other side of the Irish Sea. The principal source of revenue accruing to the Consolidated Fund is Northern Ireland's share of reserved taxes, which is paid over from Whitehall, with a smaller amount raised from transferred taxes. From 1926 on there was a Government Loans Fund; capital expenditure, and the debt created to finance it, were borne on this fund and on the Northern Ireland Consolidated Fund. Part of this loan money used to be raised, until the troubles of recent years, from the London capital market, as well as by local bond issues and Northern Ireland savings, which still continue. In addition, the Department of Finance and Personnel has access to the UK National Loans Fund, on which it now relies for a greater proportion of its capital requirements.

In the early years Northern Ireland came reasonably close to financing its internal public services out of these resources, and also made a small Imperial Contribution, under the provisions of the 1920 Act, towards the cost of the national debt, defence and other imperial services. In form, the system was presided over by a Joint Exchequer Board, consisting of one representative from the Ministry of Finance and one from the Treasury, with an outside chairman, which met once a year to approve the allocation of reserved tax revenue and the imperial contribution. In practice, matters were handled on a day-to-day basis between the Ministry of Finance in Stormont and the Treasury in Whitehall.

As time went on, the growth of public expenditure in Northern Ireland outstripped the growth of revenue. This arose from the need, in pursuance of parity of services, to keep in step with the increase in Great Britain in public expenditure generally and in particular on welfare services and on schemes of assistance to the Development Areas, which were matched in Northern Ireland by 'Development-Area-plus' treatment. This reflected the fact that unemployment in Northern Ireland had been consistently higher than elsewhere in the UK. The financial arrangements had to be shored up by various forms of support, including an annual transfer from the National Insurance Fund in Great Britain to its Northern Ireland counterpart which still continues. At one stage the gap was partly filled by basing Northern Ireland's share of Customs and Excise Duties on its share of the population of Great Britain, i.e. 2.75 per cent, instead of on the proportion of those duties actually raised in Northern Ireland.

In 1972 the problem of law and order and the political impasse in Northern Ireland led to the resignation of the Northern Ireland government, the suspension of the Stormont Parliament and direct rule from Westminster, administered by a Northern Ireland Office which was hived off from the Home Office for the purpose. By the following year it had become impossible to keep Northern Ireland in funds through the existing arrangements, and a grant in aid from a Northern Ireland Office Vote was introduced under the Northern Ireland Constitution Act 1973, which mopped up some of the previous forms of assistance. This grant is paid into the Northern Ireland Consolidated Fund.

In 1974, following the Sunningdale Conference, a Northern Ireland Executive was created, consisting of representatives of a number of the political parties, which for a brief time, from January to May, exercised a degree of administrative autonomy. Although the Executive was not given powers of taxation, or the power to increase total expenditure on those transferred services for which it was given responsibility, it was to have discretion to switch expenditure from one programme to another. A Council of Ireland was also planned as an umbrella for joint action by the governments in the North and the South of Ireland, but it never came into operation. There was not enough time to see how the financial arrangements for the Executive would work out before the Executive was disbanded as a result of resistance and industrial action by the Protestant workers, partly out of alarm at the prospect of the Council of Ireland. The government then reverted to direct rule. The events of 1974 did not affect the financial machinery.

In 1982 a new Northern Ireland Assembly was elected, intended as the first step on the path to fresh devolution of power to Northern Ireland institutions. Initially the Assembly's main task was the scrutiny of the activities of government; in reaching decisions on public expenditure, the government was to take careful account of the Assembly's advice, but the formal machinery for handling public expenditure remained unchanged pending devolution. However, the Social Democratic Labour Party declined to take up their seats in the Assembly, and late in 1983 it was further depleted by the withdrawal of the Official Unionist Party from its proceedings, at least for the time being.

The amount of subsidy going to a Northern Ireland population of 1½ million in 1982–83 was something like £0.8 billion, excluding the cost of maintaining law and order – that is, over £500 per head or over £2000 for a family of four. The total amount, if the cost of law and order is included, was about £1.2 billion. We should of course get the same sort of result for other parts of the United Kingdom with below-average GDP per head and above-average unemployment if they too had separate budgets and accounts.

Under the Scotland Act 1879 and the Wales Act 1978 the Scottish and Welsh assemblies were not to have any powers of taxation but were to be financed by a block grant related to their expenditure needs. A special unit had been set up in the Treasury to work out criteria for determining the required amounts in consultation with the Scottish and Welsh offices. Over a wide range of programmes which were thought not to impinge too directly on the rest of Britain the two assemblies were to have discretion to switch expenditure between programmes. Here too we do not know how the arrangements would have worked in practice but, in spite of the absence of taxation powers, they embodied the principle of parity of taxation and of services, since the same tax system was to continue to apply to the whole of Great Britain while services in Scotland and Wales were to be at least on a par overall with those in the rest of Britain.

This principle can be contrasted with the budgetary arrangements for the European Economic Community. On the revenue side, the Community receives the proceeds of all import duties and import levies on agricultural products, plus the equivalent of a Value Added Tax not exceeding 1 per cent of the GDP of each member country. On the expenditure side, roughly three-quarters of the budget has been spent on subsidies to farm prices under the common agricultural policy. Thus contributions to the budget bear no relation to ability to pay and receipts from it bear no relation to need.

These arrangements work out particularly badly for the United Kingdom, which is a major importer in general and a major importer of food in particular. Under the system of agricultural support which we operated before entry into the EEC, agricultural imports came in at world market prices, which thus set the level for UK farm prices. Farm incomes were made up by deficiency payments to the farmer, geared to guaranteed prices worked out at an Annual Review of Agriculture, but the consumer still bought his food at world price levels. Under the CAP, farm incomes are maintained by raising market prices through levies on imports and buying up domestic surpluses, thus creating the notorious butter mountain, wine lake, and so on. In this way public expenditure in the Community is used to make food dearer instead of cheaper, and Britain suffers a balance of payments cost on top of the budgetary cost.

Clearly the extension of the principle of parity of taxation and parity of services to the whole of the Community is not a practical proposition in the foreseeable future. Nevertheless, if the Community, the most ambitious attempt at supranational government in modern times, is not merely to survive but to develop, a more suitable

budgetary system is likely to remain an important long-term requirement. The section headed 'On the Eve of the Landslide' in chapter 6
describes the crisis over the EEC budget in 1979, when the Community's
financial resources fell short of its mounting commitments, to which
the Commission responded by proposing an increase in VAT-based
contributions to 1.4 per cent. This issue remained unresolved at the
end of the period covered by this book. Prediction of the outcome
would at that point have been a self-inflicted hazard, but a long and
acrimonious negotiation appeared certain.

Appendix III: The Mechanics of
Public Expenditure

Provision for the cash required for public expenditure is made in Britain, as it must be in practically any country, on a year to year basis, through the system of annual budgets. The Budget presented to the House of Commons by the Chancellor of the Exchequer every spring is concerned primarily with the finances of the central government for which he has direct responsibility, but it does also involve in various ways all three main elements of the public sector – that is, central government, then local government, and thirdly the nationalised industries and other public corporations. The flow-chart in this appendix shows how the finances of the rest of the public sector interact with central government finance.

Central government finance operates mainly through two principal accounts – the Consolidated Fund, largely for current account transactions, and the National Loans Fund, largely for transactions on capital account. These two accounts are controlled by the Treasury and managed for them by the Bank of England. Two other important accounts, the National Insurance Fund and the Exchange Equalisation Account, are shown in the flow-chart, but are not discussed in detail here.

All national tax receipts, including the national insurance surcharge while it has been in force, but excluding normal national insurance contributions,[1] flow into the Consolidated Fund. The bulk

---

[1] National insurance contributions are paid into the National Insurance Fund and are topped up by a supplement from a DHSS Vote, originally equivalent to 18 per cent of contributions, but reduced to 14½ per cent with effect from 1981, and reduced again to 13 per cent on 1 April 1982. In his Autumn statement of 17 November 1983 the Chancellor of the Exchequer announced that this 'Treasury supplement' to the Fund would be further reduced to 11 per cent in the following April. The money in the Fund is used to pay national insurance benefits.

of the outflow is accounted for by Supply Services, as they are called; that is to say, the expenditure programmes of the various government Departments, for which money is approved by Parliament, exercising its traditional function of 'voting supply'. Estimates for the services to be financed in this way are put to Parliament shortly before the beginning of the financial year, classified by Votes and broken down into Subheads. Legislative authority for the appropriation of money for Votes from the Consolidated Fund is secured by an annual Appropriation Act. Meanwhile there is a system of Votes on Account to make enough money available until the Appropriation Act is passed. Additional provision for particular services may be made in the course of the financial year by means of Supplementary Estimates. These increases may be offset by reductions in the original provision for services which are found not to require the full amount. The money for some services, however, is paid directly from the Consolidated Fund without going through a Departmental Vote and thus without having to be approved each year by Parliament. The point of this arrangement is to commit the country to honouring these obligations willynilly and independently of political events at a particular time. The Consolidated Fund standing services include, among other things, the service of the national debt to the extent that it cannot be met from the National Loans Fund, judges' pay, and our contribution to the budget of the European Economic Community. This last arrangement was made out of deference to the concept that this money belongs to the Community, as of right, as part of its *ressources propres*, but no doubt the government, as distinct from Parliament, could find a way to withhold these payments, amid some uproar, if a failure to resolve the dispute with the Community about the size of our contribution drove it to such a desperate measure.

The National Loans Fund did not come into being until 1 April 1968, as a result of the National Loans Act 1968. Thus, when the nationalised industries started to get their loans from the government in 1956, instead of directly from the capital market, at that stage the money was channelled to them from the Consolidated Fund through *ad hoc* accounts, such as were set up for a variety of below-the-line transactions. In substance, there was no radical difference – in terms of control, for instance – between the arrangements before and after 1968, but the National Loans Fund did represent a useful rationalisation. One fairly important provision of the 1968 Act stipulates that all borrowers from the Fund must reimburse the full interest costs incurred in raising the money for the Fund. Thus any subsidy to the interest rate has to be provided separately as an overt grant through Votes.

CENTRAL   GOVERNMENT

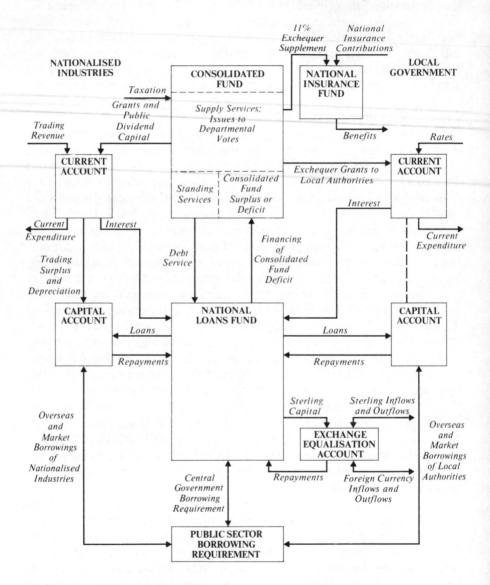

Financial flows in the UK public sector

The National Loans Fund, since its inception, has been the channel for all the government's borrowing and thus for the raising and the servicing of the national debt. It is also the channel for most government lending, though some loans on special terms (e.g. overseas aid loans) are still made through Departmental Votes.

There is an interplay between the Consolidated Fund and the National Loans Fund. If the tax revenue, etc., coming into the Consolidated Fund is not enough to meet outgoings from the Fund, and there is thus a deficit in the Consolidated Fund, the deficit is met by a transfer from the National Loans Fund, which borrows for the purpose, thus increasing the national debt above what it would otherwise be. In other words, current revenue is topped up out of capital account. In 1982–83, for instance, the topping up was about £8 billion. Accumulated borrowings to finance Consolidated Fund deficits constitute the deadweight national debt, in relation to which there is no incoming stream of interest receipts to meet the outgoing interest payments.

Money is raised through the National Loans Fund for on-lending to local authorities as well as to nationalised industries and other public corporations. The Fund charges interest on these loans at the same rate as it itself pays for borrowings of similar duration. Thus a substantial proportion of the service of the national debt is automatically offset by interest payments from the nationalised industries and local authorities. To the extent that the service of the national debt is not financed in this way, it is a charge on the Consolidated Fund. In 1982–83, as an example, the service of the national debt was about £11.6 billion, of which well over £6 billion came from offsetting receipts and over £5 billion from the Consolidated Fund.

Thus we have a circular situation in which the National Loans Fund borrows to cover the deficit in the Consolidated Fund, and the Consolidated Fund in turn contributes to the National Loans Fund to help service the national debt – and this contribution accounts for a large part of the Consolidated Fund deficit. In principle, the arrangement can work the other way round. If taxes, etc., more than cover outgoings from the Consolidated Fund, a surplus is produced which is paid into the National Loans Fund and can be used to pay off part of the national debt. But the last time that there was a surplus in the Consolidated Fund was 1971–72; and the last time that there was a reduction in the national debt, taking all transactions into account, was in 1969 and 1970 following the expenditure cuts when Roy Jenkins was Chancellor of the Exchequer.

So when we say that the service of the national debt is a charge on the Consolidated Fund, in practice this has tended to mean that new debt is raised to service old debt as well as to cover the new deficit. However, the government's ability to go on borrowing in this way depends on its taxation powers; and, in the last analysis, to be a charge on the Consolidated Fund is to have a guarantee of payment out of taxation.

All the transactions which I have described form part of the Budget arithmetic as a whole in the annual *Financial Statement and Budget Report*. Popularly known as the Red Book, this document brings together all public spending, whether out of Votes or the National Loans Fund or through other accounts, together with all the tax revenue and public sector borrowing which go to finance it. The function of the Red Book is purely presentational; it is not a document requiring Parliamentary approval. Though the tax proposals which it reflects have to be approved through a Finance Act, and Vote expenditures have to be approved in the manner already described, provision for the issue of money from the National Loans Fund in the course of the year is not subject to any corresponding arrangement and does not require specific Parliamentary approval. The total amounts which can be issued from the National Loans Fund over time to, say, the various nationalised industries are prescribed in the Acts relating to those industries, but within these totals there is no statutory limit on the amount which can be lent in a single year. These loan figures can therefore be varied in the course of a year in a more flexible way than is possible with Vote finance.

In terms of the 'PESC system', the components of planned public expenditure can be summarised, in a highly simplified way, in the following four lines:

> funtional programmes
> + debt interest
> + contingency reserve
> − allowance for shortfall

We can then move on to the following little equation which matches this PESC-type analysis with the financial flows analysis in this appendix and brings together all the Red Book transactions:

functional programmes
+ debt interest

+ contingency reserve
− allowance for shortfall
+ market and overseas
borrowings of public
corporations
− sales of public assets

$=$

central government taxation
+ national insurance contributions
+ local rates
+ the public sector borrowing
requirement (PSBR)

Postscript

The first version of this book was completed in the second half of 1981 and took the story of public expenditure since the war up to that date. The book was conceived as a definitive explanation of the public expenditure system and its development, but it was then suggested to me that I should at the same time try to show what it was like to be involved in these events as a civil servant. The book therefore alternates between semi-technical analysis and semi-personal narrative, in which some issues, such as the investment grants scheme, receive attention because they loomed large at that time in my official life rather than on the national scene – though there was great expenditure of Whitehall passion as well as Exchequer money on that scheme.

This version of the book was completed two years later and carries the story on up to the end of Margaret Thatcher's first term of office in the summer of 1983. Since one or two of the generally favourable reviews of the first version hinted that it was a bit on the technical side for the general reader, I have tried to make the going a bit easier by transferring the semi-technical description of 'The Mechanics of Public Expenditure', together with one or two other pages, to the appendices; I should have liked to make the book easier still for the general reader, but that would have required too extensive a re-write. In other respects, I have not found it necessary to alter anything in the previous version except to correct a couple of factual mistakes which I spotted for myself – the size of the post-war American loan, and the effect of pay settlements on cash limits in 1978–79 and 1979–80 – and, in the transition to the fresh events now covered in the final chapter, to give more weight to the second major rise in the oil price in 1979.

However, it should be noted that further light has been shed on many of the events with which I deal in the life of the 1974–79 Labour government by Joel Barnett (who was Chief Secretary throughout that time) in his book *Inside the Treasury* (Andre Deutsch, 1982), which appeared at much the same time as *Getting and Spending*. My book refers, for instance, to the fact that, in the July 1976 package of cuts, the extra capital expenditure of BNOC was, on the advocacy of the Secretary of State for Energy, treated as a 'special case'. Joel Barnett, with greater licence, rightly describes this as a presentational 'fiddle'. Or again, I have referred to the fact that, in the Labour government's final months, the idea was in the air that the increase in cash limits might be 2 per cent less than pay increases; Joel Barnett discloses that this 'n−2' formula was passed in Cabinet on 22 February 1979. Though his account of events and mine differ in ways such as this, I do not think that they conflict at all.

In order to deal with events in which, though they took place in my time in the Treasury, I was not involved, I spoke to various people who were so involved, including a number who had been Chancellor or Permanent Secretary at the relevant time. In general, my account of events has not been criticised as inaccurate or unfair. However, in dealing with the balance of payments deficit of 1972, I wrote that '. . . Anthony Barber was unwilling to have his Chancellorship associated with a devaluation involving a straightforward downward change of parity. In June 1972, therefore, he adopted a floating rate for the pound'. In his review of the book in *The Banker* in January 1983, Terence Higgins, who for the most part had kind things to say of it, commented of this passage that '. . . in fact, the Chancellor had made it clear throughout that he did not regard the exchange rate as sacrosanct and that, if necessary, the government would float it as a consistent part of its overall policy'. Though I have not, in the body of the book, altered the account given to me of the floating of the pound, I am glad to record this further view.

I take this opportunity to thank the friends and former colleagues who gave indispensable help in the preparation of this book both in the first place and in its revision. So far as is humanly possible, all the figures and other details have been brought up to date as at the beginning of November 1983. But of course not only will new events take place and systems change, but statisticians will continue to revise the numbers relating to the past, let alone projections of the future, and definitions will continue to be altered by successive administrations according to the circumstances of the time but with retrospective effect on all the series of figures. So I am resigned to the fact that it is not possible to be finally definitive for all time, and I have settled for trying to be provisionally definitive at the time of writing.

Index

Officials with knighthoods are shown as such in the index irrespective of the stage in the narrative at which they were knighted.

The principal offices held by Ministers at the time of their appearances in the narrative are shown against their names in the index. These brief references do not cover all the appointments held in the course of their political careers.